Selected Correspondence of Bernard Shaw

Bernard Shaw
Theatrics

General Editor: J. Percy Smith

Editorial Advisory Board

Ronald Ayling
Leonard Conolly
S.F. Gallagher
Christopher Newton
Ann Saddlemyer
John Wardrop
J.L. Wisenthal

Selected Correspondence of Bernard Shaw

Bernard Shaw Theatrics

Edited by Dan H. Laurence

UNIVERSITY OF TORONTO PRESS

Toronto Buffalo London

Bernard Shaw Letters
© 1995 The Trustees of the British Museum,
The Governors and Guardians of the National Gallery of Ireland
and Royal Academy of Dramatic Art

Introductory and Editorial Matter © 1995 Dan H. Laurence

Published by University of Toronto Press Incorporated

Toronto Buffalo London
Printed in Canada
ISBN 0-8020-3000-9

Printed on acid-free paper

Canadian Cataloguing in Publication Data

Shaw, Bernard, 1856–1950
    Selected correspondence of Bernard Shaw

    v. 1. Theatrics / edited by Dan H. Laurence.
    Includes bibliographical references and index.
    ISBN 0-8020-3000-9 (v. 1)

    1. Shaw, Bernard, 1856–1950 – Correspondence.
    I. Smith, J. Percy.   II. Title.

    PR5366.A4 1995   826'.912   C95-930151-8

University of Toronto Press acknowledges the
financial assistance to its publishing program of the
Canada Council and the Ontario Arts Council.

The Press also acknowledges a generous subvention
from Mr John Wardrop.
We also thank the Academy of the Shaw Festival and the
University of Guelph for their support.

A Standing Ovation

to the memory of

RAYMOND MANDER

and

JOE MITCHENSON

whose lasting contribution to

British theatre studies

is immeasurable

Contents

General Editor's Note

What is astonishing about Bernard Shaw's correspondence is not its sheer abundance. That a professional author with wide interests should in the course of a long life write a great many letters – even into the thousands – is not remarkable. That one should do so in unfailingly athletic prose, invariably directing at his correspondent a fund of detailed knowledge and a combination of forthrightness, penetrative argument, teasing wit, and good humour – in short, invariably projecting the persona of the author – is extraordinary indeed. These qualities appear when Shaw is writing to friends and adversaries, public personages, and private citizens, from the world of theatre, of letters, of political affairs.

Obviously, any item in Shaw's correspondence projects one voice in a dialogue that might be long-continued, involving another voice often capable of responding to Shaw in terms as forthright and downright as his own – if seldom as witty. The volumes in the present series are intended to make available some of the longer dialogues that GBS had with particular friends and colleagues in various fields: fellow workers in literature or socialism, translators of his plays, the film producer Gabriel Pascal, the illustrator John Farleigh, and so on. Other volumes will comprise letters written exclusively by Shaw to a large number of individuals focusing on particular aspects of his career, such as the theatre and publishing.

The Selected Correspondence of Bernard Shaw series has been planned by an editorial advisory board made up of senior Shavian scholars. The aim of these volumes is to present accurate texts of letters almost all of which are previously unpublished and situate them in the context of Bernard Shaw's life and career.

J. Percy Smith

Introduction

There was never a time, Shaw said, when he could not read; he could recall black-bordered reports of the death of Albert the Prince Consort and headlines relating to the American Civil War that drew his attention when he was only five.[1] He was equally precocious in regard to his theatre-going experience. His first play, at seven and a half, he reminisced, was Tom Taylor's crime drama *Plot and Passion*. As with his reading, Shaw's theatre indoctrination came so early that it seemed thereafter a natural part of his life. Recollections of boyhood excursions to the playhouse abound in his writings, not only, as expected, in his professional music and drama criticism, but also in book prefaces, lectures, interviews, correspondence, and conversation.

From these we learn that *Plot and Passion*, a three-act play, starring Frank Huntley and Sidney Bancroft, was performed in a single bill at Dublin's venerable Theatre Royal following a full-length pantomime *Harlequin Puss in Boots, or, the Fairies of the Gossamer Grove*. The latter, a hodgepodge of vaudeville, mime, ballet, and farce, starred the popular Mrs Burkinshaw as Puss and the versatile clown Hildyar, who, Shaw recollected, shot a policeman into multiple segments, and featured 'roller skaters who crashed together in the middle of the stage and disappeared shrieking down the grave trap.' The child's escort on this January evening in 1864 presumably was his mentor George John Lee, his mother's singing teacher, with whom the Shaw family shared a residence in Hatch Street, and who almost certainly would have obtained complimentary seats from his sometime partner J.M. Levey, musical director of the Theatre Royal. Shaw could not recall whom he had seen perform that evening, he said, because at the time 'it seemed all real to me.' Moreover, he 'had to be removed forcibly from the theatre at the end because after the falls of the curtain three times in *Plot and Passion* I could not be persuaded that it would not presently go up again.'[2]

Further theatre attendance was curtailed when the Shaws and Lee set up residence in 1866 in Torca Cottage, Dalkey, along the sea coast about seven miles south-east of central Dublin; but in March 1868, Shaw recalled, 'I went by myself and saw T.C. King in [Dion Boucicault's] *The Corsican Brothers*,' this being the first Dublin performance in twelve years given by 'Handsome' King, in the dual role of the twin brothers Louis and Fabien Dei Franchi. This time, Shaw remembered, 'there was illusion, but no deception: I knew that the ghost was a man painted white on a sliding bridge, lighted by a green lantern, and that Château-Renaud [the villain] was not really killed [by Fabien in a duel], though I enjoyed the fight all the more.'[3]

This maturation may have been the result, at least in part, of Shaw's exposure in the interim to opera. The initial operatic experience paralleled that of the pantomime visit, and may have occurred very shortly thereafter. 'I did not then know what an opera was,' Shaw reminisced, 'though I could whistle a good deal of opera music.' Having seen photographs of opera singers in evening dress in his mother's photo album, he assumed all the fashionably clad ladies and gentlemen in the gilded dress circle were opera singers, and focused on one 'massive, dark lady' who, he decided, was the evening's star performer, 'and wondered how soon she would stand up and sing. I was puzzled by the fact that I was made to sit with my back to the singers instead of facing them. When the curtain went up, my astonishment and delight were unbounded.'[4]

His sophistication developed rapidly with introductions to Gounod's *Faust* in 1867 and to Mozart's *Don Giovanni* in 1868. At a performance of *Il Trovatore* on 19 September 1867, to which he had been brought by Lee, he was surprised, he recalled when he was ninety-four, 'to hear in the second scene a voice from behind the scenes: Manrico singing the serenade. I asked the adult who had brought me ... "What is that?" He replied, "A pig under a gate."' It was Shaw's first experience of music criticism. 'I forbear,' he concluded charitably, 'to rescue that tenor's name from oblivion.'[5] One additional performance that must have affected him was an amateur production of *Il Trovatore* on 31 March 1868, conducted by Lee, in which he witnessed his mother performing as Azucena.

Until he left school in 1871 and entered employment in the land agency of C. Uniacke Townshend, Shaw's theatre attendance was meagre. His acquaintance with Douglas Jerrold's nautical melodrama *Black-Ey'd Susan* may have been made through T.C. King's production late in 1869. On 21 November 1870 he watched Kate Bateman re-create her greatest London success, *Leah the Forsaken* by Augustin Daly. By a happy coincidence, when Miss Bateman elected to emerge briefly from retirement in 1907 it was to appear as Mrs Dudgeon in the first West End production, at the Savoy, of Shaw's *The Devil's Disciple*.

Lack of accessibility to Dublin's theatre centre during the years divided between Dalkey and school did not, however, retard Sonny Shaw from finding an imaginative ingress to the drama in a world of dreams that rapidly became his only reality. 'The eye, born anew,' says Ibsen's John Gabriel Borkman, 'transforms the old action.' The incipient playwright, before he was ten, acquired a table-top toy theatre, for which he purchased cut-out cardboard scenery and characters in a small shop across from the Queen's Theatre, manipulating these to create from imagination dramatizations of novels he had read and of Shakespeare's plays, and to re-create performances stored in his mind, undertaking all the parts and, presumably, improvising dialogue he could not recall. 'Whether it be that I was born mad or a little too sane,' he confessed in a preface to *Immaturity* that he drafted in 1921, 'my kingdom was not of this world: I was at home only in the realm of my imagination, and at my ease only with the mighty dead. Therefore I had to become an actor, and create for myself a fantastic personality fit and apt for dealing with men, and adaptable to the various parts I had to play as author, journalist, orator, politician, committee man, man of the world, and so forth. In this I succeeded later on only too well.'[6]

At Dalkey, too, Shaw 'painted the whitewashed wall in my bedroom ... with watercolor frescoes of Mephistopheles,' his taste running 'strongly on stage villains and stage demons.' Having decided he would be a 'wicked baritone' when he grew up, he 'revel[led] in the exercise of dramatic invention.'[7] Throughout his life Shaw would continue to conflate music and drama, and to play devil's advocate, commencing at fourteen with a demonic verse play (probably in panto tradition) he called *Straw-berrinos: or, The Haunted Winebin.*

When his clerkly position at the land agency began to provide him with pocket money he at last could indulge to the full his craving for theatre, attending virtually every week, at two shillings a performance. Pressing anxiously towards the theatre entrance he would, as the doors were flung open, lunge down the stairway to the pit (there were no stalls) to guarantee himself a front seat on the long rows of hard benches, emerging from the crush 'with all my front buttons down the middle of my back.'[8]

Voraciously he absorbed whichever attraction was available to him. Week after week, or for brief multi-week seasons, the Theatre Royal headlined international stars in scratch performances with its under-rehearsed, barely competent resident stock company, interspersed with visits by full touring companies. In the five years of his employment in Dublin, until he emigrated across the channel, Shaw viewed every major touring performer: Madame Céleste, queen of melodrama, in *The Woman in Red* and Buckstone's *Green Bushes* (these at the Gaiety); the celebrated light comedian Charles Mathews in the farce *Cool as a Cucumber*; Henry Irving, at the top of his young form, as Digby Grant in James Albery's *The Two Roses*; E.A. Sothern in his most popular role as Lord Dundreary in Tom Taylor's comedy, *Our American Cousin,* and, with John Buckstone, in T.W. Robertson's *Home.*

Shaw saw too Hugo's *Lucrezia Borgia* with the American-born Gene-viève Ward; Adelaide Ristori's Italian version of Schiller's *Maria Stuart*; Tom Taylor's *Joan of Arc* in a bill with Philip Massinger's *A New Way to Pay Old Debts*; Gilbert and Sullivan's *Trial by Jury* (at the Gaiety); Mrs Dion Boucicault, supported by Shiel Barry, in her husband's Irish melo-tragedy *The Colleen Bawn*; Craven Robertson's Company in T.W. Robert-son's *Caste* and Richard Young's Company in Robertson's *Ours* and *The M.P.* He saw the legendary Charles Calvert in Byron's *Sardanapalus*; the low comedian J.L. Toole in *Paul Pry* and *Oliver Twist*; the performance of Madge Robertson (later Mrs Kendal) with John Buckstone and the Hay-market Company in *Pigmalion and Galatea*; and in 1895 he recalled 'the deep conviction and pathos' of Ada Cavendish as Mercy Merrick, relat-ing her life story at the outset of Wilkie Collins's *The New Magdalen,* lamenting her fall from society and her conviction that 'I can't get back;

I can't get back,' which ended in 'the memorable fit of hysterics which swept away the audiences of the seventies with the undercurrent of rich, passionate, indignant emotion which was Ada Cavendish's chief gift.'[9]

When the illustrious provincial tragedian Barry Sullivan made his first Dublin appearance in April 1870, billed as 'the leading legitimate actor of the British stage,' Shaw was there to see his *Hamlet* and to be 'reduced' by the performance of a local Ophelia in the Theatre Royal stock company 'to such paroxysms of laughter that I narrowly escaped ejection from the theatre.' He was there again in December 1870 (when Sullivan brought his own Ophelia) – and in 1871 – and once more in 1873. Sullivan was, in Shaw's words, 'a great actor.' Seventy-seven years after first experiencing his Hamlet, Shaw remembered Sullivan as having 'majesty and power ... For boys like me he was irresistible.' His stage walk 'was by itself worth going to the theatre to see. When [as Hamlet] he killed the king by dashing up the whole depth of the stage and running him through again and again, he was a human thunderbolt.' He saw Sullivan's Macbeth, Sullivan's Richelieu, Sullivan's Richard III ('a monster of truculence'). He also witnessed Daniel Bandmann's Hamlet and Othello, his Romeo and Richard III, as well as his production of Bulwer-Lytton's *The Lady of Lyons*; and saw too the Hamlet of Alice Marriott. Sullivan, in his eyes, ever was unequivocally the best: 'when I was a very impressionable boy he became my model of personal nobility.'[10]

On the first day of April 1876 Shaw forsook Dublin for what he later would call 'the great stage of London,' because 'all that Dublin offered to the enormity of my unconscious ambition' was 'failure ... poverty ... obscurity ...' and 'the ostracism and contempt which these imply.'[11] He joined a mother and sister, in straitened circumstances, who had abandoned him, his father, and Dublin in 1873, and who were mourning the death a week earlier of another sister, whose fresh grave Shaw visited in the Isle of Wight. At first opportunity, however, he gravitated to the West End for tempting glimpses of Ernesto Rossi as Lear and the brilliant Tomasso Salvini as Hamlet and a visit to the Alhambra for a performance of Offenbach's *Le Voyage de la Lune*. Being unemployed (and not particularly anxious to abandon this new-found freedom) resulted, of course, in a paucity of funds for entertainment. When he did eventually find something congenial enough to accept, it was as a ghost-writing music critic for a satiric weekly *The Hornet*, which confined him to the concert halls and opera houses for nearly a year.

In 1878, at twenty-two, he commenced writing in earnest, filling composition books and quires mostly with unsaleable short stories and *belles lettres*, though in February of that year he actually made an attempt at a play. Called provisionally *The Household of Joseph*, it was an iconoclastic attempt to convert the romantic 'five acts and in verse' theatrical formula to a cynical, profane Passion Play, in which Jesus, described in the cast of characters as 'the illegitimate son of Mary,' is the antagonist, with Judas Iscariot as a rational philosopher, who by process of ironic inversion becomes the first Shavian anti-hero. The concept soon palled: before the would-be dramatist had reached the end of the second act he had cast aside the manuscript, never to return to it.

In its stead, in March 1879, he commenced composition of *Immaturity*, the first of five novels, written at the rate of one a year, having forsaken theatre as 'being mentally dust and ashes.'[12] Much autobiography may be discerned in the novels, especially as regards the theatre: in *Immaturity* Shaw himself is limned as an unfledged youth discovering London life and the stage; in *The Irrational Knot* (1880) the actress Lalage Virtue is drawn from his sister Lucy, who had turned to the theatre in light opera and pantomime; in *Love Among the Artists* (1881) Lucy again is the model for an actress, Madge Brailsford, whose experience as a member of a provincial theatre company is graphically depicted, Shaw most effectively utilizing his extensive knowledge of Dublin stock-company performers and performances, anticipating by nearly two decades Pinero's rather more roseate and sentimental treatment of the subject in the play *Trelawny of the 'Wells'* (1898).

It was not until 1884 that Shaw took another stab at dramaturgy, under pressure from a recently acquired friend, William Archer, already at twenty-eight (the same age as Shaw) an established drama and art critic. They agreed to collaborate on a play tentatively titled *Rhinegold*, to be adapted from a French play, *La ceinture dorée*, by Guillaume Augier. Again Shaw got no further than Act II; Archer lost interest; and the play was abandoned. Two years later, after attending a performance on 22 February 1886 by the celebrated Mr and Mrs Kendal, supported by John Hare and Linda Dietz, Shaw was inspired to draft a hasty shorthand outline he headed 'Plan for St James's Piece':

HARE: Pessimist. He takes a frightful view of human nature, but is cheerful, benevolent, wise, witty and hospitable. Maintains that all men are liars, but is indignant when his word is doubted. When in love takes up a looking glass, admires himself in it, and suddenly shouts Grr, you old profligate, at himself.

Mrs K is a widow who wants to marry him, but he does not dream of this, and supposes she wants to marry K. He disappoints her frightfully by scheming to bring this about. K. also annoyed, because he is afraid of being disinherited if he refuses to marry a woman his uncle chooses, and on the other hand, he is in love with another (LD) whose jealousy of Mrs K may be worked on by a rival admirer, the villain of the piece.[13]

There is no evidence that Shaw pursued the idea beyond the brief outline, nor did anything come of a more prolonged effort in 1889–90 to work at a play *The Cassone*, several fragments of which survive. From 1884 to 1892, however, Shaw continued sporadically to tinker with *Rhinegold*, drafting a third act, rewriting, discarding, then further revising. At last the play, newly titled *Widowers' Houses*, was completed, in 1892, at the behest of the critic and journalist J.T. Grein for performance in the second season of Grein's private society, the Independent Theatre.

With incredible self-confidence Shaw undertook to stage the production himself, and, having accomplished the task creditably (though Archer insisted he was not and never would be a playwright), proceeded to work at a second play, scribbling for his own guidance a memorandum 'that unless I could produce at least half a dozen plays before I was forty, I had better let playwriting alone.'[14] Though he did not complete his first play until he was nearly halfway into his thirty-seventh year, he met the quota with a play and a half to spare by his fortieth birthday on 26 July 1896.

As *Theatrics* opens, in mid-1889, Shaw is a music critic and practical journalist, as well as a Socialist organizer and street orator. The persona has germinated and commenced to emerge in 'G.B.S' and 'Corno di Bassetto.' But he has not yet completed his first play and is five and a half years away from the strategic drama criticism in the *Saturday Review* (1895–8) that would make his voice 'heard upon the high places' as he set to work to 'raise the theatre from the dead.'[15] In June 1889 Shaw alone knows what the world would eventually discover: that a single man by unyielding determination can alter the course of the theatre, creating through the magic of his genius a glorious phoenix of intellect and imagination to rise from the 'dust and ashes' to transform the theatre of his boyhood.

Dan H. Laurence

San Antonio
November 1993

NOTES

1 Hesketh Pearson, *Bernard Shaw: His Life and Personality* (1942), 22. Spoken prologue for American audiences preceding the film *Major Barbara*; in Shaw, *Collected Plays with Their Prefaces*, III (1971), 65.
2 Roy Nash, 'The Theatre To-day and Yesterday According to George Bernard Shaw,' *Manchester Evening News*, 6 December 1938, 6:3–7. 'I believe,' Shaw noted, 'the performance began and ended with a farce; for that was the length of entertainment the public expected in those days at the old Theatre Royal.' In this instance, however, no farces were announced in newspaper advertisements, or alluded to in critical notices.
3 Ibid.
4 'How the Theatre Fared,' preface to *Heartbreak House*; in Shaw, *Collected Plays with Their Prefaces*, V (1972), 45–6.
5 'We Sing Better than Our Grandparents,' *Everybody's* (London) 40 (11 November 1950); in *Shaw's Music* (1981), III, 768. The luckless vocalist was the long-forgotten Signor Tombesi, in his first and last Dublin appearance.
6 Preface to *Immaturity* (Standard Edition, 1931), xliii.
7 Ibid., xx.
8 'The Theatre of My Childhood,' *Evening Post* (Bristol), 3 December 1946; in Shaw, *The Matter with Ireland* (1962), as 'Preface: Fragments of Autobiography,' 11–12.
9 'The New Magdalen and the Old,' *Saturday Review* (London), 2 November 1895; in *Our Theatres in the Nineties* (Standard Edition, 1932), I, 234.
10 'Barry Sullivan, Shakespear and Shaw,' *Strand Magazine* (London), October 1947; in *Shaw on Theatre* (1958), 273–8.
11 Preface to *Immaturity*, xxxiii and xliv.
12 *Everybody's Political What's What?* (1944), 188.
13 Shorthand manuscript (transcribed by Barbara Smoker) on a correspondence card: Dan H. Laurence Collection of Bernard Shaw, University of Guelph Library. Published by permission of the University of Guelph and the Estate of Bernard Shaw.
14 Preface to *Plays Unpleasant*; in Shaw, *Collected Plays with Their Prefaces*, I (1970), 11.
15 Autograph letter signed, to Henry Wilson, 10 August 1915; in Shaw, *Collected Letters 1911–1925* (1985), 306.

Editor's Note

The intent in this volume is to focus on 'theatrics,' an American usage that connotes not only activities of a theatrical character but behaviour that manifests itself as theatricality. The correspondence selected for the volume – most of it hitherto unpublished and none of it previously 'collected' – relates to Bernard Shaw's theatre dealings and theatrical interests, at the same time attesting to the 'histrionic instinct' and 'theatrified imagination' (his own phrases) of the man who penned them. The letters reveal a consummate man of the theatre, one man in his time playing many parts: dramatist, director, actor, designer, publicist, financial backer, translator, critic; immersed in such varied concerns as play licensing, censorship, theatre politics, box-office prices and ticket sales, managers, royalties, rehearsal secrecy, cutting of texts, prying journalists, 'blacklegging' playwrights, amateur societies, early-door policy, theatre staffing, condition of playhouses, programs, and wireless and television performances.

One hundred and fifteen correspondents are represented. (To avoid duplication of correspondence scheduled for other volumes in the Toronto edition of Shaw's correspondence, letters to William Archer, Gilbert Murray, and Augustin Hamon, Shaw's French translator, have been excluded.) Correspondents are addressed according to their needs, reflecting Shaw's perceptiveness of individual personalities and psyches, as he teases or mocks or cajoles, or soft-pedals with blarney. The letters, under his dramatic skill, are shaded with histrionic tones of assumed anger, of irritation, of anguish. The style invariably is colloquial, free-flowing, ebullient – and personal.

No effort has been made to place the correspondence in historic or social context or to give it a biographical locus. The outside world intrudes into or impinges on the theatrical otherworld of 'G.B.S.' only by occasional reference in the correspondence and necessitous brief annotation relating thereto.

Shaw's texts, as has become customary in scholarly editions of his work, retain his idiosyncracies of spelling and punctuation, though a few instances of careless spelling or grammar have been silently corrected. As Shaw habitually misspelled proper names these are left unaltered in the text, with corrected spelling provided in editorial head- or endnotes. Unless otherwise stated, the dates given for plays are dates of composition. Years of birth and death, when ascertainable, are supplied for contemporary personages, and selectively for others, omitting dates for major historical figures like Henry VIII and Disraeli, Shakespeare and Ibsen. The correspondence has been judiciously trimmed to eliminate non-theatre-related subject-matter, repetitions, or inconsequential references that would have demanded extensive wasteful annotation. Omissions in the text are indicated by ellipsis marks; a few postscripts have been silently lopped off. Shorthand transcriptions are the combined work of John Wardrop and Barbara Smoker, to whom I am, as on several previous occasions, much indebted.

Provenance has been provided for correspondence so far as it has been possible to do so. In several instances, however, correspondence transcribed more than thirty years ago by courtesy of the recipients or their heirs and executors has later been dispersed through auction houses and autograph dealers, vanishing into private collections. I have identified these as 'present source unknown.'

Material sufficient to place each letter in its context is provided in the form of a headnote preceding the letter. Less-essential annotative matter follows the letter, the subject of each annotation (as referred to in the letter) being in boldface type. Necessary editorial interruptions – where, for example, a word or phrase must be conjectured or a name completed – are placed in square brackets, with conjectured text in regular type and editorial italicized.

Acknowledgments

Over the past thirty years I have received the generous cooperation and inestimable assistance of many individuals, among whom are several, now deceased, whom I should like once more to salute for contributions posthumously valuable to *Theatrics*: the inordinately generous Bernard F. Burgunder, who built a superb Shaw collection for Cornell, and who was for two decades a Shavian surrogate parent and unbilled collaborator; Raymond Mander and Joe Mitchenson, longtime colleagues and friends, whose vast British theatre collection and prodigious knowledge of British theatre have enriched every Shaw work I have produced; Ivo L. Currall, Lew David Feldman, T. Edward Hanley, David M. Holtzmann, Donald F. Hyde, Harry Mushlin, and Robert H. Taylor.

I gratefully acknowledge also the assistance of the late Virginia Ackert, Dr Sidney P. Albert, Dr Jacques Barzun, Patrick Beech, Winton Dean, Robin Dower, Geraldine Duclow (Head, Theatre Collection, Free Library of Philadelphia), Dr Bernard F. Dukore, Samuel N. Freedman, Professor Reavley Gair and the J. Nugent Monck Estate, Jack Hall, Sir Rupert Hart-Davis, Mary Hyde (Lady Eccles), Caroline Jones (Deputy Archivist, St Bartholomew's Hospital), John Kirkpatrick (Bibliographer, Harry Ransom Humanities Research Center), Professor Margery M. Morgan, Paul S. Newman, Richard O'Donoghue (former Administrator-Director of the Royal Academy of Dramatic Art), Kate Perry (Archivist, Girton College, Cambridge), Ellen Pollock, Charles Sachs of The Scriptorium, the late Philip Sang, Lewis Sawin, Leo T. Sides, Donald Sinden, Dr Samuel A. Weiss, and the staffs of the Billy Rose Theatre Collection, New York Public Library for the Performing Arts; the Honnold Library, Claremont, California; the Elizabeth Coates Maddux Library, Trinity University, San Antonio; and the University of Guelph Library (especially its Special Collections librarian, Nancy Sadek).

And to the patient and pragmatic General Editor of this series, Dr J. Percy Smith, whose wise judgment and eagle eye have provided guidance in the preparation of *Theatrics*, I offer most sincere thanks.

Grateful acknowledgment is made to the following institutions for permission to publish correspondence from their collections; and to the directors, curators, and librarians who have provided much-valued assistance:

Boston University: Mugar Memorial Library. Howard B. Gotlieb, Director.

British Broadcasting Corporation (BBC): Written Archives Centre. Jacqueline Kavanagh, Written Archives Officer.

British Library (BL): Department of Manuscripts. Dr Anne Summers, Curator for Shaw Archive; Kathryn Johnson, Curator in charge of Lord Chamberlain Papers.

Churchill Archives Centre: By permission of the Master, Fellows and Scholars of Churchill College in the University of Cambridge.

Colgate University: Leverett Needham Case Library, Richard S. Weiner Collection of George Bernard Shaw. Melissa McAfee, former Head, Special Collections.

Cornell University: Carl A. Kroch Library. Bernard F. Burgunder Shaw Collection. Dr James Tyler, Curator of the Burgunder Shaw Collection.

Dartmouth College Library. Philip N. Cronenwett, Head, Special Collections.

Folger Shakespeare Library, Washington, DC.

Free Library of Philadelphia: Rare Book Department.

Garrick Club, London. Enid M. Foster, Librarian.

Hampden-Booth Theatre Library, Players Club, New York. Raymond Wemmlinger, Curator and Librarian.

Harry Ransom Humanities Research Center (HRC): University of Texas at Austin. Cathy Henderson, Research Librarian.

Harvard College Library: Harvard Theatre Collection. Jeanne T. Newlin, Curator.

Hofstra University, Hempstead, New York. Axinn Library. Barbara M. Kelly, Curator of Special Collections.

Honnold Library of the Claremont Colleges, Claremont, California.

Hyde Collection, Somerville, New Jersey.

King's College Library, Cambridge. Jacqueline Cox, Modern Archivist.

Manchester (England) Central Library.

National Library of Ireland: By permission of the Trustees.

National Library of Scotland: By permission of the Trustees.

New York Public Library (NYPL) for the Performing Arts: Billy Rose Theatre Collection. Bob Taylor, Curator; Mary Ellen Rogan, Archivist.

New York University (NYU): Elmer Holmes Bobst Library, Fales Library. Frank Walker, Fales Librarian.

Pierpont Morgan Library, New York City. Charles E. Pierce, Jr, Director.

Princeton University Library: Robert H. Taylor Collection and George
    C. Tyler Collection. Margaret M. Sherry, Reference Librarian/Archi-
    vist, Rare Books and Special Collections.
Shubert Archive, New York City. Dr Brooks McNamara, Director.
Theatre Museum, London. Claire Hudson, Director of Library Services.
    By permission of the Trustees of the Victoria and Albert Museum.
Universal City (Texas) Public Library.
University of Delaware Library, Newark, Delaware. Timothy D. Murray,
    Head, Special Collections.
University of Newcastle upon Tyne and The Trustees of the Trevelyan
    family papers.
University of North Carolina at Chapel Hill: Southern Historical Collec-
    tion. Richard A. Shrader, Archivist.
University of Pennsylvania: Van Pelt Library, Ada Rehan Papers. Nancy
    M. Shawcross, Curator of Manuscripts.
University of Virginia: Alderman Library, Edwin A. Alderman Papers,
    Department of Special Collections. Michael Plunkett, Curator of
    Manuscripts and Archivist.
Washington University Libraries: Olin Library, Department of Special
    Collections. Kevin Ray, Curator of Manuscripts.
Yale University: Collection of American Literature, Beinecke Rare Book
    and Manuscript Library.

The Editor also acknowledges with thanks the cooperation of the Honnold Library, in supplying a transcription of a Shaw letter to Ellen Terry
in its Norman Philbrick Collection, and to the Royal Academy of Dramatic Art (RADA), London, for a photocopy of a Shaw letter to an unidentified correspondent (no. 109) in its Ivo L. Currall Collection
(Scrapbook no. 31, f 58).

D.H.L.

Abbreviations

ALS	Autograph letter signed
APCS	Autograph postcard signed
HD	Holograph draft
inc	Incomplete
LCP(C)	Lord Chamberlain Papers (Correspondence), BL
mic	Microfilm
p	Photocopy
t	Typewritten signature
TLS	Typewritten letter signed
u	Unsigned

Letters

1 / To Janet Achurch   29 Fitzroy Square W
                                            21st June 1889

[ALS: HRC]

Shaw, attending the first performance of Henrik Ibsen's A Doll's House *in the William Archer translation, was hopelessly smitten by the actress Janet Achurch (1864–1916), who, with her husband Charles Charrington (1860?–1926), had produced the play out of pocket on 7 June. At the end of the brief engagement at the Novelty Theatre the Charringtons departed for a two-year Australian tour, which was negotiated to provide funds, by mortgaging their salaries, for the production costs of the Ibsen play. Shaw viewed the play for a second time on the 11th, again on the 20th, and once more on the 29th for the closing performance. His letter of 21 June, he confided to his diary, had taken 'all the forenoon' to write.*

Dear Miss Achurch

The world has vanished: the gardens of heaven surround me. I thought I was old – that youth was gone – that I should never be in love again in the starry way of the days before the great Disillusion; and lo! it is all back again, with the added wisdom to know my own happiness. I desire nothing: I hope for nothing: I covet nothing: I possess, enjoy, exult: the coward rejoices and is brave: the egotist loves and is not jealous. Come: set me some hard, squalid, sordid drudgery – twenty years of it to gain an inch of ground. Away with you to Australia – for ever, if you will. See whether that prospect will dash me one jot! I have drunk the elixir of life – twice – a quarter to nine and a quarter past eleven; and now Time is vanquished. Change, fade, become a mere actress, spoil, wreck yourself, lose yourself, forget yourself: I shall still possess you in your first perfection. I have enjoyed: now let me work for the rest of my life.

All this is by kind permission of Charles Charrington Esquire, the burden bearer and harvest reaper: lesser than Macbeth, & greater: not so happy, yet much happier.

I should have answered your letter last night; but I was afraid of writing extravagantly; so I slept over it.

In proof of my sobriety, here are two pieces of advice which proclaim the inflexible intelligence behind the intoxicated, enamoured will. 1. There are certain very natural and expressive facial tricks which involve a slight, whimsical screwing of the mouth to one side. You tried one of them last night in the 1st act. Avoid them as you would the plague. They always evolve into horrible paralytic distortions . . . 2. Keep your chin loose. Never let emotion concentrate itself in your lower jaw. Your remote ancestors, when strongly moved, always prepared *to bite*; and it is that bad habit which makes it so difficult to teach dramatic natures how to sing or speak. No power and beauty of touch and tone can come from between jaws that are *set*. If you want to steady your voice by setting something, set the back of your mouth round and open, and pull against it by setting *down* your diaphragm (a sort of shelf with which your inside is provided a little above the waist).

Will you send me Herman Vezin's address; and will you, at the same time, incidentally mention when you are going away; so that if I call I may not arrive too late and be driven to walk straight down to the bridge and over the parapet? And will you thaw Archer & tempt him to write a play? He wants to; they all want to; but he could do it if he were first broken in pieces and melted up – a quite possible consummation. . . .

Heavens! the day is half gone: am I mad to waste my time like this, writing absurd letters to spoiled young women? Well, well: there is Australia ahead: that is one comfort . . .

G. Bernard Shaw

Hermann **Vezin** (1829–1910), American-born leading man with the Henry Irving (1838–1905) company, played Eilert Lövborg in the production. The translator, William **Archer** (1856–1924), was dramatic critic of the *World*; he did not write a successful play until *The Green Goddess* (1920).

2 / To Tighe Hopkins   29 Fitzroy Square W
                                                        2nd September 1889

[ALS: Cornell]

Tighe Hopkins (1856–1919), journalist and novelist, was a contributor to the New Review, *whose editor was Archibald Grove (1854–1920). Hopkins had been introduced to Shaw by Jane Patterson (1840?–1924), whose affections and bed had been shared by both.*

Dear Hopkins

. . . What is this you say about Grove? Does he want an article? Will he pay? How much? I will see him boiled in hissing hell sulphur before exhibiting my dialogues to him; but for greed of gain I do not mind writing for his pestiferous rag, ruined as I am by days spent in proof reading of Fabian essays, & Sundays in spouting to raise the wind for the dockers.

Never fear: my comedy will not be unactable when the time comes for it to be acted, though perhaps it may be obsolete then. I have the instinct of an artist; and the impracticable is loathsome to me. But not only has the comedy to be made, but the actors, the manager, the theatre & the audience. Somebody must do these things – somebody whose prodigious conceit towers over all ordinary notions of success – somebody who would blush to win a 600 nights run at a West End theatre as a duke would blush to win a goose at a public house raffle – some colossal egotist, in short, like

yrs in hot haste

GBS

The **comedy** was *The Cassone*, commenced in June 1889, which Shaw never completed. *Fabian Essays in Socialism*, edited by Shaw, was published in December. The **dock workers** had begun a thirty-day strike for better wages, which resulted in an increase of sixpence per hour. Although Shaw was a frequent orator at the London docks, there is no evidence in his diary that he spoke for the dockers during the strike, though he attended (and perhaps addressed) a dockers' meeting in Hyde Park on 8 September.

3 / To Elizabeth Robins   Aerated Bread Shop, Strand WC

After Hedda Gabler

30th April 1891

[ALS: NYU]

The American actress Elizabeth Robins (1862–1952) gained attention in London through her productions of, and performances in, Ibsen's plays, commencing with The Pillars of Society *(1889). She and Marion Lea (1861–1944) presented William Archer's translation of* Hedda Gabler *at the Vaudeville Theatre on 20 April, with Robins as Hedda, Arthur Elwood (1850–1903) as Lövborg, Marion Lea as Thea, and Charles Sugden (1850–1921) as Judge Brack. Shaw attended the opening performance. His impressions, after a second viewing on the 30th, are scrawled in pencil across 18 small leaves extracted from a pocket notebook.*

Dear Miss Robins

Thank you for the stalls: I brought my mother, and gratified myself at the same time by going to see Hedda giving Lövborg the pistol with love in her eyes – a thing which has haunted me ever since Monday week. However, no living woman shall turn my head as you have turned Archer's: I have infinite fault to find. I declare before high heaven that you are guilty in the blackest degree of playing more and more up to the conventional villainess conception of Hedda. The first act today was perfect Richard III all through; and in the third you did not give him the pistol with love in your eyes worth a cent: I wanted my money back. I demand the following modifications of your play. In Act I, when Thea tells about the woman with the pistol whose shadow came between her and Lövborg, a keen pang of delight on Hedda's part should shine through Richard III for a moment. In Act III, when Thea leaves the stage deceived, and Lövborg turns to Hedda with the words 'To you I can tell the truth' the heavens should open for another moment, beginning the celestial transport in which alone she could give him the pistol (with love in her eyes, remember).

(I am no longer in the Aerated Bread Shop, but in an underground railway carriage; and consequently my writing deteriorates in point of legibility.)

In Act II, at the cue 'of the mistress of the house – and of the master too,' your play implied the conventional 'SIR!!!' Why should you hoist the flag of outraged virtue by that half rising, that proud shrinking? I assure you that Hedda is perfectly callous in the security of her contempt for Brack and her sense of having the pistol ready for him if he becomes troublesome. Besides, she is a woman who will talk about anything: she has absolutely no delicacy in that sense: she is the Englishwoman rather than the American. Note, for instance, the brutality of her remark to Brack that she would like to overhear the conversation at the orgie. Your omission of that line is a piece of what Lövborg calls Thea's 'stupidity.' I do not suggest that you should stab yourself every day by restoring it; but I do plead against any sensitiveness with Brack's proposals. On the other hand, it would not be amiss to squirm a little when you are described in Act I as 'looking flourishing.' Would not 'flourishing,' by the bye, supply the wanted synonym for 'filled out'?

I still protest vehemently against 'Do it gracefully.' Archer has reproached me for doing you the injustice of offering you a sordid motive for restoring the original text; but I maintain that a woman who would alter that passage would do anything. If ever I take to the stage and play Lövborg to your Hedda, then, if you say 'Do it gracefully' I will at once reply, 'Yes, madam: it shall be done in the best style, regardless of expense. I shall be careful to brush my hair, scent my handkerchief, wear a new pair of gloves and my best hat.'

The people in the pit behind me today could not make out the stove in the first act. At last one lady explained that it was a safe. Elwood was quite inaudible in the album scene, as you probably gathered from the agonized remonstrance of the far back pittite. . . .

I congratulate you on your transfer to the evening bill. Judging from the fate of the solitary anti-Ibsenite who hissed at the end of the first act today, you have nothing to fear from any opposition that may be organized except redoubled applause by way of counter demonstration.

yrs very truly

G. Bernard Shaw

4 / To Amy Lawrence 29 Fitzroy Square W
27th January 1893

[APCS: Swann Galleries, New York; sold 6 May 1976]

Amy Lawrence, a young postal worker and socialist lecturer, became a member of the Fabian Society in July 1893. She has hitherto been confused by Shaw research-ers with an unrelated Girton College graduate of the same name (1872–1934).

Widowers' Houses is in the printer's hands; but when it will be out of them is more than I can say.

What on earth do people mean by 'types'? I suppose you and I are types of the people who are just like us; but that seems hardly worth say-ing. There was no intention to make anybody in the play more of a type than that. When you read it you will find Blanche natural enough. Owing to difficulties which the public knew nothing about & which were the fault of circumstances alone, the representation was not quite successful in bringing out the provocation under which the young lady acted.

GBS

Widowers' Houses was published in May 1893 as No. 1 of the Independent Theatre Series. The young lady who performed **Blanche** in the Independent Theatre production staged by Shaw at the Royalty Theatre on 9–10 December 1892 was Florence Farr (1860–1917), who since late 1890 had shared an amorous relationship with Shaw.

5 / To Oscar Wilde

29 Fitzroy Square W
28th February 1893

[ALS: Mary Hyde]

Oscar Wilde (1854–1900) and Shaw never were friends, but maintained a cordial relationship for several years, exchanging books on publication.

My dear Wilde

Salomé is still wandering in her purple raiment in search of me; and I expect her to arrive a perfect outcast, branded with inky stamps, bruised by flinging from hard hands into red prison vans, stifled and contaminated by herding with review books in the World cells, perhaps outraged by some hasty literary pathologist whose haste to lift the purple robe blinded him to the private name on the hem. In short, I suspect that they have muddled it up with the other books in York St.; and I have written to them to claim my own.

I have always said that the one way of abolishing the Censor is to abolish the Monarchy of which he is an appendage. But the brute could be lamed if only the critics and authors would make real war on him. The reason they wont is that they are all Puritans at heart. And the coming powers – the proletarian voters – will back their Puritanism unless I can lure the Censor into attacking the political freedom of speech on the stage. I enclose you a red bill to shew you what I mean. That bill was designed by the active spirits of the dock district at the east end. Observe the H stuck into the middle of my plain Bernard (I wonder they did not make it Bernhardt), and the title 'Democratic IDEALS,' all their own 'taste.' There is political life and hope in the bill; but as far as Art is concerned, there is all Maida Vale, with the great Academic desert beyond, for them to pass through before they enter into the Promised Land – an ocean of sentimentality, dried up on the farther coast into a Sahara of pedantry. That is what we have to half fight down, half educate up, if we are to get rid of Censorships, official and unofficial. And when I say we, I mean Morris the Welshman and Wilde and Shaw the Irishmen; for to learn from Frenchmen is a condescension impossible for an Englishman.

I hope soon to send you my play 'Widowers' Houses,' which you will find tolerably amusing, considering that it is a farcical comedy. Unfortunately I have no power of producing beauty: my genius is the genius of intellect, and my farce its derisive brutality. Salomé's purple garment would make Widowers' Houses ridiculous; but you are precisely the man to appreciate it on that account.

I saw Lady Windermere's Fan in its early days, & have often wished to condole with you – since nobody else did – on the atrocious acting of it. I except Marion Terry, and I let off poor Lilian Hanbury, whose fault was want of skill rather than want of enlightenment; but all the rest were damnable, utterly damnable. I hope you will follow up hard on that trail; for the drama wants building up very badly; and it is clear that your work lies there. Besides, you have time and opportunity for work, which none of the rest of us have. And that reminds me of the clock; so farewell for the moment.

GBS

The **red prison vans** were postal trucks, in one of which the not-yet-received copy of *Salomé* had travelled. **World cells** refers to the cramped offices of the weekly journal in York Street for which Shaw supplied music criticism and reviews. The **red bill** enclosed by Shaw was a flyer for a lecture scheduled for delivery at the Poplar dock gates on Sunday morning, 26 February. Shaw's diary entry indicates he 'went down to the Docks, but it was too wet for the meeting.' Shaw and Wilde were devotees of William **Morris** (1834–96), writer, artist, reformer, publisher. Shaw was attracted principally by Morris's political and social philosophy, Wilde by his poetry and aesthetics.

Lady Windermere's Fan was first presented at the St James's Theatre, 20 February 1892; Shaw and Florence Farr had seen it on 6 April. Marion **Terry** (1852–1930), sister of Ellen Terry (1847–1928), created the role of Mrs Erlynne. Lilian (later Lily) **Hanbury** (1874–1908) was a theatre newcomer to whom Shaw was considerably less kind in his notice in the *Saturday Review* (19 October 1895) of her performance in the A.W. Pinero (1855–1934) play *The Benefit of the Doubt* than he was in his private comment to Wilde.

6 / To Lady Colin Campbell   29 Fitzroy Square W
                                                   4th May 1893

[ALS: Paul S. Newman]

Irish-born Gertrude Blood (1858–1911), widow of Lord Colin Campbell, fifth son of the Eighth Duke of Argyll, from whom she had been judicially separated since 1884, earned her living as a journalist, succeeding Shaw as art critic of the World. *Oscar Wilde's* A Woman of No Importance, *at the Haymarket Theatre since 19 April, had apparently vexed her. Shaw was prevented by his music-reviewing commitments from seeing the play, though he made an abortive effort in May. It was Lady Colin Campbell who labelled Wilde 'the great white caterpillar.'*

You are wrong to rail thus at Oscar. One of the first lessons that Socialism has to teach you is always to play up for your own side. There are only two literary schools in England today: the Norwegian School and the Irish school. Our school is the Irish school; and Wilde is doing us good service in teaching the theatrical public that 'a play' may be a playing with ideas instead of a feast of sham emotions compounded from dog's eared prescriptions. Compare his epigrams with the platitudes of the rest – and this is taking him beyond all bounds in his praise. No, let us be just to the great white caterpillar: he is no blockhead and he finishes his work, which puts him high above his rivals here in London. . . .

GBS

7 / To Elizabeth Robins 29 Fitzroy Square W
14th November 1893

[ALS: NYU]

'Heilige Elisabeth
Bitte für mich' ['Saint Elizabeth, pray for me']: I am at my wit's end about this unlucky play of mine. Oh, if you were only fifteen years older: I would have you in that part in spite of General Gabler's pistol. I read the great scene to Mrs Wright; and she rose up; declared that not even in her own room could she speak the part to herself, much less in public to a younger woman; delivered a magnificent impromptu tirade which I will certainly dramatise some day; rushed out of the room in disorder; and came back in ten minutes to hear the rest of the play. Do you know any woman between forty and fifty who wants such another chance as Mrs Wright got in Ghosts and will be able to make the most of it? . . . Grein is bent on having a play by me; and I really haven't time

to write a third one this season. Of course it would be easy to get some-body who would play the part out of sheer callousness; but such a per-son will not do: the play is not an *immoral* one, and the right woman ought to have the courage for it. You *must* think of someone: otherwise you will simply have to make up middle-aged and do it for me yourself.

GBS

Shaw's **unlucky play** was *Mrs Warren's Profession*, completed a fortnight earlier. **General Gabler's pistol** is a teasing allusion to Robins's threat, when Shaw interviewed her the previous February, to shoot him if he published anything she did not approve of (see Shaw, *Diaries*, ed. Stanley Weintraub, 1986, p. 902). Mrs Theodore **Wright** (1846?–1922) was Mrs Alving in the Archer translation of Ibsen's *Ghosts* staged on 13 March 1891 by the Independent Theatre Club, newly founded by the critic and playwright J.T. **Grein** (1862–1935).

8 / To Charles Charrington

[21 Elm Park Road SW
21 March 1894]
3.55 [p.m.]

[ALS: HRC]

Arms and the Man *was hastily completed for Florence Farr's season at the Ave-nue Theatre, where it opened on 21 April. Shaw was not privy to the secret involvement of Annie Horniman (1860–1937) as financial backer of Farr, hence his reference to the 'mysterious management.'*

Dear Charrington

I want to know what terms I should exact from the mysterious manage-ment at the Avenue. A proposal has been made, as follows: – 5% on gross receipts for 50 nights, 6% on subsequent nights; £25 down, to be deducted from percentage, if any; and my British rights to be assigned for a term of years. To this I have replied provisionally that I will assign nothing but the London rights for the run, and that I am prepared to forego all fees if the piece fails. The £25 I repudiate wholly. What, under these circumstances, ought I to demand in the way of percent-age, assuming that the piece succeeds? I want to drive a fair bargain, as on the one hand I do not want to use my influence with F.F. to get more than my due; and on the other I do not want to blackleg dramatic authordom by taking too little & running down prices. Being new to the trade and its customs I should like to have your opinion (which ought to be an exceptionally judicial one as that of an author-actor-manager) as to what I should propose.

When I had altered the third act after our late discussion of it, I read it to Stepniak, who greatly terrified me by inviting the admiral of the Bulgarian fleet to assist. I fully expected to get my throat cut; but he fortunately turned out to be a Russian. The play proved impossible from beginning to end. I have had to shift the scene from Servia to Bulgaria, and to make the most absurd alterations in detail for the sake of local color, which, however, is amusing & will intensify the extravagance of the play & give it realism at the same time.

I am staying down at Oxted just now . . . and must return by the 5 train from Victoria: otherwise I should wait & communicate these details by word of mouth. . . .

GBS

Sergius **Stepniak** (pseudonym of Sergei Kravchinski, 1825–95) was a Russian nihilist resident in London. The **admiral** was a Russian naval defector and nihilist, Esper Aleksandrovich Serebryekov (1854–1921), who had sought asylum in Britain. Shaw wrote the letter at Charrington's flat.

9 / To Max Hecht

29 Fitzroy Square W

27th June 1896

[ALS: present source unknown]

Max Hecht (1844–1908) was a financier and theatrical investor, whose syndicate, after receiving a script of Shaw's You Never Can Tell, *contracted with actor-manager Cyril Maude (1862–1951) and his new partner Frederick Harrison (1853–1926), manager of the Haymarket Theatre, for a production of the play.*

Dear Mr Hecht

Charrington has sounded me on the subject of my new play at your suggestion. However, there is no difficulty in the matter. You will understand that my position as critic makes it very difficult for me to offer a play to a manager; but, as it happens, the difficulty was removed in this case by Cyril Maude taking the initiative. When the play was finished in the rough, I offered to read it to him, thinking that he might possibly like to get that much beforehand with it. But he either could not face that ordeal (a horribly disagreeable and inconvenient one usually) or else was not in a hurry: at all events he elected to read it himself, which involves waiting until I have worked out all the stage business and procured half-a-dozen duplicate prompt copies, a thing not easily to be done in the thick of the season. The only man who had the gumption to face a reading was Alexander, who will accordingly have the first peep. I very much doubt whether I shall be able to get the copies ready until it is too late for the winter season. I have to go to Bayreuth for the first set of Ring performances there; then back for the International Socialist Congress here; then to Brittany & perhaps to Italy for an absolutely necessary holiday. All that is not favorable to finishing the stage detail of the play. All I can do meanwhile is to read it if required to anyone who will stand it.

yrs sincerely

G. Bernard Shaw

George **Alexander** (1858–1918) was one of London's leading actor-managers, at the St James's Theatre. Though Shaw on several occasions negotiated with him, Alexander never produced or appeared in a Shaw play. Shaw attended the **Bayreuth** *Ring* cycle 19–22 July, returning for the International Socialist Trades Congress, in London, 27 July–1 August. The visits to Brittany and Italy were cancelled.

10 / To Sir Henry Irving

29 Fitzroy Square [W]

12th July 1896

[Shorthand: HRC]

Sir Henry Irving, knighted in 1895 (the first actor in modern times thus honoured) was the most celebrated actor-manager of the 19th-century British stage. Shaw and Irving's leading lady Ellen Terry had, since November 1895, engaged in an epistolary conspiracy to inveigle Irving into scheduling a Lyceum Theatre production of Shaw's play The Man of Destiny *(1895).*

Dear Sir Henry Irving

Miss Ellen Terry has asked me to communicate with you about The Man of Destiny.

What I propose is this. (1) That you give half a dozen performances of the play in London in 1897, in addition to any preliminary trial you may wish to make in the provinces, you playing Napoleon and Miss Terry the Strange Lady. (2) That if these performances do not take place until the winter season, you will publicly announce them before the end of the summer season, not necessarily [officially], but in some sufficient way – a speech before the curtain, for instance. (3) That the six performances be given within three consecutive weeks, and be advertised beforehand as limited to that number; so that their discontinuance cannot be mistaken for a withdrawal in consequence of failure. (4) That if the result of these six performances or any provincial preliminary ones be unsatisfactory, you hand me back the play as of no use to you, without any further responsibility in connection with it. (5) That if you decide to place it in the Lyceum repertory, you have the right to do so on the following terms. In 1898 you will, in the course of the year, give not less than 16 performances of the piece (on consecutive nights or not just as you please), at least six of them being in America. (6) That you pay me 3 guineas for each performance, including those in 1897. (I say guineas so as to make the minimum authors' fees come to £50 a year.) (7) That the part of Napoleon is to be played by you, and that of the Strange Lady by Miss Terry. (8) That outside the area affected by your English and American tours the rights are to be still at my disposal. (9) That copyright – as distinguished from stage right – remains with me. (10) That my name appears in all programs, advertisements, and other announcements of the play. (11) [That] you [are] to have the option of renewing the agreement from year to year under the like conditions, the understanding being that if you do not give me notice to the contrary before the 1st October in any year, the agreement shall hold good for the following year, and so on from year to year for 5 years beginning 1st January 1898. (12) That in the event of the stipulated number of performances not being given in any year I am to receive fees as if the full number had been given, and to have the option of terminating the agreement at the end of the year.

If this will do, send me the briefest word on a postcard, and I will draft an agreement and submit it to you. If I have forgotten anything from your point of view, as I very likely have, I can add the necessary clauses if you will make note of them for me. Or if you prefer to draft the agreement yourself, that will suit me equally well – I have only proposed the conditions to save you as much trouble as possible.

I am taking it for granted that America will henceforth be a regular part of your program; but if I am wrong we can leave America out of the question.

I am heartily sorry that the play is so trivial an affair; but when I wrote it I had no idea it would be so fortunate. Even now I am not quite persuaded that it is more than a fancy of Miss Terry's. If so, and a performance or two on some special occasion – a benefit or anything of that sort – would meet the case, I should of course be delighted to license any such representation without any question of terms.

[unsigned]

'As I daresay you know,' Irving replied on 15 July, 'the exigencies and conditions of management are such that it is an almost impossible thing to undertake to produce a one-act piece at any given time; so if you will allow me what I would suggest is this: I shall do my best with the play if you care to entrust it to me and I think that you will feel quite safe in such case. For the sole rights for Britain (and her colonies) and America I would pay you for three years commencing with 1897 a minimum sum of £50 per annum calculated at three guineas for each performance so that if in any year your play was given more than sixteen times you would receive proportionately. After the third year I should pay you three guineas for each performance. Your name would of course be always duly announced. It is of course my intention that I should play Napoleon and Ellen Terry the Strange Lady but of course in case of death or illness we should have to do the best we could. You will understand that I would do my best to carry out your wishes in all ways. I only mention these points in case of contingencies' (Shaw's typewritten transcription, British Library of Political and Economic Science).

11 / To Sir Henry Irving   29 Fitzroy Square [W]
17th July 1896

[HD: HRC]
Shaw, in the knowledge that actor-managers were notorious for bribing drama

critics by buying outright, then shelving, their plays, was being cagey in his nego-
tiations.

Dear Sir Henry Irving

Your proposal is quite reasonable, and yet it raises a host of difficulties
for me. You cannot secure me £50 for 1897 without performing the
play, because I have to make my living as a dramatic critic, and it is
impossible for a critic to take money except for actual performances
without placing both himself & the manager in a false position. That is
why I propose six performances in 1897 without any guarantee as to
fees. If it were inconvenient to give exactly 16 performances, I should
of course not mind taking £50 for a smaller number, provided the play
were really alive & in the repertory; but if I were to take it for a play
which simply lay on the shelf, I should be doing just what I have often
vehemently declared should never be done.

Again, it is a matter of very little consequence to you whether the
play is produced next year or in 1900 (say). Your battle is won: my
attack is only beginning. A production this winter would be worth far
more to me than one next winter, and one next winter than one in
1898. It is my business to get Napoleon done as soon as possible, and, if
no better way be [found], to write a new play for you for 1898 if you will
not be ready for me until then.

Yet another reason. I want Miss Terry to create the Strange Lady soon
after Imogen, because in both parts there is the same change of dress.
Of course if Cymbeline were to run all the year like Macbeth & Faust it
would alter the case; but that is hardly possible: the play is too childish,
and there is no adequate part for you in it. And, except in the case of a
run in a play already put up, the public must take what you choose to
give it.

There is another point. You say you want the rights for Britain & her
Colonies & America. But I am convinced that you dont realize how
large the world is – I only realize it myself because I have some friends
in the Colonial Office. Why, for instance, should you bargain for the
right to prevent the inhabitants of the Virgin Islands from ever seeing
the play performed by local talent? Then there is Australia, India, & the
Cape. You may never go there. If you do, you should guarantee me half

a dozen performances in each in addition to the 16 for England & America. And even in England & America there are many places where you will not only never play, but where a performance could no more emerge from obscurity or touch your interests than one given in Siberia. That is why I propose the areas affected by your tours. I am quite willing that you should have every particle of the rights that you can use, or that can be used by others to your disadvantage or annoyance, for as long as it is worth your while to use them; but dont let us *waste* anything.

In all other respects my proposals, I think, cover your points. They enable you to drop the play at any time; and if, in renewing for the fourth year, you propose to discontinue the guarantee of £50, that is easily done. To save trouble, it can be expressed in the agreement so. The fact is, if the play proves worth anything, the part will be so identified with you, and my interest in it so bound up with yours, that if you will only guarantee me the production next year, the rest will follow automatically from our good understanding & common interest, agreement or no agreement.

I leave for Bayreuth this evening & will not be back until the end of next week.

very truly yours
[*unsigned*]

PS. As to 1897, I will make one concession. If you produce a play by Ibsen – say Peer Gynt or The Pretenders (you playing Peer or Bishop Nicholas) – then I will not only consent to a postponement of The Man of Destiny but will hand over the rights for all the world to you absolutely to do as you like with until your retirement, without fee or condition of any kind. But if you will excuse my saying so, I'm hanged if I'll be put off for Shakespear. Take him away: he lags superfluous.

Irving added *Cymbeline* to the Lyceum bill on 22 September. The friends of Shaw in the **Colonial Office** were Sidney Webb (1859–1947) and Sydney Olivier (1859–1943), both members with Shaw on the Fabian Society executive. Negotiations between Irving and Shaw were broken off, finally, in May 1897, a month after Irving presented a rival Napoleon play, *Madame Sans-Gêne*, by Victorien Sardou (1831–1908) and Émile Moreau (1852–1922). In his review Shaw described its Napoleon as 'rather better than Madame Tussaud's [*waxwork dummy*], and that is all that can be said for it' (*Saturday Review*, 17 April 1897).

12 / To Charles Charrington

The Rectory. Stratford St Andrew
Saxmundham
22nd August 1896

[ALS: HRC]

Shaw, who spent several weeks at Stratford St Andrew holidaying with Sidney and Beatrice Webb (1858–1943) and his future wife Charlotte Payne-Towns-hend (1857–1943), had that day completed the 'stage business' of You Never Can Tell *and arranged for the typing of a final prompt copy for Max Hecht, with a duplicate to Cyril Maude. His casting was premature and, as was almost always the case, more ideal than realistic. Eventually, after Evelyn Millard (1871–1941) had refused the role of Gloria, Maude's wife Winifred Emery (1862–1924) chose to play it, with Dolly assigned to Eva Moore (1870–1955).*

The game is as follows. Ever since Cyril Maude spoke of the possibility of Winifred Emery doing Dolly, my powerful mind has been playing more or less on the problem of how to enable her to do it without getting cut out as leading lady in her own theatre. With Evelyn Millard as Gloria this would inevitably occur, or with Julia Neilson, or anyone regularly in the popular fashionable ranks. But if somebody in a quite special position could be got – somebody whose engagement would be recognised on all hands as quite exceptional and relevant only to the advancedness of the play – then the matter might be arranged. Janet [Achurch] would not do, because she would wipe the floor not only with Dolly, but probably with the play as well – Winifred would quite certainly play Gloria ten times over sooner than let her have such a chance. But Elizabeth is supposed to be an entirely unsympathetic actress, playing from her head alone; and she would develop the proud, opinionated, unpopular side of Gloria – in fact, she would *be* Gloria. She would thus be rather a foil to the popular Dolly than otherwise. I do not think that Gloria can hurt the play if Valentine is a success; for the less sympathetic she is, the better she will feed him on the purely laughable plane. If he is a failure she cannot save the play no matter how good she is. On the other hand it is essential that Dolly should be thoroughly popular, which Winifred *is*. I do not think that Winifred will let Gloria slip – I could not honestly advise her to do it from her own point of view – but if she thinks otherwise, and Elizabeth plays Gloria as well as she played Hilda, that will do for me very well. A success would mean that there was money in the Ibsenite actress plus a play by Shaw; and that might smooth the obstacles out of the way of Candida. I fully expect that Winifred will receive my suggestion that she should not play Gloria by simply laying her finger alongside her nose; but if by any chance she should prefer to reaffirm her youth and prettiness as Dolly, then I think Elizabeth stands a rosy chance if I insist on her. This is entirely my own conception, born of the fact that Gloria is just as much a realistic study of the American woman as a poetical conception. Both Shakespear and I know what we are about better than you think. As to 'the obstacles with which she has surrounded her valuable &c &c,' have no concern about them. The great Boyg does not fight: he conquers. We are on excellent terms. I never allow my nonsense to interfere with my business, or anyone else's. . . .

GBS

Julia **Neilson** (1868–1957) had made a huge success in 1896 in *The Prisoner of Zenda* following her appearance opposite her husband Fred Terry (1864–1932) in Wilde's *A Woman of No Importance* (1893). **Elizabeth** Robins played **Hilda** Wangel in Ibsen's *The Master Builder.* The **great Boyg** is a character in Ibsen's *Peer Gynt.*

13 / To Max Hecht   Stratford St Andrew Rectory
                                        Saxmundham
                                        28th August 1896

[ALS: present source unknown]
A 'syndicate' in Shaw's day was theatre parlance for any group of investors in stage productions. Today these investors are known as 'backers' or 'angels.' Syndicates were formed for a single production, for a single theatre management, or for investment in multiple enterprises.

Dear Mr Hecht

I presume you have the play by this time: Miss Dickens sent me a copy the day before yesterday.

My difficulty about the syndicate is not at all in reference to the payment of tantièmes. That will be all right. The point that concerns me is the possibility of my play getting locked up in such a way that it belongs to neither myself nor to anyone else; but to a number of people who are making no use of it. Suppose the syndicate were to drop their enterprise after a few months' trial. They could dispose of their scenery & costumes easily enough by simply selling them to the highest bidder. But no author in his senses would enter into an agreement giving a manager power to dispose of a stage right without the author's approval. Therefore it might easily happen that every one of the parties might have the power to prevent the others from dealing with the stage right, whilst at the same time he would have no power to deal with it himself.

Now if the transaction were an ordinary business one, you would dispose of this by simply saying that business cannot be conducted at all except on the assumption that men will be reasonable enough to consent to act in their own interest and not to obstruct the sale of their own property wantonly. Unfortunately, there is this peculiarity about theatrical business – that managers, when they are actors, will refuse all offers and disregard all interests sooner than allow a good part or a good play to get into the hands of a professional rival. The fact is, there is hardly an actor-manager in London who is not sitting tightly on some play which he will neither produce himself nor let anyone else produce. Under these circumstances an author is forced to stipulate that the play shall be produced within a given period, that if the management suspends business the rights shall thereupon revert to the author, and that there shall be no right of assignment or transfer or subletting without the author's approval. The agreement is, in short, not an assignment of the stage right, but a licence to perform during such & such a period and on such & such conditions.

Do not be alarmed at all this bargaining: I only put it to you because the peculiar nature of theatrical business makes it necessary to provide against contingencies which are contrary to the very nature of ordinary commercial business. If you give up the enterprise after a year or so & wind up the syndicate, you will find that Cyril Maude will take a much more complicated view of the disposal of stage rights than you will. If, for example, the assets of this nature include a play in which he has made a striking personal success, and another in which Miss Winifred Emery has done the same, it will be your interest simply to get the best terms in the market for those rights. But it will be Mr Cyril Maude's interest before everything to prevent those parts falling into anyone's hands except his own & Miss Emery's. That interest might very easily conflict seriously with yours and the author's. For my part I wish the law as to property of this kind could be entirely altered; but that is too long a story to go into here.

I strongly advise you to get that other £5,000. The truth is, £10,000 is not enough, except for a strictly limited experiment with non-commercial aims. It is appallingly possible to lose £10,000 in three months. The current expenses at the very lowest (and it is not your interest to keep them down to that) will be £500 a week; and nobody knows, unless they have counted the returns, how desperately little the public pay when they do not rush to the opposite extreme. If you only have £10,000, the attractiveness of the play with which you open becomes a matter of first-rate importance; and I doubt whether you ought to venture without a dramatist of established reputation – Pinero, Grundy or Jones. However, no doubt you have considered all this. Only, I should not like to become associated in your memory with a disappointment of any sort.

yrs sincerely
G. Bernard Shaw

Ethel **Dickens** (1864–1936), granddaughter of the late novelist, was the proprietor of a typewriting copy service, who supplied all of Shaw's prompt copies from the longhand drafts. Arthur **Pinero**, Sydney **Grundy** (1848–1914), and Henry Arthur **Jones** (1851–1929) were at the peak of their careers in the last decade of the century. They shortly would be supplanted by Shaw, J.M. Barrie (1860–1937), and John Galsworthy (1867–1933).

14 / To Janet Achurch   29 Fitzroy Square W
                                              7th September 1896

[ALS: HRC]

In 1895 the American actor-manager Richard Mansfield (1854–1907) engaged Janet Achurch to perform opposite him in Shaw's Candida *in New York. Mansfield, however, soon had second thoughts about the play (it was, he informed Shaw, 'of the impossible . . . three long acts of talk – talk – talk – no matter how clever that talk is – it is talk – talk – talk') and was repelled by the 'fuzzy-haired' actress ('I couldn't make love to your Candida . . . if I had taken ether' [14 April 1895: Shaw,* Collected Letters 1874–1897 *(1965), pp. 523–4]). When he cancelled the production Shaw informed him: '[Y]our acquaintance with my future plays will be acquired in the course of visits to other people's theatres' (19 April 1895; ibid., p. 522). A year later, however, he negotiated with Mansfield for* The Man of Destiny, *and in 1897 Mansfield staged the world première of* The Devil's Disciple.

. . . I have just had a long letter from Mansfield, very clever & very friendly. At present it seems to me that he will get Napoleon after all; for I have not heard further from Irving, and it seems possible that when I ask him to make up his mind, as I shall do when Cymbeline is launched, he may either be unable to do it or say no, in which case I shall send it to Richard without further ado. My chief anxiety is to conduct the matter without shewing any want of regard for H.I.: in fact, if he really wanted it for immediate use I should make him a present of it without hesitation, only unfortunately that would be quite the least advantageous way of settling the matter for him.

You Never Can Tell is now in the hands of the Haymarket syndicate, with all its stage business complete down to the details of the table service in the second act. Maude declares that he is delighted with it: Hecht, who has not heard it read, is, with respect to some of it, in much the same condition as Alexander. I have not heard from Harrison. Hecht urges me to come to his holiday retreat at Weybridge to discuss the matter at grand council. I, having spent as much time & pains on the wretched thing as I intend to spend without very solid reasons, point out that they can discuss it much more freely from their own standpoint in my absence, and, in effect, invite them to make the next move. If the affair falls through it will only renew my interest in the business and enable me to breathe more freely. What I want is a few more completed plays in hand. Then we could feel about for a syndicate to try a Shaw theatre, where we could all seriously learn our business. However, no more of that, or you will announce that you expect the project to be on foot and the Shaw theatre open before the end of October. . . .

GBS

Maude contracted for *You Never Can Tell* with a stipulation that Shaw direct the play. Dissatisfied with the casting and with the attitude of the performers towards their roles in rehearsal, Shaw suddenly asked to cancel the production, to which Maude, with alacrity, agreed.

15 / To Ellen Terry   29 Fitzroy Square W
                                                31st January 1897

[ALS: present source unknown; transcript: Honnold Library]

The frequently revived Olivia *by W. G. Wills (1828–91), from Oliver Goldsmith's novel* The Vicar of Wakefield, *had been restored to Henry Irving's stage the previous evening.*

Beautiful, beautiful – I cried like mad. Far better than in 1885, far, far, *far* better. (Only dont *slam* the window when you're running away: the Vicar might hear you.) I'll tell you all about it in the Saturday.

By the way, *do* make Thornhill cut those ridiculous, impossible, old fashioned asides.

Oh my heart! you and I were children again. And this time with the child's heart that real children – the little animals! – never have.

What a capital play it still contrives to be, even after Ibsen! I wonder will it run: all London, it seems to me, should crowd to see that third act. (By the way, dont push him aside merely: *hit* him as you did at the Court: otherwise the line 'I have lost even my womanhood' is unintelligible – you must really be angry & violent for the moment, with a quick revulsion.) . . .

Miss Milton did that remonstrance over the pistols very rightly. Vezin is better than H.I. as the Vicar. I do not say that he *does* better – always; but that he *is* better. H.I. could not resist putting on a beautiful dignity and looking hungrily round the room for you, and then saying 'I forget you sir' without the least beauty or dignity; but [Vezin], with perfect worried, indifferent-to-appearances *truth*, was more touching than you can imagine. H.I., breaking down in the attempt to lecture you, was shocking: he embraced you with the passion of a lover – even of a stage lover. He made the Vicar in the other scenes so *fine* by his execution, that he destroyed his credibility. Vezin is the very man; and with you as the veriest woman, the play resumes its old Court charm, which was lost when I saw it in 85. . . .

                                                            GBS

PS. After the play I wrote you a note begging you to let me come round and kiss you just once; but Stoker, whom I asked to deliver it, said that he had sworn to H.I. to prevent my communicating with you in any way if he could, and that the note should only reach you over his dead body. So I tore it up and crept weeping home.

Maud **Milton** (1855–1945) played Mrs Primrose, the Vicar's wife. Hermann Vezin succeeded Irving as the Vicar, with Frank Kemble Cooper (1857–1918) as the new Thornhill. In Shaw's notice in the *Saturday Review* on 6 February he reminisced, as in his letter, about the first production he had seen, at the Court Theatre in 1878 (two years after his arrival in London), reflecting his extraordinary ability to store and retrieve subtle details of theatrical performances viewed in his early theatre-going years. He had also seen it in 1885 at the Lyceum. In Act III the Vicar tells Thornhill: 'In my agony I cursed you – now sir I forget you.' Bram **Stoker** (1847–1912), author of the still-celebrated novel *Dracula*, published in 1897, had for 20 years been Irving's business manager and adviser.

16 / To Richard Mansfield

The Argoed. Penallt. Monmouth
[8 September 1897]

[HD: BL 50543, ff 84–7]

The letter as sent by Shaw to Mansfield has not survived. A few lines included in Paul Wilstach's biography of Mansfield (1909) were reproduced in the Shaw Collected Letters 1874–1897 (1965), as was a draft of an extended postscript located in the Humanities Research Center (not reprinted here). The draft text is published in extenso for the first time.

My dear Mansfield

In a month or two will appear, in England and America simultaneously, a couple of volumes of my plays, including Arms & the Man, Candida, The Man of Destiny and You Never Can Tell, as well as three earlier plays, Widowers' Houses, The Philanderer, & Mrs Warren's Profession. My description of Bluntschli will beat your best efforts off the stage, and as for Candida, your reputation will not survive the discovery of your monstrous error and sin in letting it slip through your fingers. I have made one or two slight alterations in the text of Arms and the Man, mostly affecting Petkoff; but I am more than ever convinced of what I told you from the beginning – that Sergius is the part that requires playing.

The publication of this book may boom me a little; so have The Devil's Disciple ready in case anything of the sort occurs. Never mind the third act: it will probably fail – *certainly*, if it is not played with perfect conviction and careful attention to military routine – but no matter: I shall not be able to alter it to any purpose for three or four years; and even then I shall make it impossible instead of merely difficult as it is now. Forbes Robertson wants me to write a suitable last act, in which Mrs Patrick Campbell's charms will not be resisted; but I wont. I maintain that if Burgoyne is played by a man capable of believing, or seeming to believe, in him, and if you can get clean beyond all sentimental love rubbish and give the full force and mystery (to the public) of the man to whom neither Judith nor Anderson are more than other women & men, and who yet goes to the gallows for them by the law of his own nature, then it will be all right. Its quite simple: get all the drill & uniforms as smart as in Verestchagin's picture of Blowing the Indian Mutineers from the Guns (where the gay sunlight and the pleasant, paradelike look of the men & guns make a prosaic horror by the absence of horror); stand still and say the things as if you believed them; and nothing worse can happen to you than financial ruin, which is one of the inevitable accidents of your profession.

Shakespear is popular here now: the public have just grown up to him, and at last his plays are making their way on the stage much as he wrote them. Even Timon would draw for one night, as many people like to add to the number of Shakespear's plays they have seen acted. But I dont advise you to meddle with it. As there is no woman in it except an unmentionable one who does nothing seductive, it has to stand by its poetry & philosophy; and as the philosophy is a depressing sham, ending in nothing, and the poetry is not irresistible, it would only have a brief success of curiosity even if you spent thousands on a banquet scene.

I was much hurt by your contemptuous refusal of The Man of Destiny, not because I think it one of my masterpieces, but because Napoleon is nobody else but Richard Mansfield himself. I studied the character from you, and then read up Napoleon and found that I had got him exactly right. Felix's notion of a bill consisting of 'Chand d'Habits & The Man of Destiny was not a bad one. But you will never get over your difficulties until you become the master & not the slave of your profession. Look at me, enviable man that I am: I act the real part of Bernard Shaw, and get you, or anyone else stagestruck enough, to dress up as Bluntschli or any other of my figments and fakements. It is as an organizer of the theatre that you really interest me; and here I find you paralyzed by the ridiculous condition that the drama must always be a Mansfield exhibition. I wanted Candida done. Why didnt you send for Courtenay Thorpe, who has just 'created' Eugene here? If you set your mind to it you could teach all the necessary tricks to the first dozen able bodied human shells you meet in the street. I dont believe a bit in your own acting: you're too clever, too positive, and have imagination instead of what people call 'feeling'. Why not hire a specimen of the real actor-article – the true susceptible, hysterical, temperamental, somnambulistic, drunk-on-air nothingness – and put ideas into the creature's head, and hypnotize him with a part. He'll act your head off, because you have to be yourself, whereas he has no self and can only materialize himself in the delusive stuff spun out of another man's fancy. For you acting is only intentional madness, like David drabbling in his beard. Harden your heart against it, and manage, manage, manage. Bless you, I know by your letters: I miss the hollowness, the brainless void full of tremulously emotional chaos waiting for a phantom shape in a play – bah! it's no profession for you. The people come because they are curious about the interesting man, Richard Mansfield, and because you have imagination enough to strike *their* imaginations with stage effects; but that's quite another thing. You may ask me whether these spooks of people will ever understand my plays. I reply that I dont want them to understand. If they did theyd be dumfoundered. Besides, my plays never will be played, though they *can* be. I'll write them & print them; and the right people will understand. Meanwhile play the Devil's Disciple, and then retire & write to the papers explaining (as above) why you scorn to act any longer, except in an emergency as Marcellus or Bernardo and devote the rest of your life to the organization of victory all over the States – ten companies at a time – instead of to broadsword combats.

Do not shew this letter to your wife: she will blow me up for allowing the winds of heaven to visit your face too harshly.

Irving's son has written a play about Peter the Great of which I hear high praise. The younger generation is knocking at the door: nephew Alf has played Osric to Tree's Hamlet here – at least I saw him announced for the part. I did not see the performance, as I am in the country for August & September.

Any chance of seeing you over here[?]

yrs sincerely

G. Bernard Shaw

The two-volume edition of Shaw's first seven plays, *Plays Pleasant and Unpleasant,* was published in Chicago by Herbert S. Stone and in London by Grant Richards in April 1898. Johnston **Forbes-Robertson** (1853–1937) was performing Shakespeare with Mrs Patrick **Campbell** (1865–1940) as his leading lady; in 1900 he undertook a provincial tour with *The Devil's Disciple* (1896), but with his new wife Gertrude Elliott (1874–1950) as Judith. Shaw reviewed an exhibit of the realistic war scenes of the Russian painter Vasily **Verestschagin** (1843–1904), including his 'Blowing from the Guns in British India,' in the *World,* 12 October 1887.

Felix **Mansfield** (1852–?), based in London, served as brother Richard's agent and adviser. **'Chand d'Habits,** a mimed musical play by Catulle Mendès and Jules Bouval, was staged in London the previous spring. Laurence **Irving** (1871–1914), Sir Henry's younger son, was an actor and playwright. Courtney **Thorpe** (1854–1927) was a member of the Achurch-Charrington company who performed Marchbanks in the première performance of *Candida* on 30 July 1897. **Alfred Mansfield** (1877–1938), son of Felix, played Osric on 12 August for two scheduled performances of *Hamlet* with H. Beerbohm Tree (1853–1917) at Her Majesty's. In 1901 he played Cashel Byron in the copyright reading of Shaw's *The Admirable Bashville.*

17 / To Elisabeth Marbury

[29 Fitzroy Square W
c. November 1897]

[HD: BL 50527, ff 145–51]

Elisabeth Marbury (1856–1933) was a New York play-broker and literary agent, head of the American Play Company, who dealt principally with Shaw's American amateur rights, licensing performances and collecting royalties. The dictated draft of Shaw's letter is in the hand of Charlotte Payne-Townshend.

My dear Miss Marbury

How can I ever learn my business if I don't do it myself? Someday, when I have found out all that is to be found out about it, & come to know all the managers & actor-managers in the market by personally driving bargains with them, then I shall hand the whole business over to you; but for the present I am death on negotiating all my contracts myself. It is not lack of confidence in you, but the certainty that you would take my work off my hands so efficiently that I should never master it for myself, that makes me so determined to make everybody deal straight with me. Suppose you were to marry a millionaire & retire from the business, as you very likely will some day, where should I be then? I assure you that is the whole secret of it & nothing else.

As to Mr Palmer's complaints of what I take out of Mr Mansfield's share, tell him with my compliments that I take nothing out of anyone's share. I take my own share from the public, & not from Mr Mansfield or the manager. The arrangements they may make as to the division of the 80% which constitutes their very handsome share are not my business. The manager provides the theatre: Mr Mansfield provides the company: I provide the play. That means at least six months difficult work for me before either of them spend a farthing; & if the play is a failure they can both clear out of it without, to say the least, any heavier loss than mine. Under these circumstances it is absurd for Mr Palmer to represent me as the rapacious party in the transaction, because I claim ten dollars out of every 100 paid by the public to witness a performance of my play.

Whether it is good business for me to fix that figure is another question; & if Mr Palmer would talk business instead of talking nonsense I might be disposed someday to listen to him, though for the present I have no intention of departing from the terms of the agreement about the Devil's Disciple. It is clear that if companies seeking theatres are easier to get in New York than theatres or plays, Mr Mansfield will find himself squeezed between the theatre proprietor and the author. That is the fortune of commerce; & since the position of the theatre proprietor is so strong, the only result of the author conceding part of his percentage would be that the theatre proprietor would grab it in the long run. . . .

The chief obstacle to a readjustment of terms appears to me to be the American form of the sliding scale, which is really a graduated scale & not a sliding scale at all. If Mr Palmer were to suggest, for instance, that when the receipts do not exceed $500 I should be content with 5%; that when they exceed $500 but do not exceed $1000 I should take 7½% *on the gross*; & that over $1000 I should have my full 10%, all through, then there would be a genuine sharing of the luck. That is the English way; & I do not see why it should not be applied to American theatrical business. I do not, of course, commit myself to accepting this or any other proposal; but if we do come to readjust the terms when the novelty of the play wears off, I shall probably be readier to readjust it in that way than by the elaborately graduated American scale.

You will understand that what makes me rather stiff-necked just now is my desire to make managers understand that agreements made with me, whether judicious or not on my part, are made to be kept & not to be broken. Mr Mansfield knew perfectly well last April what his company would cost him, & what terms he would get in New York. You suggest that he did not foresee the success of the play, & was willing to offer 10% for an occasional performance; but I can assure you that he has been arguing the case with me himself with Mr Palmer's assistance, & that his contention has been that nothing but a very big success could make the 10% reasonable. So I think we may as well stand to our guns for the present.

My correspondence with Mr Mansfield had become so volcanic before the production of the Devil's Disciple, that he returned my last letter unopened; & this is the sole communication that has passed between us since September.

Remember me affectionately to him if you meet him; & believe me, dear Miss Marbury,

yours very sincerely

[*unsigned*]

Albert M. **Palmer** (1838–1905), veteran theatre manager, was a business associate of Mansfield.

18 / To Beatrice Mansfield

29 Fitzroy Square W

1st January 1898

[ALS: Free Library of Philadelphia]
Beatrice Cameron (1868–1940), leading lady to Richard Mansfield, who married him in 1892, played Raïna in Arms and the Man *(1894) and Judith in* The Devil's Disciple *(1897) in the American productions. The photographs she sent were of herself in the latter role.*

My dear Mrs Mansfield

The photographs are capital: if you look like that you have nothing to do but insist on that fall (as to which I observe your guilty silence – *his* guilt and *your* silence) and you will make a tremendous success.

What am I to do? – I must abuse him to somebody, or I shall burst; and you dont want me to abuse him to other people, do you? If you hadnt married him I shouldnt have breathed a word of my sentiments to you; but you *did* marry him, and now you must take the consequences.

The situation is made very difficult for me by the fact that Mr Mansfield (you see I speak of him with perfect propriety, to please you) hasnt a theatre of his own, and does not get the full value of his engagements in the way of sharing. He drives me out of my senses by referring me to Mr A.M. Palmer. I daresay his complaints are well founded – that he only gets 50% of the receipts & provides both the play & the company; that he makes less out of the performances than I do and so on. But do you suppose he would get a farthing more in the long run if I gave him my plays for nothing? Not a bit of it: there would only be so much the more to squeeze out of him for the theatre trust. Next time I shall demand 20% and *force* him to get the same terms that comparative nobodies are able to get here without any trouble. Besides, it is on tour that he will reap the harvest sown by the New York success.

I know all about his acting, and his imagination & genius and so on. I have imagination & genius myself; and I know how much and how little they mean. But I will not hear of peace & goodwill as long as I hear of other people's business being spoiled. I'm not satisfied – not a bit in the world. I quite understand that the last scene is so arranged that nobody watches Judith, & that the spectacle of Richard Dudgeon making Sydney Carton faces keeps the theatre palpitatingly indifferent to everything else. And that's just what I object to: it's all wrong: the audience ought to see *everything* – the frightful flying away of the minutes in conflict with the equally frightful deliberation of Burgoyne & the soldierlike smartness of the executioner: they ought to long for a delay instead of that silly eagerness to see whether the hanging will really come off or not & so on. No: I wont see the other side of it: I'll fight & complain & extort royalties and be a perfect demon until the parts are *all* successes.

I have succeeded in baffling all the plans for producing the play here. One of them was Charles Frohman's for producing it with Drew. I insisted on Terriss, and said that if an American actor did it, why not Mansfield? Now Terriss is dead; and I am supposed to be negotiating with Waring & Bourchier (Richard & Burgoyne). But Waring seems to have plenty of things on hand. I do not see how a Mansfield production here could be arranged without an unearthly loss to me, which my rapacity can ill consent to; but there is such a whacking lot of money to be made in the English provinces by anyone who has conquered London (Tree & Irving are finding that out), that if I could only civilize Dick (excuse a bad habit caught from the disinherited Felix) and get him out of his obsolete, ill tempered Macready–Barry Sullivan ways, he might put in half his year very profitably in this country. In London particularly the sudden upspringing of suburban theatres in all directions has changed the whole situation, and acting is coming into fashion again. By the way, why doesnt Dick secure the American rights of Peter the Great? And why didnt you send me some of *his* photographs?

yours sincerely

G. Bernard Shaw

Sydney **Carton** is the self-sacrificing hero of Dickens's *A Tale of Two Cities* (1859). Leading men of the London stage included John **Drew** (1853–1927), American actor under the management of Charles **Frohman** (1860–1915); Herbert **Waring** (1857–1932), the Helmer of the Charringtons' *A Doll's House*, a frequent member of George Alexander's company at the St James's; and Arthur **Bourchier** (1863–1927), English actor who became manager of the Garrick Theatre in 1900. William **Terriss** (1847–97), noted for his production of melodramas at the Adelphi Theatre, had commissioned Shaw to write *The Devil's Disciple*. He was murdered by a disgruntled actor at a private entrance near to the Adelphi stage door, on 16 December 1897. William **Macready** (1793–1873) and Barry **Sullivan** (1821–91) were tragedians of the British stage, the one in London, the other in the provinces. Henry Irving had recently presented a new play, *Peter the Great*, by his younger son Laurence Irving.

19 / To Charles Charrington

29 Fitzroy Square W

8th June 1898

[ALS: HRC]

Shaw had married Charlotte Payne-Townshend on 1st June. Although they spent the next year in Surrey, and then, after a Mediterranean cruise, returned to Charlotte's flat at 10 Adelphi Terrace, Shaw kept up an appearance of residing in Fitzroy Square (actually his mother's home), to qualify him for retaining his position as an elected member of the St Pancras Borough Council (until 1903).

Your letter went clean out of my head last night. I should have answered it by return.

There is no objection to a single night of Candida here any more than in Manchester; but there are serious obstacles. If you dont give away all the stalls to the press, you will make them your enemies for life. If you do, and the thing is properly advertised, you will have to turn away money & lose it into the bargain. And you will spoil all the interest of a real first night if the play ever goes up afterwards. Not to mention the horrible aggravation of being unable to follow up an *apparent* success, since Esmond will not be available for a run, even if he can get away for the one night. Why not wait for a real chance? Have you no thrift in you?

GBS

Henry V. **Esmond** (1869–1922) was a young actor and playwright, whom Shaw had been wooing since 1896 to play Marchbanks in *Candida.*

20 / To Beatrice Mansfield

In the Mediterranean
Malta to Algiers
S.S. 'Lusitania'
21st October [1899]

[ALS: Free Library of Philadelphia]

Following an 18-month siege of illness caused by a necrosed bone in his foot and a subsequent fall that shattered an arm, Shaw embarked with Charlotte on 21 September on a cruise to the Holy Land. Brief portions of the text of the letter were obliterated by the scissoring of Shaw's autograph for a collector.

Dear Mrs Mansfield

Your letter reached me at Malta; and the deterioration in my handwriting is due to a slight swell off the African coast and an abominable scirocco.

It is quite true that I have written a play called Captain Brassbound's Conversion; but it is tied up for the present. I wrote it to fulfil a promise to Ellen Terry; and she wants to bring it to America. So I have promised to hold the American rights at her disposal until she returns from her present American tour with Irving. She is to see about dates &c so that she may make me a definite proposal when she comes back. I am myself rather sceptical as to whether she will be able to produce the play at all, even in England, as it is not clear how she can do that without to some extent breaking away from the Lyceum. However, I must let her do her best, as the play was written to please her and not as a matter of business. There is only one woman in it – a very [*text cut away*] part for a brilliant and tender comedian. Captain [Brass]bound is rather of the Devil's Disciple order; but without [the] humor & penetration & rightmindedness: the lady gets the [best] of him & converts him, the conversion consisting in his renunciation of a terrible scheme of revenge which he has foolishly cherished all his life. The scene is in Morocco; and the play is full of everything that is *de plus* Shaw in his geniallest vein. But the woman has so much the best of it, and the low comedian has such a hold of the audience as far as laughter goes that I very greatly doubt whether R.M's virtue would have brooked such rivalry even if I had been able without spoiling the tribute to Ellen to put it at his disposal.

There is no difficulty about You Never Can Tell except the difficulty of getting it acted. The end of the second act requires a consummate comedian; and that comedian has never been available. At the Haymarket here we rehearsed the play for some time; but that scene beat us; and finally I told the management that they must give it up – that the failure of that scene would wreck the play. So it has never been produced, though everybody is resolved to produce it – chiefly because everybody wants to play the waiter. You would find the same obstacle – no Valentine. Another very difficult part to fill is Mrs Clandon. Of course the waiter & the twins are safe; and Crampton is not beyond the available talent in that line; but they could not save the play. John Drew, or Wyndham (20 years younger) could manage Valentine; but they are out of your reach. It is a pity; but unless you saw the play rehearsed as I did, you could never realize the utter impossibility of that scene even to a practised & popular farcical young comedian, accustomed to play leading parts in London. It was not that he did it badly, or tamely, or wrongly: he simply could not do it at all; and we had to tell all sorts of stories to account for the withdrawal of a play which had been paragraphed on all hands. Of course the most obvious explanation was that the play had proved a failure at rehearsal on its own demerits; and I was quite willing to let this get current so as to spare the Valentine as much as possible; but of course the publication of the play made an end of that.

We have left Hindhead, as I am now practically well again, or was until I was dragged on the conventional voyage to restore me completely. Anything better calculated to destroy me, body & soul, than a Mediterranean cruise in a pleasure steamer in October & Sept. (the scirocco months) it would be hard to devise; but I shall probably get back to London at the end of the month alive, if not much more. My wife has had a very bad time of it, suffering so much from a mild form ,of cholera (as it seems to me) that it was with difficulty that I got her ashore at Constantinople for a couple of hours to see the mosques. The reason this letter is so dull is that we are sailing along the African coast through a sickly blue sea, breathing scirocco, steam & cigar smoke. I feel thoroughly out of sorts. Never before have I felt so keenly the force of the saying that life would be tolerable but for its pleasures.

I hope Mansfield the younger is flourishing after his recent initiation into Christian rites. Archer saw Cyrano during his American visit & gave me some account of R.M. I cordially approve of the matinee scheme; but you should go a step further & have a separate theatre. Husband & wife always ruin one another on the stage – either the one or the other has to sacrifice every chance. However, the matinees will do to begin with.

The D's D was produced in London the other day at a suburban theatre during my absence. It seems to have made a great press sensation; but I dont know whether there was any solid success.

[*unsigned*]

Ellen **Terry** eventually performed Lady Cicely in *Captain Brassbound's Conversion* (1899) on an American tour, but not until 1906, a year after Sir Henry's death. Charles **Wyndham** (1837–1919), a light comedian with few equals, was for many years manager of the Criterion Theatre. The **young comedian** in the aborted *You Never Can Tell* was Allan Aynesworth (1865–1959), the original Algy in *The Importance of Being Earnest* (1895).

Mansfield **the younger** was George Gibbs Mansfield, born in 1898, who later was known as Richard Mansfield, Jr. He died at 19, of meningitis, during military service at Fort Sam Houston, San Antonio, in 1918. Mrs Mansfield retired from the stage in February 1898, but may have yearned for a return in special matinees (which apparently did not occur). On 8 January Mansfield scheduled a special farewell performance of *Arms and the Man* to enable his wife to appear one last time as Raïna. One of Mansfield's greatest successes was as Rostand's **Cyrano** de Bergerac in 1898–9. *The Devil's Disciple* was produced on 26 September at the Princess of Wales, Kennington.

21 / To Beatrice Mansfield 10 Adelphi Terrace WC
11th February 1900

[TLS: Free Library of Philadelphia]

In spite of Mrs Mansfield's tentative negotiations for You Never Can Tell, *no further Shaw play made its way into Mansfield's repertory. Eventually it was licensed to Arnold Daly (1875–1927), who had a moderate success with it in New York in 1905.*

Very well, Mrs Mansfield, very well. Have your own way; I see that I shall not have mine. Play 'You Never Can Tell' by all means, and cast Richard for the Waiter, to shew that he is not losing his versatility.

But now that you have carried your point, what use is it to you? You will have a lot of trouble, and a matinée, and that's all. You can repeat the matinée, I suppose, until the matinée audiences are exhausted, which will occur in about five afternoons on the most favorable supposition. And what then? You cant put the play up at night, because Richard will want the theatre. You cant take another theatre and start an opposition management to him, because you will be wanted for your parts in his repertory. Or if you *can* do these things, you wont, which comes to the same thing as far as I am concerned. Now suppose your matinées are a tremendous success. Suppose at the same moment Frohman or somebody has a failure on hand and is at his wits' end for a new piece to put up. He makes me an offer for You Never Can Tell – for a regular evening production. I shall hand it over to him, of course, since the alternative would be to let it drop through your inability to do what Frohman would do. At the utmost I could only stipulate that he should engage your company – and even that might be extremely unreasonable if he had a company of his own eating their heads off – without any likelihood that you would consent to become Frohman's leading lady and abandon Richard to strange Judiths and Raïnas. You would be frightfully angry with me, whereas if I refused flatly now to let you touch the play, you would only be disappointed. True, this may not happen. But then it may; and I want you to realize it beforehand, so that you may know exactly what you are taking your chance of.

Let me point out, too, that the problem is complicated in a diabolical manner as long as you and Richard are in the same theatre. The fact that you had one play of mine and Richard two others (not to mention future ones) might result in your play playing his off the stage, and so destroying me by my own competition.

However, if you choose to take your chance of all these disagreeable possibilities, and rely on the improbability of any manager touching a play with the gloss of novelty rubbed off it, even under the persuasion of the vigilant Elisabeth Marbury, I shall be only too willing to see you get what fun there is to be got out of the play. I do not think there is much real risk: the play is too witty to be popular with the multitude. The probability is that it will be left to you as long as you care to play it. And though you will have no hold of me with regard to it, on the other hand I will have no hold of you; and it may be that this arrangement, all the chances considered, may be the best for you. For if you lock up the play, you will have to enter into all sorts of engagements as to exploiting it fully – engagements which you could not possibly fulfil without definitely going into management on your own account, or else casting Richard for the Waiter as aforesaid and making the play the next regular Mansfield production. Better take advice and think it over carefully.

As to terms, you can either pay me the usual 10%, or, if you prefer it, agree to an English sliding scale, as follows. If the receipts at any performance do not exceed $250, you pay me 5% on the gross. If they do not exceed $500, you pay me 7½% on the gross. Not exceeding $1,000, 10% on the gross. Exceeding $1,000, 12½% on the gross. Please explain to Mr Palmer, or anyone whom you may consult about this, that it does not mean the usual American arrangement of 5% up to $250, 7½% from 250 to 500 &c. It means 5% when the house is small, 7½ when it is middling, 10 when it is good, and 12½ when it is very good. You will lose 2½ by this if the play is so successful that all the houses exceed $1,000; but if they are less than $500 – which is rather probable, I am afraid, you will save 2½, whilst if they are less than $250 you will save 5%. That is, against the 10% all through plan.

It will really rest with yourself and your luck as to how tight you can hold the play when it is once committed to the boards by you. If it fails, nobody will dispute its possession with you. If it succeeds, you have only to play it for all it is worth to secure yourself against my running the risk of a change of cast and theatre for no mortal reason (for the terms are by no means low enough to be likely to be outbidden, nor should I risk a change for the sake of another two and a half per cent, or a sum down which I am in no need of). On the other hand, I repeat that if you find that your situation makes it impossible for you to follow up a success, you must not then be angry with me if I allow somebody else to follow it up.

Think this over with due solemnity, and take the advice of some competent man of business.

To change the subject, I must correct what I said about Tree's business being like Richard's. In theatrical language business unfortunately means two quite different things. What my critic meant was not that Richard's financial position or methods were the same as Tree's, but that their lines of dramatic business were the same, or more nearly the same, than that of any other English manager than Tree. To put it unmistakeably, that if Richard were forced to exchange repertories with any London manager, or Tree with any New York manager, they would have to exchange with one another. Their artistic methods are very different, Tree being a scatterbrain and Richard a concentrated person.

If Richard can fill his theatre without the advertisement of London, there is no mortal reason for his coming here. London is exactly what I explained in my last – advertisement and nothing more. Irving will hurry back to America next October to repair still further his London disasters. Miss Terry will return with him; and the result of that may be a change in the destination of Captain Brassbound's Conversion.

I hope Mansfield junior is flourishing. Why dont you bring him over here for a trip? All the rest of America comes here every summer. I am much more amiable in person than on a typewriter.

yours sincerely
G. Bernard Shaw

Charles **Frohman** was a leading American theatre manager, active on both sides of the Atlantic. The **critic** who had seen Mansfield perform was William Archer, who told Shaw, as reported to Mrs Mansfield on 7 January 1900, that Mansfield 'was the nearest thing in America to Tree (I am now speaking of his business position, not his artistic one)' (*Collected Letters 1898–1910* [1972], p. 132). Mansfield's contemplated second London visit (the first was in 1889) did not occur.

22 / To George Alexander   [10 Adelphi Terrace WC

c. 25 February 1900]

[HD: BL 50528, ff 1–7]

Dear Alexander

I have just had a glimpse of the Statutes of the new London University. They will be published in a day or two.

You will naturally here interject, 'Well, what the devil has that to do with me?'

I will tell you. Sir Henry Irving, in insisting on being made a knight, has done nothing really solid for his profession. Knighthoods are too cheap, as the throwing of an extra one to Bancroft proved. Now I propose that you shall end as Sir George Alexander on a granite Eddystone basis. The first step is to read the following extracts from the Statutes. [*Circled instruction in draft: 'Copy here the extracts.'*]

Now observe. Music, in the Platonic sense proper for University use, means physical training, declamation, elocution, dancing (in the solemn Greek sense) and a great deal more besides – enough to completely cover a School of Dramatic Art. Henry Neville's school, or Malvina Cavalazzi's, wont do, because they are carried on 'for the private gain or profit' of Henry & Malvina aforesaid. But if you could call a meeting of the leading managers, appeal for endowments, hunt up titled patrons, start a library, knock up a handsome building somewhere, and so get into existence an imposing school of Physical & Artistic Cultivation – a sort of poetic Sandow institute (I'd bring Sandow into it) – you could finally get it admitted as a School of the University of London under the Faculty of Music. The result would be that the graduates of the University in the faculty would become the actors of the future; and acting would then at last be a learned profession. Nothing but this can make it so: mere knighthoods alone can never distinguish it from brewing or railway directing. And the man who carries this through will become the head of his profession in a sense that Irving has never attained to.

Of course I do not propose all this as an amusement for your spare hours during the next fortnight. The war is not good for such projects.

But stow it at the back of your mind (if it seems worth entertaining) and wait for your opportunity, always remembering that if you wait too long somebody else may jump the claim. I have not mentioned it to anyone else, and do not propose to do so at present unless you think it hopeless.

I shall not meddle with the matter myself: the mere mention of my name would scatter all the managerial forces. Besides, it's not my busi-. ness. It *is* yours; and when the unpublished Statutes were shewn to me yesterday, I thought I might as well drop you this hasty line, knowing how little chance your two performances a day are leaving you of catching on to these matters which are always drifting past me.

I still think, by the way, that you are the man for the Endowed Theatre, which might very well form part of the scheme of a University School. But you will have to train a staff & delegate a lot of your work before you can make yourself into six men instead of one. I quite recognize the killing difficulty of finding time & energy to do more than keep the St James's going.

yours sincerely
[*unsigned*]

Alexander replied on 26 February, 'I do not think the idea at all hopeless,' in fact, I think it an excellent one, and I will work at it. You say you will not mention it to anyone else, and I take it that you are a good keeper of secrets' (BL 50528, f 9).

Squire **Bancroft** (1841–1926), knighted in 1897, and his wife Marie Wilton (1839–1921) created the vogue for drawing-room comedy in London at their intimate Prince of Wales's Theatre. After decades of adulation Bancroft retired in 1885. Henry **Neville** (1837–1910), veteran actor-manager, ran a drama studio in London. Malvina **Cavalazzi** (d. 1924), Italian dancer who performed at the Metropolitan Opera at its opening in 1883 and at London's Alhambra, operated a school of dance in London until summoned in 1909 to open a ballet school at the Met. Shaw's ideas for a fully developed school of dramatic art came to fruition when Beerbohm Tree founded the Academy of Dramatic Art in the dome of His Majesty's Theatre in 1904. The school, later Royalised, flourishes in Gower Street today as the RADA. Shaw, who served on its governing council for 30 years (several as chairman), bequeathed one-third of his residuary estate to the school at his death in 1950. Eugene **Sandow** (1867–1925) was a professional strongman and physical-culture exponent. Britain had been at war in South Africa since the siege of Mafeking began in October 1899.

23 / To Margaret Halstan   10 Adelphi Terrace WC
                                                    28th April 1900

[TLS: U. of North Carolina]

Yorke Stephens (1860–1937), Shaw's 1894 Bluntschli, and James Welch (1865–1917), the Lickcheese of Widowers' Houses in 1892, had scheduled a series of matinees of You Never Can Tell at the Strand Theatre commencing 2 May. Shaw recommended Halstan (1879–1967), a young actress he had taken a shine to, for the role of Gloria (which she had performed for the Stage Society in November 1899). When he was informed by the managers that she had a conflicting engagement, Shaw consented to a substitute hiring. 'I should certainly have insisted that the part was yours by right of artistic conquest,' he informed Halstan on 25 April, 'if I had known that you could have played it. However, you must bear in mind that the engagements were made at a time when they were counting on Easter week to begin with; so you must judge by that, and not by the postponed date' (ALS: UNC).

Dear Miss Halston

This is certainly very exasperating, but you had better accept the lateness of the telegram (too close to Easter week) as the explanation. You will of course form your private conclusions for yourself; but it is much better for you that the reason given by Y.S. and J.W. – namely, that when the engagements were made for the old date, you were not at liberty – should be the public reason. In a sense, it was the real reason, as I should not have sanctioned the change on any other ground.

If you complain, you will suffer in three ways. 1. You will appear in the character of a person with a grievance, which is always a mistake. 2. You will create an impression that an engagement for a few matinees (probably unsuccessful) at the Strand is a matter of importance to you. 3. You will force Y.S. and J.W. to disparage your acting in order to justify themselves. So smile on them and say nothing, making a silent note for your future guidance in such matters. This is the wisdom of the serpent. I wish I could find you a remedy instead; but they have got the better of us this time.

yours sincerely
G. Bernard Shaw

PS. [*Handwritten*] Sydney Warden has suffered in just the same way.

Phil and Dolly have been changed also; so that four important parts will be newly filled. There can therefore be no question of playing with the original cast.

Sydney **Warden** (d. 1901) played Finch M'Comas in the Stage Society production, in which Roland Bottomley (1880–1947) and Winifred Fraser (1868–1951) were the twins **Philip and Dolly**.

24 / To Frederick Kerr

Piccard's Cottage
St Catherine's. Guildford
6th January 1901

[ALS: present source unknown]

Frederick Kerr (1858–1933) performed only once in a Shaw play, as the piratical captain in Captain Brassbound's Conversion, *opposite Ellen Terry (1906).*

Dear Mr Kerr

I am much obliged to you for your letter and your suggestion that I should write a comedy for the Court under your management. But although I think that if I were seven years younger I could fit you exactly, I am afraid that if I write you a play now, the time will not be ripe for it until 1908. Arms and the Man, for instance, which I wrote in 1894, would, if it were new, produce the effect of an up-to-date topical play, with the Queen's chocolate prominent in it, and a perfect part for you. In 1894, produced as a stopgap after a failure, it drew a steady £25 a night or thereabouts; and the chocolate passed as an Offenbachian joke. Two or three years later I wrote You Never Can Tell for the Haymarket, at Cyril Maude's request. I mentioned certain names to the management for the part of Valentine – yours prominently among them. But they did not see the part as I saw it; and I had to withdraw the play to save them from a fiasco. Again, I complied with a request for a play from William Terriss (The Devil's Disciple) which, but for its success in America, would be on my hands to this day. Mr Forbes Robertson liked one scene in The Devil's Disciple, but wanted something better. I wrote him a big play in which he could have played Julius Cæsar to Mrs Campbell's Cleopatra. It has never been performed and is not likely to be. My last play was produced by The Stage Society the other night, after it, too, had lain on my hands for 18 months.

In short, for the last eight or nine years, I have written a play whenever anyone asked me to – ten in all. Not one of these plays has been produced by the people for whom they were written: in fact, except for a few scratch matinees, a provincial tour which had to take a play of mine because it could get nothing else, a flutter at a suburban theatre, and the shows of forlorn hopes like the Independent Theatre &c &c, they have not been produced at all. Nobody was to blame; but the fact remains that nothing ever came off. Managers very seldom know what they want. They sometimes thought they wanted a play by me until they saw the prompt book; and then they knew well enough that they didnt want *that*. So I published the plays, and gave up the theatre as a bad job.

I tell you this long story because I owe you something franker than a polite refusal for your very sensible and friendly letter. I have had enough of it: that is all; and I can do more good by going hard ahead and making the advance easier for younger men than by simply using the stage skill I have picked up in manufacturing popular successes.

As to writing for my own amusement in the sense of asking managers to spend their money and actors their time and talent on deliberate trifling, the extent to which I have been accused of that only shews how few people there are in the theatrical world who have good sense enough to really mean business and understand when other people mean it. I have never done less than my best; and though I believe that the public should always have a sense of something over their heads, and will stand a great deal from anybody who gives it to them, yet I should be sorry to send an audience away without a sense of having thoroughly enjoyed its evening.

I wish you success at the Court. I never go to the theatre now; but I broke the rule lately to see Frank Harris's play. Nobody else on the stage could have done Daventry as you have done him. Whoever you get to write a play for you, tell him that he must put a *man* behind the comedian, or the man in you will smash his play. Remember how it smashed that play of Parker's at the Lyric when it tailed off into sentimental *comedietta* after the second act. You burst it like a charge of lyddite in an ironmonger's pistol. If I were young enough to write the play you want, I am by no means sure that it would be a comedy. There would be a pretty stiff back to the comedy, at all events.

Excuse my writing so long a letter. I very seldom have a sensible correspondent on this particular subject.

> yours faithfully
> G. Bernard Shaw

The **Queen's chocolate** was a gift from Queen Victoria distributed to British troops in South Africa in November 1899, adding credence to Shaw's 'chocolate cream soldier' in *Arms and the Man.* The **Stage Society** produced *Captain Brassbound's Conversion* on 16 December 1900. Frank **Harris** (1856–1931), journalist and writer, was the author of *Mr and Mrs Daventry* (1900), based on a plot supplied to him by Oscar Wilde (for a fee). The **scratch matinees** were of a single performance of *Widowers' Houses* by the Charringtons at the Crystal Palace on 1 May 1900 and the six performances of *You Never Can Tell* at the Strand Theatre in May 1900. *Candida* was performed a few times by the Charringtons in their 1897 **provincial** tour. The **suburban** production was *The Devil's Disciple* by actor-manager S. Murray Carson (1865–1917) at Kennington in September 1899, for 13 performances. The sole play by Louis N. **Parker** (1852–1944) in which Kerr had appeared was *The Happy Life* (1897), which was, however, presented at the Duke of York's Theatre, not the Lyric.

25 / To George Alexander [10 Adelphi Terrace WC]
15th October 1901

[HD: HRC]

Dear Alexander

You have been listening to the voice of the siren. However, the siren's proposition seems reasonable in both our interests.

The difficulty about the Man of Destiny is its inconvenient length – a good hour – too long for a curtain raiser & too short for a whole bill. Unless the Wilderness is a shortish play, the only way out of the difficulty is to cut either one piece or the other. It is my custom to say, when that proposal is made to me[,] 'Certainly: what do you want cut?', knowing very well that I have already cut the play to the bone. I spare you that little comedy; for though I am quite willing to consider any cut or other improvement you can suggest, yet it is, according to my experience, so unlikely that any serious alteration is feasible, that we had better assume that the play must be given as it stands. If it cannot be done that way, you will find that it cannot be done at all.

As to terms, my agreement with Irving (who regards fifteen shillings an act as the natural remuneration of a West End playwright) was for three guineas a performance; but I will cheerfully take six if you prefer it. The most sensible arrangement seems to me to be that you should try the piece quietly on your tour and see how you like it, leaving the question of a London production an open one.

Will you send me your itinerary, so that I may see whether I could run down to a few rehearsals. As the piece has been through my hands lately I could save you a lot of trouble. Let me know also who you have on tour with you, as the casting of the lieutenant & the innkeeper is important.

> yrs ever ·
>
> [*unsigned*]

After Alexander had pressed Shaw to cut ten to fifteen minutes out of the play, offered a fee of £1 per performance, and eliminated himself from the role as being too tall, Shaw responded on 17 October: 'What! You arent to play Napoleon! Million millions! Even Irving stopped short of this outrage. Never mention The Man of Destiny to me again. All is over' (shorthand note: HRC).

The **siren** was Margaret Halstan, a member of George Alexander's company, who performed *The Man of Destiny* with Harley Granville Barker (1877–1946) for a *Sunday Special* (weekly newspaper) matinee on 29 March 1901. *The Wilderness*, for which Alexander desired Shaw's play as a curtain-raiser, was a three-act comedy by H.V. Esmond, an actor in the company, produced at the St James's Theatre on 11 April.

26 / To W.J. Douglas

10 Adelphi Terrace WC
19th March 1902

[ALS: HRC]

An amateur production of Candida, directed by fellow Fabian Millicent Murby (1873–1951), a postal clerk, was performed at Cripplegate Institute on 15 February, and repeated in Bayswater on 19 March. Shaw, who had attended the first performance, informed Charles Trevelyan (1870–1958), Liberal (later Labour) MP, the next day: 'They really contrived to make it very tolerable – all the more so as they mostly didnt know how to act. ... [S]omehow the performance was a successful one on the whole – more so than old professionals could have made it' (ALS: University Library, Newcastle upon Tyne). In writing to Douglas, who played Candida's father Mr Burgess, Shaw apparently was oblivious to the fact that the next performance was to occur that very evening.

Dear Sir

Go to the nearest Town Hall and sit in the ratepayers' gallery during the next meeting of the Borough Council. You can pick out your Burgess among the councillors & copy his dress.

If you cannot do this, wear a black frock coat of substantial stuff & cut, a double breasted waistcoat of the same stuff with a solid looking watchchain, with enough opening in front to show a gold stud, a black necktie, and very respectable shirt & collar. Trousers either black or of some very ordinary color. The suit must not be slim and elegant, but solid & prosperous. In fact, the whole make-up & dress should be such as would seem exactly natural at a service in the nearest chapel if worn by one of the principal men in the congregation. Take yourself very seriously.

At Cripplegate your dress was grotesque: it suggested a music hall knockabout. Your acting was very successful for one of your age and inexperience: in fact, I should have taken you for an older & more practised hand but for the dress, which betrayed the amateur. You must remember that amateurs always try to make themselves like the figures they have seen on the stage, whilst actors always strive to make themselves like the figures they have seen in the street. Grip that difference, and you will do very well.

In the second act, do not bring in your hat. You are spending the afternoon in the house & have been for some time with Candida – long enough to be able to tell the poet what she is doing upstairs – consequently you must come in without any air of having just called.

yrs faithfully

G. Bernard Shaw

27 / To Gertrude Elliott   10 Adelphi Terrace WC

17th June 1903

[ALS: BL 61998, f 4]

Gertrude Elliott, who married Forbes-Robertson in 1900, was his leading lady until his retirement in 1913, after which she performed under her own management. Though their four-month provincial tour of The Devil's Disciple *(1900) was a critical and modestly economic success, Shaw allowed it to approach no*

*nearer to the West End than a week's engagement at Notting Hill Gate. It did
not reach London's theatre centre until 1907.*

. . . I shall always do my best to prevent HIM from producing the D's D
in London, because I have no faith in it financially. If he were a beginner at leading business, needing an advertisement & a discussion above
all things, I should say risk it and hang the expense. But he is past all
that: Dick Dudgeon cannot add to the reputation of our only Hamlet;
and there is really no reason why he should touch the play except as
matter of business. The right cast would be expensive, and, in his opinion, unnecessary; and he would loathe the proper melodramatic treatment of the last act, with an enormous crowd (horribly troublesome to
drill) and a big band &c. And the part, though he appreciates the effec-
tiveness of the first act and of the middle of the second, would not
really reconcile him to the bother of the thing. Only a passionately religious man, who could read William Blake and Bunyan and the Bible
hour after hour, could really feel Dick enough to enjoy him and *be* him.
Dick's diabolonian saintliness leaves Hamlet cold and even slightly disgusted. All this tells against the prospects of a return to the D's D. in
London. But of course if he insisted and faced it, the thing is not mine
to refuse: the artist has his rights and the author his duties; and if he
were really serious about it (which, by the way, I dont think he ever will
be) it would be impossible for me to stand on my legal right to say no. I
have far too much respect for him to consider myself free in the matter
– not to mention my natural feelings as a dramatist. You understand,
dont you?

> yrs sincerely
> G. Bernard S
> h
> a
> w

Forbes-Robertson's *Hamlet* (1897) was his crowning achievement in the theatre; he revived
it for his farewell tour, 1912–13.

28 / To Violet Vanbrugh
Maybury Knoll. Woking
28th December 1903

[ALS: Leo T. Sides]

Shaw's first choice for Ann Whitefield in Man and Superman *was Violet Vanbrugh (1867–1942), wife of Arthur Bourchier, who, even before she had read the play, accepted his invitation to perform in the anticipated Stage Society production. The performance was, however, rescheduled for the following season. By May 1905 Vanbrugh was unavailable and the role was given to Lillah McCarthy (1876–1960), a vivacious young actress who had been leading lady to Wilson Barrett (1846–1904) since 1900.*

Dear Mrs Bourchier

You will find somewhere in the book I am sending you (Man and Superman) a play. Will you, when next you have an hour to spare, read that play, or as much of it as you can bear. My reason for asking you – at least my immediate, practical, business reason – is that the Stage Society wants to perform this play. Now by cutting out the dream in the third act, and possibly the whole third act, and by cutting almost all the man's talk in the scene between the hero & heroine in the first act, an acting version can be made, reasonable in length, and endurable in dramatic quality. BUT—

Where is my heroine to come from? The part of Ann is no ordinary leading lady's business. Where is the person who can be this cat, this liar, this minx, this 'something for which I know no polite name' (this is the hero's description of her) and yet be perfectly irresistible and perfectly dignified? You see, unless the lady is vital enough to reduce all these abusive epithets to the most unreal moral claptraps by simply living them down as a much more important & fascinating fact in nature[,] her own self, the play would be unbearable. Now – I desire to approach the point delicately – do you think that *you*, for instance, would care to – or at least – not that I would suggest that – well, in short, would you play Ann for the Stage Society? If you wont, I am greatly afraid there will be no performance; for I really cannot bear the idea of anybody else in the part. You are a very difficult person to fit; and it follows that what fits you doesnt fit anybody else.

Playing for the Stage Society is a labor of love, usually made meritorious by experiences which are known only to performers in booths at fairs. The Society is homeless: it rehearses where it can, performs where it can, disappoints, postpones, breaks down, picks itself up, and finally achieves performances which have a quite peculiar nervous quality (highly effective from the front) owing to the fact that the whole cast has been driven to madness & distraction during the rehearsals. The artists are solemnly presented with two guineas each for 'expenses.' I think Henrietta Watson once got a butter muslin shirt as well; I am not sure of this. In fact, nobody but real good people will stand it, though it is much better now than it was at first. At all events, you know the worst in advance. *Will* you?

G. Bernard Shaw

Henrietta **Watson** (1873–1964) played Lydia in the Stage Society production of Shaw's *The Admirable Bashville* in May 1903.

29 / To Charles Frohman   [The Old House. Harmer Green. Welwyn
c. 11 July 1904]

[HD: BL 50514, ff 191–3]

Ada Rehan (1857–1916), Irish-born comedian of the American stage, was leading lady to the actor-manager Augustin Daly (1839–99) for twenty years, becoming one of the most celebrated actresses on the New York and London stages, principally in classic roles: the shrew Katharina, Lady Teazle in The School for Scandal, *and Rosalind in* As You Like It. *Shaw, in his preface to the Shaw–Terry correspondence (1931), recalled that she spoke Shakespeare's lines 'so harmoniously that, when listening to her, it was impossible to care much about anything but the mere music of her voice and Shakespear's.' Since Daly's death Rehan had performed on her own, with little success, and in May 1905 made her final stage appearance.*

Acting on a suggestion of the agent Elisabeth Marbury, Shaw wrote to Rehan, who was visiting London, to ask if he might read to her Captain Brassbound's Conversion, which had waited five years for her. The reading occurred on 2 July. Rehan reacted favorably, suggesting she might include the play in a contemplated American autumn tour under Shubert management. Shaw, however, overwhelmed and frightened her with grandiose ideas of a London engagement and

extended tours. Negotiations stretched out for more than a year, until Rehan put
an end to the matter by pleading illness and retiring from the stage. Ellen Terry
at last carried the play to America as the jewel of her Jubilee tour – under Charles
Frohman's management.

Dear Sir

A few days ago I happened to read a play of mine called Captain Brassbound's Conversion in the presence of Miss Ada Rehan, with the result
that she has induced me to allow her to play the principal part in America during her winter engagement under the Shubert management.
This arrangement, however, is in my opinion by no means an ideal one,
especially as Arnold Daly's production of You Never Can Tell will give
New York as much Shaw as it will need for the moment. Then, too,
although Mr Shubert seems to have found out at last that Miss Rehan is
one of the two or three greatest actresses in the world, and that in more
modern hands than those of the late Augustin Daly, she has in her ten
or fifteen years of work of a class quite beyond any of the usual popular
leading ladies, yet I am not satisfied that Mr Shubert can handle a play
of mine unless I am there to direct it (Miss Rehan herself owned that
she had read it herself without seeing what could be done with it). Now
I dont want to cross the Atlantic to rehearse it, as I should be bothered
out of my life with interviews & invitations & visits & so forth. Besides, I
dont know the American stage well enough to choose a cast for it. I
should very greatly prefer to have it produced in London next spring &
then taken to America as a London success – or even a London failure[.]
    There is no other manager who can do this so well as you. If you were
to engage Miss Rehan & Edwin [*error for John*] Drew for a season next
spring, the old enthusiasm of the Daly days would revive, and not be
crushed by the hopeless obsolescence of Daly himself. If Brassbound
failed it would not fail *much* – it would not lose more than you could get
back by reviving the old repertory – The Taming of the Shrew, As You
Like It, School for Scandal &c &c. I have not ventured to suggest this to
Miss Rehan, because I take it for granted that she is one of the old
guard who resisted the Trust. I should have had Brassbound produced
in America years ago had not Mr Fiske quarrelled with me for telling

him that the Trust was ten times better than the rotten system it had replaced, & defending my opinion publicly. At that time, to the great discredit of my argument, you were a baby in London management, heaping business blunders on artistic crimes & artistic crimes on business blunders. Today your theatre is the most advanced theatre and your management the most advanced management in London. So if there is any old quarrel between you and Miss Rehan surviving from the long drawn agony of Daly's extinction, you can very well afford to shew her that you can find better work for her & make more of her than the old system did.

Captain Brassbound's Conversion is, after all, not an essential part of my suggestion. Barrie could write an enormously popular Rehan-Drew play if you set him at it, and if he could see for himself, as I have seen, how absurd all the talk about Miss Rehan being out of date is. Brassbound can wait for its turn.

Will you kindly let me have a line to say whether this strikes you as possible? Miss Rehan is leaving town at the end of the week; and I could probably induce her to hold her hand as regards Shubert if I can get you round on the subject.

Excuse the bluntness of the proposal. The truth is, the whole idea jumped into my head readymade half an hour ago when I was writing to Miss Rehan; and I hardly know whether it is a happy thought or an absurdity.

yours faithfully
[*unsigned*]

Sam S. **Shubert** (1877–1905) was one of three young brothers who had recently entered into a managerial rivalry with America's monopolistic Theatrical Syndicate (also known as the Theatre **Trust**). The latter comprised leading theatre owners and managers (later called producers, a term that in England hitherto had denoted what now would be called directors), including the powerful duo Marc Klaw (1858–1936) and Abe Erlanger (1860–1930), George C. Tyler (1867–1946) and his partner Theodore Liebler (1852–1941), and Charles Frohman. The Trust had flourished since 1896. Harrison Grey **Fiske** (1861–1942), journalist and manager of the actress Minnie Maddern Fiske (1865–1932), for whom he had in 1900 sought American rights for *Brassbound*, was a virulent enemy of the Trust, which, as a consequence, barred Mrs Fiske from performing in their theatres, obliging them in 1903 to buy their own New York theatre.

30 / To Ada Rehan   The Old House. Harmer Green. Welwyn
[*c.* 11–12 July 1904]

[ALS: HRC]

The 'enclosed' possibly was a copy of the letter Shaw had just written to Charles Frohman.

My dear Miss Rehan

Read the enclosed; and dont fly out at me. You do it very nicely; but it ruins my nerves.

The first thing to consider is whether Shubert can do as much for you with the play as Frohman or Klaw & Erdlanger. Does he control as many theatres? Above all, can he do anything for you in London? – probably not. That, of course, is not conclusive; but still, if you could make a great London success and an American success *for the same management* at your first stroke with a really modern play on the new business scale, you would have them all at your feet and enter into your kingdom with a gorgeous Restoration after the commercial revolution made by the Trust. So do not be in a hurry to decide.

If you *do* decide to produce Brassbound during your engagement with Shubert this winter, then you can deal with him or send him to me, whichever you prefer. A good deal will depend on whether you intend to alter your contract with him – to demand a larger salary or percentage from him in consideration of your bringing the play. He would of course say yes if you were to pay my royalties out of your winnings. As you must on no account agree to this, and must leave him to pay me exactly as if he were dealing with me directly, he may prefer to depend on your old repertory. You are worth as much to him without Brassbound as with it. That is at once your glory and your commercial disadvantage as the monopolist of Lady Cicely. You might just as well leave all the trouble to me.

You have no idea what a lot of things I have thought of that you havnt, and how exactly I know what is going to happen. Have you an agent or a lawyer or a friend or anyone whom I could worry & argue with (he must have a strong constitution) instead of spoiling your holiday? I hate to bother you; but what can I do? I will try not to write oftener than ten times a week.

yours sincerely
G. Bernard Shaw

31 / To Ada Rehan   The Old House. Harmer Green. Welwyn

16th July 1904

[ALS: HRC]

My dear Miss Rehan

Your telegram reached me in the open country, too late to reassure you by wire. I am full of remorse; but you will soon get used to me. I quite understand about the syndicate, and have not involved you, and will not involve you, in any advances I may make to them. Whatever I do without your knowledge and authority will be done with the full knowledge on the other side that I am acting without your knowledge and authority, and will not commit you in any way.

You must remember that I am only an innocent author & politician (in the English sense of the word – not the American). I know nothing of any quarrel you may have with anybody; and I never quarrel myself. Even when other people quarrel with me, it is not because I quarrel with them, but because I wont quarrel with somebody else. Once, to my great terror, Miss Terry delivered Brassbound into the hands of Mrs Tess D'Urberville Maddern Minnie Fiske, who proposed to usurp Lady Cicely. Though I was waiting for the only possible Lady Cicely (I never saw the Maddern lady act, and imagined her, without the slightest reason, to be an acidulated, genteel, intense amateur) I could not quarrel. Fortunately Mrs Fiske had a husband, poor lady, who was amusing himself with a benightedly impossible and wrongheaded campaign against the theatre trust instead of taking care of his wife's interests. Now I had foretold the trust years before it was formed, and done my utmost to warn all my friends against any attempt to hold back the clock or put it back to the year 1870. I gave Fiske such excellent advice, & tried so hard to shew him what a delightful creature Charles Frohman was, that he finally wrote me that my terms were reasonable and my play excellent, but that sooner than allow his wife to appear in a play by a scoundrel who had no sense of chivalry to WOMAN nor of honor among men, he would slay her with his own hand. Whereat I breathed again, Lady Cicely being saved, dear lady, for you. But I did not quarrel with Fiskerandos Furioso. He sometimes sends me notes from the Dramatic Mirror on the iniquities of the syndicate; and I write him the kindest letters in return, to the general effect that if he will not allow me to convince him that he is a hotheaded idiot, and if he is determined to devote his life to fighting the XX century singlehanded, at least he ought not to make his unfortunate wife march in front of him.

Now I daresay you have, as a proud and generous person with a fine character, occasionally taken up your friends' quarrels, and perhaps burst out into a quarrel or two of your own, besides inevitably inheriting from the old system some bias against the new system, with its rampant financial blackguardism and the atrocious ignorance, vulgarity, and venality of its first attempts at theatrical art. It is therefore very important that you should be in touch with somebody who is on speaking terms with the opposite camp. I owe nothing to the old school and the old regime. Never, never, never shall I forgive it for Dollars & Cents. That it was stupid about Ibsen was nothing; for it hated Ibsen; but that it should have been stupid about *you* shewed that the gods were tired of it, and that the sword was falling on its devoted neck. On the day that Irene Vanbrugh comes to me and says that the syndicate has done to her anything so wicked & wasteful as that, I will apologize to Fiskerandos; but until then I shall regard Charles as a possible heir to salvation.

In short, then, do not let my tentative negotiations trouble you. You can always repudiate them when you please. Nobody can make you sign an agreement: nobody can prevent you withering, blasting, and blighting Charles if he dares propose an engagement to you. You are free; you are great; you are adored; you are independent: he, poor devil, is clinging to the edge of an abyss, with his fifty theatres all straining to tear him to pieces the moment he ceases to cram them with money and 'attractions.' Let us be a little pitiful to a fellow creature.

I will now write to Alexander; but I do not see my way there. *Can* I make a Brassbound of him? However, all the stones shall be turned for your sake.

your very respectful Agent
G. Bernard Shaw

Harrison G. Fiske was owner and editor of the New York *Dramatic Mirror*, in which he furiously lambasted the Theatrical Trust. Irene **Vanbrugh** (1872–1949), after major successes as Gwendolyn in *The Importance of Being Earnest* and Rose in Pinero's *Trelawny of the 'Wells'* (1898), came under Charles Frohman's management in 1902, remaining with him until his death in 1915.

32 / To Harley Granville Barker   Firthview. Rosemarkie
                                            Fortrose. N.B.
                                            25th August 1904

[APCS: HRC]

.It has only just occurred to me that it would be very bad business to produce Rule Britt. before parliament meets again. In fact, it mustnt be done. You will sell a lot of stalls to the political people; and the Irish M.Ps will fill the pit. I forget the exact date of the next session – early in November, I think.

The revision threatens to take longer than I thought. After two days hard, I am not yet *half way through the first act.*

I am sending a card concerning the date to Vedrenne.

                                                        GBS

Rule Britannia, Shaw's newest play, would soon be re-christened *John Bull's Other Island.* Granville Barker and John E. **Vedrenne** (1867–1930) had joined forces in April 1904 to present a series of matinees of *Candida* at the Royal Court Theatre, which Vedrenne was managing for a wealthy amateur Shakespearean actor-scholar J.H. Leigh (1858–1934). The success of the venture led to a partnership, financed by Shaw (eleven of whose plays were presented, for a total of more than seven hundred performances), in a repertory that ran for three years and carried over briefly to the Savoy Theatre in the Strand before funds were exhausted.

33 / To Annie Horniman   North British Station Hotel
                                   Edinburgh
                                   14th September 1904

[ALS: Central Library, Manchester (mic)]

Annie Horniman provided the subvention for the Irish Literary Theatre that enabled it in 1904 to set up shop in Dublin's Abbey Street Theatre under a patent royal. Shaw had offered John Bull's Other Island *to the theatre; it was rejected as too ambitious a production for the Abbey's limited stage facilities and mostly amateur performers.*

Dear Miss Horniman

A 20′ stage will be enough for John Bull's Other Island; and it will have the advantage of not being outrageously large for Irish interiors.

But my question to Yeats did not refer to the size of the stage. There are things called cuts and bridges in stages which are used in transformation scenes in pantomimes, and in scenes where the actors go down a ladder into the cellar to produce the illusion of going down a hill, or going down steps to the water's edge or the like. The removal of a strip of the stage floor to make such a descent possible is called a cut. If, in addition to the cut, which is a simple affair, you have the removable strip of stage mounted on hydraulic pistons so that it can be raised and lowered with immense weights of scenery or people on it by one man, then you have a hydraulic bridge, which, though a costly thing to instal, saves the wages of many carpenters and also saves their elbow room behind the scenes. If the I.L.T. deals much with fairy plays and with plays generally which involve much scene changing, it might be worth while to venture on a hydraulic bridge. I asked Yeats whether anything of the sort was available because I could greatly improve the handling of my play if I could depend on such devices. But of course it can be done without.

It is rather difficult for me to say anything about the last paragraph in your letter, as it seems to allude to something which I should never have dreamt of mentioning to you for fear of putting you in the dilemma of Sir Walter Scott when the question of the authorship of Waverley was raised. All that I need say now is that in the year 1894, I was concerned with Yeats and Miss Florence Farr in a theatrical enterprise which involved the keeping of a secret from me. The secret was duly and faithfully kept, all the more easily because I am remarkably stupid at guessing. Years afterwards, when the matter had been out of my mind for months, and nothing whatever had occurred to remind me of it or suggest what followed, I had a dream in which the solution suddenly flashed on me. Now a dream is no warrant for a conviction; and I have no other warrant and do not propose to seek any. But since then I have always assumed, in conversation or correspondence with Yeats and Miss Farr, that the dream was inspired; and they – or perhaps I should say only Miss Farr; for I do not know whether Yeats was in the secret or not – have of course neither affirmed nor denied anything concerning it. The matter went no further; and the only effect of it was to suggest to me that I might be under a considerable obligation to a person whom I had met once or twice, and to whom I was perfectly content to be under an obligation.

The matter may be left at that until the history of the dramatic revival (such as it is) comes to be written, or longer – for ever, in fact – if it is desirable to keep the secret so long. But I am very glad that there is no secret about the I.L.T. enterprise. Believe me, no public enterprise should have money that it cannot account for, especially when it is conducted by a woman. I have never doubted that there were weighty reasons for the secret in the other case; but I *have* sometimes doubted whether the enormous weight of the reasons against secrecy were fully appreciated. There! that is the very worst I have to say or have ever said.

yours faithfully
G. Bernard Shaw

Sir Walter **Scott** published his first novel *Waverley* (1814) anonymously, his biographer J.G. Lockhart alleging that Scott considered fiction writing to be beneath the dignity of a law clerk of the Court of Sessions, a post he held for 25 years (*Memoirs of the Life of Sir Walter Scott,* 1837–8).

The **theatrical enterprise** was the Avenue Theatre venture in 1894, underwritten secretly by Horniman, in which Shaw's *Arms and the Man* was double-billed with *The Land of Heart's Desire* by W.B. **Yeats** (1865–1939). The Horniman **letter** to which Shaw alludes does not appear to have survived. In a letter to Florence Farr in 1905, however, she wrote: 'My circumstances in life have so changed that secrecy is no longer necessary' (Josephine Johnson, *Florence Farr: Bernard Shaw's New Woman,* 1975).

34 / **To Ellen O'Malley**

10 Adelphi Terrace WC
10th November 1904

[ALS: HRC]

Ellen O'Malley (d. 1961) rose to fame with her radiant performance as Nora in the Vedrenne-Barker production of John Bull's Other Island, which began its series of six matinees on 1 November. Almost immediately she received an offer from a prestigious management (probably from Tree). As no plans for additional performances of Shaw's play had been firmed, he did not wish to discourage O'Malley from embracing a lucrative assignment. In advising her, however, he had tactlessly made a remark he belatedly realized was unethical, and hastened to amend it. O'Malley returned to John Bull for nine additional matinees in February 1905.

Dear Miss O'Malley

I should not have said today that if you accepted the part you mentioned you could easily get off if anything better offered. There is no doubt that if you accept, you will be tied up for the whole run of the piece. That is of course not any reason why you should refuse it; but do not accept it on the strength of my muddle headed remark about it. You will not add to your prestige by playing a bad part in a bad play even at that majestic theatre; and if the salary is no object, you can afford to please yourself. At the same time the engagement might lead to something better; for I am sure that the more people you work with the more you will have wishing to work with you again.

This is not advice – only to withdraw a stupid word which has stuck in my conscience somehow.

yrs sincerely
G. Bernard Shaw

35 / To Kate Rorke   10 Adelphi Terrace WC
                                                    26th November 1904

[ALS: Garrick Club]
Candida, with Kate Rorke (1866–1945) in the title role, had been restored to the Royal Court bill for matinees and evenings on 26–7 November and six matinees from 29 November to 9 December.

My dear Miss Rorke

Dont try to be as good again tonight as you will kill yourself. The last act – *your* last act – was immense: if I had met you immediately after it I should simply have eaten you; so I ran away.

yrs enthusiastically
G. Bernard Shaw

36 / To Lyman J. Seely   The Old House. Harmer Green. Welwyn
                                                    28th December 1904

[ALS: Pierpont Morgan Library, MA 2993]
Lyman J. Seely (1877–1933), a young journalist in Rochester, New York, later became publicist for the Curtiss Aeroplane Company and publisher of a chain of

weekly newspapers. Arnold Daly's national touring production No. 1 of Candida *(there was another in the west) performed in Rochester on 8 December.*

Dear Sir

What a pity it is that Shakespear is not alive to be asked what his idea of Hamlet or Lear might be!

However, you may not be so stupendous an imbecile as your putting the same question as to Marchbanks & Candida would suggest to any ordinary observer, though the question is not on that account less trying to the temper of a just now sorely overworked man.

The difficulty is not in the play, which is explicit and straightforward to an extent which clearly violates nature, but in the prejudices & stupidities which people bring to the theatre with them. For example, there is the convention that a man who loves another man's wife could not possibly tell him so, and that if he did, the husband must instantly offer him bodily violence and kick him out of the house. The only foundation for this in fact is that a certain sort of man will, if he becomes jealous, tell his wife that if he catches his rival in the house again, he will kick him out, thereby throwing on her the disagreeable task of getting rid of the unwelcome visitor, who nevertheless may count on meeting the husband personally with perfect safety. It may be that some of the robuster critics of Candida may imagine that they would really explode with volcanic violence on such an occasion; but my business as a dramatist is not with what men romantically think they would do, but with what as a matter of fact they *do* do, which is a very different matter.

Candida tells her father in the play that when Morell found Marchbanks homeless & apparently destitute in London, he actually had a seven days bill for $275 in his pocket, imagining that he would have to wait until the seven days were up before he could raise any money on it. That incident is taken straight out of the life of De Quincey, whose shyness, whose sense of 'the burden of the incommunicable,' are also reproduced dramatically in the scene between the poet and the typist. If you had written Candida, and I had gone to see it, I should have put my finger on De Quincey at once as one of your models for the figure of Eugene. The fact that nobody has done so in America shews a most deplorable Philistinism in republican journalism. Occasionally one hears a suggestion of Shelley, who was not in the least like Eugene, and who at Eugene's age would have insisted on arguing about the existence of God with Morell, who could not easily have throttled a poet six feet high. Of course half a dozen good men have written sensibly and feelingly about the play; but an appalling number, even of its admirers, clearly cannot understand why Morell did not behave like an average billiard marker and Eugene like a phthisical hairdresser – in saying which I imply nothing worse of billiard markers & hairdressers in general than that they are admittedly not spiritual leaders and poets.

yours faithfully

G. Bernard Shaw

Like Marchbanks, whom Morell found camping on the Thames Embankment, Thomas De Quincey (1785–1859), essayist and critic, as a destitute and shy teenager survived in his early peregrinations in London and Wales by sleeping 'abroad,' with only the sky for a roof. I have not, however, discovered in his prodigious autobiographic writings the situation to which Shaw alludes, involving the seven-day bill for £55 (as mentioned in Act I of *Candida*, but translated by Shaw into dollars for his American correspondent).

37 / To Millicent Murby   10 Adelphi Terrace WC

13th February 1905

[ALS: HRC]

Millicent Murby's amateur New Stage Club, which had performed Candida *in 1902, was about to present the first staged performance of* The Philanderer *on 20 February.*

Dear Miss Murby

I have been so overdriven lately that I have only just realised from your letter the imminence of The Philanderer.

I think you had better let me see a rehearsal or two. There are always a few points, of which the author has the trick, which cannot be made clear in a prompt book, however intelligently it is studied. And as I presume you are playing yourself, I should like to give you what help I can, as I was much interested by your performance in Candida. I promise not to be disagreeable; and if my appearance makes your people nervous I will soon reassure them.

Tomorrow I have to speak in Leeds; but I shall be in town on Wednesday evening (I understand from Miss Florence Farr that you rehearse in the evenings); and as I shall be in town rehearsing at the Court until the 28th, I can put some work into the Philanderer for you.

yours faithfully

G. Bernard Shaw

Shaw lectured to the **Leeds** Art Club on 14 February on 'Art and Ugliness.' He was rehearsing his one-act play *How He Lied to Her Husband* for a triple bill (with plays by Yeats and Arthur Schnitzler) opening at the Royal Court on 28 February.

38 / To Ada Rehan　　　　　　　　　　　10 Adelphi Terrace WC

13th March 1905

[TLS: HRC]

Shaw's meeting with Sam Shubert was his first and, as it transpired, his last, for Shubert died two months later after a train wreck in Harrisburg, Pa. Shaw's description of Shubert as one of the 'sons of Abraham' is an allusion to the fact that many of the principal American theatre managers – the brothers Charles and Daniel Frohman, the partners Abe Erlanger and Marc Klaw, David Belasco – were of Jewish origin.

My dear Miss Rehan

I am afraid you have by this time forgotten my existence. I have almost forgotten it myself, so crushed have I been with rehearsals and business of all sorts for months past.

At last, however, I have seen the youngest and most fascinating of all the sons of Abraham, who is entered on the books of the Carlton Hotel as Sam Shubert. Sam says that if there is a play which he admires in the world it is Brassbound, and will I send him a copy to read. He says also that if there is an artist whom it is a privilege and a delight to work with, it is Miss Rehan, and that such is the harmony prevailing between them, that she has agreed with him for two years ahead.

May I take it, then, that if I give Brassbound to Sam for two years, with a proviso that you are to play Lady Cicely, this will be the best way of securing the play for you without loading you with any responsibility? If you are comfortable with him, and get, as he assures me, a guaranteed percentage, you will be on velvet by this arrangement. Please let me know the exact date of the expiration of your engagement. I shall have to draw the agreement (if it comes off) rather carefully so as to secure you the piece for your repertory without any break or overlap.

The morning after my interview with Sam, I got a letter from Charles Frohman to say that he was quite ready to approach you about it. Charles is no doubt impressed by having had to pay for a seat at a special performance of John Bull's Other Island (my latest big play) ordered by the King. The managers still regard me, as Tyler of Liebler & Co candidly told me, as 'a freak proposition'; but they argue that if I can draw the king and a whole row of cabinet ministers and smart society ladies, the king and the smart ladies will draw the mob; and money will ensue. Which is, of course, very nice for me as far as facilitating business is concerned.

Shubert wants me to allow him to produce in New York. I am very much against this, because, as he admits, he could take a London company to America, but not an American company to London. Therefore you would have to rehearse the play twice over if it were produced in America; and I should not be there the first time. Unfortunately a visit to America would be a frightfully laborious business for me, as I should have to lecture and be lionised to a murderous extent. So do all you can to have the first performance in London. Shubert ought to open his new theatre with it; but he says it will not be finished until June, which is, of course, too late in the season. He therefore wants to begin with a musical comedy. I think this is a pity as the musical comedy is more likely to fail in the hot weather than a strong play; and besides, YOUR theatre ought to begin on the high level. Possibly, however, when Sam realizes that the moment he opens his theatre [the] rates and taxes begin on a heroic scale, he may consider the expedience of delaying its opening.

I am writing in great haste, overwhelmed with correspondence and business details that wear my very soul out. Anything more horrible than to find oneself suddenly an acted playwright after years of freedom from the worries of success cannot be conceived. In future I will take care to write plays that nobody can produce, so outrageously superior to the popular taste will I make them.

I wish you were playing over here. I would go to see you and refresh my weary soul, which feels just now as if it had been beaten like a dusty carpet.

You will come over as usual in the summer, will you not? It would be nice to stay in Cumberland until it was time to rehearse Lady Cicely at the new theatre here. . . .

> yours, always devotedly
> G. Bernard Shaw

The **special performance** of *John Bull's Other Island* for Edward VII (Shaw declined to authorize a 'Command Performance') was given at the Royal Court on the evening of 11 March. The Shuberts' **new theatre** in London was the Waldorf (now the Strand) at the bottom of Drury Lane. It opened on 22 May 1905.

39 / To Kate Rorke

The Old House. Harmer Green. Welwyn
17th May 1905

[ALS: Garrick Club]

As Candida *did not return to the Court Theatre bill until 22 May, for a three-week run, this letter would appear to have been misdated, unless there was an unannounced change of bill on Monday the 15th. Shaw wrote to C.V. France on the same day: 'What is the matter with you? Why this fearful pre-occupation, this devastating absent-mindedness, this air of having an important appointment somewhere else and wishing you could get rid of Candida and Eugene so that you could go and keep it. Have you taken to betting? Are you studying Hamlet? Have you fallen in love? . . . [A]s you have boiled down Morell to a refined and delicate young clergyman, saddened by a wife who does not understand him & bothers him with effusive endearments, the balance of the play is upset quite ludicrously. Will you change parts with Barker if I arrange it for you?' (ALS: Sidney P. Albert).*

My dear Candida

I was in front on Monday night; and I was sorry to see that a coolness has come between you and James. I dont blame you for it, because he has become so completely indifferent to you that nobody could possibly care much for him; but you should not parade your domestic differences before the public.

Come! shall I get you a new husband and a new poet? You are evidently frightfully tired of them; and I dont wonder at it. Morell has become an absent minded curate; and Eugene a powerful and overgrown tragedian who might easily be your father. Will you have Calvert and Martin Harvey? Or do you think of Harben as Morell for a change? The play as it is is quite terrifying. Candida with her sentiment gone and her brains coming out brilliantly – all meaning and force of character and no feeling – a clearheaded able woman trampling on two doormats – chills the manly soul and makes the performance an awful warning. You *did* make that last speech hum.

James is very exasperating; but oh, my dearest Kate, couldnt you pretend to love him just a little for my sake?

devotedly

G. Bernard Shaw

The **Morell** was C.V. France (1868–1949), who joined the cast for the second production in November 1904. The Marchbanks was Granville Barker, who had performed with Kate Rorke in the play since its first Royal Court performance in May 1904. Louis **Calvert** (1859–1923) played Broadbent in *John Bull's Other Island*. John **Martin-Harvey** (1863–1944), former member of Irving's company, went into management in 1899 with the hugely successful *The Only Way*, a dramatization of Dickens's *A Tale of Two Cities*, and on 22 May 1905 would be playing *Hamlet*. Hubert **Harben** (1878?–1941) was a young performer playing the curate, 'Lexy' Mill, in *Candida*.

40 / To Rosina Filippi The Old House. Harmer Green. Welwyn
21st June 1905

[ALS: Cornell]

Rosina Filippi (1866?–1930) was a character actress much in demand; she created Lady Britomart in Major Barbara *the following autumn.*

My dear Miss Filippi

What is this I hear about your being engaged to Hicks for September, when Forbes-Robertson produces Cæsar & Cleopatra? Can he not be persuaded to release you? You are more important to me than anyone else in the cast. It is a perfect part, no trouble, and a colossal effect. You are the only person killed in the piece – in fact the only person ever killed in a Shaw piece! A splendid death – a moonlit altar of white marble, and BUCKETSFULL of gore – immense!

Do try to get free. There is nobody like you. All I want is the best of everything; and you are not only the best, but something more – something different in kind & quality.

yours sincerely

G. Bernard Shaw

Seymour Hicks (1871–1949), an actor-manager at home equally in comedy, musical comedy, revue, and music-hall, built the Aldwych Theatre in 1906. Forbes-Robertson was obliged to cancel the contemplated production of *Cæsar and Cleopatra* due to its immense projected cost. He did, however, tour the United States with a scaled-down production in 1906, and starred in a production for Vedrenne-Barker at the Savoy Theatre in 1907.

41 / To Siegfried Trebitsch

Derry. Rosscarbery
Co. Cork, Ireland
18th July 1905

[ALS: present source unknown]

Siegfried Trebitsch (1868–1956), an Austrian journalist and playwright, was Shaw's German translator. Dr Paul Schlenther (1854–1916), director of the Vienna Burgtheater, had sought a licence for Trebitsch's translation of You Never Can Tell. *Shaw, declining to sign the play away for a 15-year exclusivity to 'the Emperor's theatre,' sent on 6 June an agreement exclusively licensing the Burg for two years to produce in Vienna for a royalty of 10 per cent on the gross. Schlenther, though objecting to a clause calling for payment of 500 kronen as 'liquidated damages' in the event the play was not staged at the Burg within two years, eventually arrived at a compromise agreement with Shaw. The play was performed in Vienna as* Der verlorener Vater (The Abandoned Father), *on 17 March 1906.*

Dear Trebitsch

I began reading Mrs Warren last night. I observe that you call Vivie's cottage a villa with a veranda, which is absurd in view of the supper in Act II.

A villa with a veranda × ¿ × ¿

A cottage with a porch ×

The difference is important, as any air of *luxe* would completely destroy the atmosphere of Vivie's holiday studies; and modern theatres are only too glad to snatch at the least excuse for vulgar splendors of furniture &c &c.

I really must teach you to wait and fight. These big things like the Burgtheater are far easier to conquer than small affairs conducted by energetic men like Antoine, Lugné Poe or Barker. You must go straight to Schlenther and make him sign that agreement, or else you must tell him that I have refused and that you can do nothing with me. Or, if you prefer it, I will write to Schlenther direct & take the combat into my own hands. I dont in the least object to his breaking your heart & ruining you: I *do* object very strongly to allow my piece to be played on the infamous conditions cited in that agreement. The agents of Maeterlinck, Hauptmann, Sudermann, Tolstoi & Mirbeau & Barrie may sign what they like: the firm of Shaw & Trebitsch is quite another matter. I am absolutely inexorable on this point: I am fighting for all the dramatic authors in Europe against the vilest traditions of Austrian officialism; and the battle of Lodi will be a joke compared to the battle of You Never Can Tell unless Schlenther surrenders at discretion. . . .

GBS

André **Antoine** (1858–1943) and A.F. **Lugné Poe** (1869–1940) were actor-managers of coterie theatres in Paris, Antoine celebrated for his Théâtre Libre, after which London's Independent Theatre was modelled, Lugné-Poe for his Théâtre de L'Œuvre. The six dramatists cited by Shaw were theatrical giants in their time, of whom only Octave **Mirbeau** (1848–1917), French playwright who specialized in problem plays like *Les mauvais bergers* (1897), a study of the clash between capital and labour, and Hermann **Sudermann** (1857–1928), German playwright and novelist, whose *Heimat* (1893), was a hit in London as *Magda* (1896) with Mrs Patrick Campbell, have sunk into complete obscurity.

42 / To Dion Boucicault Derry. Rosscarbery. Co. Cork
22nd July 1905

[ALS: Princeton]

Dion ('Dot') Boucicault (1859–1929), son of the Irish dramatist, was director of plays, under Charles Frohman's management, at the Duke of York's Theatre. His experiment with one-act plays was confined to a triple bill of Shaw's Overruled, *Pinero's* The Widow of Wasdale Head, *and Barrie's* Rosalind *in October 1912, which survived only for 27 performances.*

Dear Mr Boucicault

I forgot to say one thing. If you try your experiment *do* spend a little of your money behind the curtain. The stages of the Scala theatre and of His Majesty's have not a single appliance – bar electric light – that would be new to Molière. If you will undertake to work six changes from one complete set to another in twenty seconds each and with five minutes between each change without any carpenters (the music halls must be training hydraulic & electric operators to this sort of work), then I will write you a play some thirtyfive minutes long which will revolutionize the theatre.

Of course ideas just substantial enough for one act occur to authors. But what do they do with them? They write the act; call it Act III or Act II; and manufacture Acts I, II & IV, or Acts I & III out of nothing so as to make it fill a whole evening. *That* is why I tell you you will have to grow your authors & not depend on the old gang.

yrs faithfully
G. Bernard Shaw

43 / To George C. Tyler Derry. Rosscarbery. Co. Cork
(until October)
21st August 1905

[ALS: Princeton]

Shaw had negotiated unsuccessfully in June with Frederick Harrison for a production of Major Barbara, *to star the English-born American actress Eleanor Robson (1879–1979). When he gave the play to Vedrenne-Barker for the Royal Court, George Tyler (who controlled Robson's contracts) attempted to negotiate with Vedrenne; the two proved to be mutually antipathetic. The result was a standoff, with the role of Barbara going to a Canadian actress, Annie Russell (1864–1936), with no production in America until 1915.*

My dear Tyler

You have made the most stupendous mess of this business. That is the worst of you Americans: you are uncommonly nice people personally; but you have no notion of practical affairs. I went into the Haymarket business with Harrison months ago; and I should have liked to go to his house if it were possible; but it isnt. Now that our project has come to grief, there is no use wasting your time in telling you why: you must take my word for it.

Vedrenne's report of your interview was virtually the same as yours; but Vedrenne of course, being, if not English, at least Norman-English, did you in the eye. He wanted Annie Russell, who had been talking to him a good deal; and he did not want Miss Robson, whom he never saw. He was prepared to pay Miss Robson a very heavy salary (probably as much or more than you give her) sooner than lose the play, because the libraries guarantee my plays at the Court (the 'command night' by the King did this for him), and he had either to get my play or else shut up shop; but of course he very much preferred to take Miss Russell at a much smaller rate if he could do so without losing me. You can imagine his delight when you – YOU, George Tyler, great baby as you are – began to play into his hands by making difficulties, and talking about the Haymarket. He had all the cards in his hands except Miss Robson – the fashionable Shaw theatre patronized by the King, the educated Shaw audience, the library guarantee, the repertory system, which makes an open failure impossible, and the knowledge that Granville Barker was absolutely indispensable to the cast, not to mention Calvert & Miss Filippi, whom Harrison could perhaps have replaced without actually wrecking the play. You see, he had heard half the play, and knew that I was depending on all the Court cards for it. So he sat tight and snorted at you; and you rose at it and snorted at him as the keeper of a twopennyhalfpenny outside theatre [*street show*]; and so he had his way; and Miss Robson lost her play and will never forgive you, and serve you right!

And now, what do you suppose will happen if Miss Russell makes a hit as Major Barbara? How can Miss Robson take the part from her in America? – how can I refuse her the part in America if she works hard for me and makes it her own? I am not committed, and will not commit myself until I see how the play turns out on the stage; but I can see what is coming, whereas you, oh buffle headed disastrous Tyler, can see nothing.

You ought to go straight into a penitentiary for six months at least.

Next time – if there ever is a next time – you may motor about the Tyrol as much as you please; but you must do exactly what I tell you to do; and the wronger you think it, the more certain it will be to be right.

Now I must make pitiful apologies to Miss Robson. She will never forgive me either; but as for you, she will never speak to you again unless she is as magnanimous as she is lovely[.]

yrs ever
G. Bernard Shaw

PS. My wife says that *you* didnt want Miss Robson to play Barbara either; and that you & Vedrenne have simply outwitted me & Miss R between you; but on consideration I reject this view, though of course if you had really wanted the thing to come off it would have come off.

---

44 / To Louis Calvert   10 Adelphi Terrace WC
                                             18th November 1905

[TLS: Sotheby Parke-Bernet; sold 6 May 1981]

Shaw had been rehearsing Major Barbara *with Calvert as Undershaft since the beginning of November. Calvert gave one of his finest performances as the old actor in the Paul Kester (1870–1933) play* Sweet Nell of Old Drury *(1900). Shaw's remark suggests Calvert had invested in, or been paid off in, shares in the production by Fred Terry (1864–1932), who had sent out multiple touring companies. Calvert's principal problem was that he was a slow study and, through lack of concentration, frequently forgot his lines or missed his cues.*

My dear Calvert

I hope I did not worry you too much today at rehearsal. The fact is, you are ruining the end of the second act by your enormous, desolating, obvious-to-everybody absent mindedness. The reason I put on an understudy for Barbara was that you had driven Miss Russell almost out of her senses by letting the scene drop when she was doing her hardest to get hold of it. She did not complain; but I saw what was happening and acted on my own initiative. You see it is all very well for you: you know that you can wake up at the last moment and do the trick; but that will not help out the unhappy victims who have to rehearse with you. And you forget your own weight. The moment you let the play go it drops. You sit there, greatly interested (except when you are asleep) by the way to manage the play and the mistakes that all the rest are making, and trying to make out what is wrong with the whole scene. Of course what is wrong is *you*. There is that frightful speech where Undershaft deliberately gives a horrible account of his business, sticking detail after detail of the horrors of war into poor bleeding Barbara to shew her what Mrs Baines will stand for £5000. Cusins, who sees it all, is driven into an ecstasy of irony by it: it is a sort of fantasia played on the nerves both of him and Barbara by Machiavelli-Mephistopheles. All that is needed to produce the effect is steady concentration, magnetic intensity. Irving, who could not do lots of things that you can do, could have done this superbly. But you are evidently thinking of Lord knows what – the returns from one of your Sweet Nell companies, or how Barker always drops his voice when he ought to raise it and emphasizes the wrong word, or what a monstrous thing it is that an idiot of an author should produce a play when he doesnt know the first rudiments of his business or – and then you suddenly realize that the stage has been waiting for you for ten minutes. There are moments when if we were not in a conspiracy to spoil you, we should rend you to pieces and wallow in your blood. Miss Russell has been working at the thing with the greatest enthusiasm, and when she tries to get into the rush of it, and is slacked down every time by your colossal indifference, she almost gives up in despair. If you were an insignificant actor it would not matter: they could run away from you; but they are not strong enough for this: the piece takes its time and intensity from you in spite of all they can do.

Mind, I quite appreciate your heroic study of lines; and I dont complain of anything except the end of the second act; but for that I have no words strong enough to describe your atrocity: you will scream through endless centuries in hell for it, and implore me in vain to send you ices from heaven to cool your burning tongue. We have only one week more; and I have set my heart on your making a big success in the part. And you are taking it as easy as if Undershaft were an old uncle in a farce. Spend tomorrow in prayer. My wife was horrified at my blanched hair and lined face when I returned from rehearsal today. And I have a blinding headache, and can no more.

> your unfortunate
> G.B.S.

45 / To Hugo Vallentin   10 Adelphi Terrace WC
                                              5th March 1906

[ALS: Dartmouth]

Hugo Vallentin (1860–1921), a journalist who became press officer for the Swedish Consulate in London, was for fifteen years Shaw's Swedish translator. Helden (Heroes) *was the German title for* Arms and the Man.

Dear Dr Vallentin

Our first duty as men of letters is to keep up prices and not make it harder for our fellow authors to live. I must have the highest royalties paid to any author in Sweden – in fact, higher, because there are two mouths – yours and mine – to be fed. Five per cent is absurd: we should have ten. Seven and a half is the very least I will consider. I know all that the managers will say; so they may as well save themselves the trouble of saying it. If they dont like my prices, let them produce plays by Swedish authors.

I strongly object to the translation of Helden from the German. The translation must be made direct from the English, and made by *you*, if you are going to be my translator. We cannot afford to have any plums picked out of our pudding.

Tell all the managers that I am a Harpagon, a bloodsucker, a millionaire; that you are ashamed of me; but that you have no power &c &c. I am not unreasonable; but I know all these marketings and chafferings by heart; and I never say 'c'est à prendre ou à laisser' ('take it or leave it') unless I have reason to believe that I can get what I ask for. Helden is [a] cheap play because it is an old one. Man & Superman will be dearer.

> yours faithfully
> G. Bernard Shaw

46 / To Ada Rehan   10 Adelphi Terrace WC
                                         4th July 1906

[ALS: HRC]

My dear Miss Rehan

Your letter came at the right moment. I had heard late on Sunday night
that a boat train had been wrecked at Salisbury. On Monday morning I
rushed for the papers to assure myself that you were safe; and lo! on
the top of the papers on the breakfast table was a letter addressed in
your handwriting. So that was all right.

   The position about Brassbound is rather strained just now. I held out
hopes in all directions of a final answer in June. Frohman is building a
gigantic air castle on Ellen Terry's Jubilee Tour in America. He is so
absolutely certain that she will draw $2000 *every time* in Brassbound that
he has actually offered me my royalty on $1750 guaranteed rather than
on the actual receipts whatever they may be. He has asked me to make
the contract at once, reserving my promise to you in case you are ready
to play Lady Cicely. Now this is of no importance to me if I can get you;
for I should make as much or more in the long run from the play in
your repertory. But it is of some importance to Ellen, as there is no
other part within her reach so well suited to America and to herself.
The fact that she never mentions the subject of America to me shews
that she is conscious of having a personal interest which she must not
push at your expense.

   Our position is rather a delicate one. My personal impulse is to wait a
thousand years if necessary; but, as I have been reminded, there are
limits to my moral right to make a monopoly for you as against Ellen;
and there are limits to your moral right (I say this because I know how
you feel about it already) to prevent her from playing her best part on
her Jubilee tour by any other means than playing it yourself. Everything
turns on whether you feel in yourself (never mind the doctors) that you
can reasonably undertake to play Lady Cicely in October. If not, Destiny
is too strong for us; for you cannot say 'I will neither play it myself nor
let Ellen play it'. That is the case for giving in.

   But before you decide there are one or two things you ought to
know. Between ourselves, the Court production has been only a moder-

ate success. The 84 performances already given have *averaged* only $362 taken at each performance; and the Court Theatre, small as it is, holds $800. This is not Ellen's fault: the play is badly flattened out & even made boresome in places by two bad mistakes in casting. But the fact remains. If you can play Lady Cicely you will not be snatching a huge success from Ellen: you will be taking a part in which, financially, she has only just held her own, though she has made an artistic success in it.

Another thing – to explain the weakening of my own backbone. I have just seen Eleanor Robson for the first time since her tour with Merely Mary Anne. I declare to you that if I saw a horse that had been so obviously overworked, I should try to get the owner prosecuted. They will half kill Ellen, since it is apparently impossible to kill her out-right. What they would do to you is more than I care to contemplate. Anyhow, you must take the impression made by Miss Robson into account too. It almost made me ask you never to play except at a Court revival of Brassb^{d}.

Having written all this I feel a strong impulse to tear it up; for I know that it all points one way; and though it is Fate that is driving us along that way, *I* am extremely recalcitrant to it; and I should never forgive you if you were not equally so. After holding on all these years, it is infu-riating to have to let go.

Dont answer too hastily. I have no belief whatever in the average doc-tor; and though Parkinson (who doctors my wife) is not an average doc-tor, he has certain crazes. He is perfectly convinced that all my failings are due to something wrong with my kidneys. All the crimes of civiliza-tion are to him mere kidney symptoms. On any other subject you may listen to him; but if ever he warns you on *that* subject, do not be too much impressed. How do you feel yourself? Is there *any* chance of your being able to play Lady Cicely before the end of October? Say yes; and let me say no to Frohman.

yours ever

G. Bernard Shaw

Ellen **Terry** performed *Captain Brassbound's Conversion* at the Royal Court for six weeks in March 1906 and a 13-week run from 16 April. *Merely Mary Ann* by Shaw's colleague and friend Israel Zangwill (1864–1926) was one of Eleanor Robson's most popular successes both in America and Britain. There were two London physicians named **Parkinson** recorded in the Medical Directory for 1906: Dr John P. Parkinson (1863–1930), at 57 Wimpole Street, and Dr (later Sir) Thomas Wright Parkinson (1863–1935), a New Zealander, at 77 Sloane Street.

47 / To Ada Rehan   10 Adelphi Terrace WC
                                          14th July 1906

[ALS: U. of Pennsylvania]

On 11 July, following another siege of illness, Ada Rehan wrote to thank Shaw for giving her 'one more chance,' and regretting that she was unable to commit herself: 'You can never understand how hard it has been for me to let it go' (ALS: HRC). Though she survived until 1916, she never performed again.

My dear Miss Rehan

Very well.
Good.
It cannot be helped.

I am not in a sullen rage. I *was* in a sullen rage. Now I am calm. I have seen Charles Frohman. That romantic baby has his imagination full of sensational matinees and gold mine returns. He sees America weeping at the tomb of Irving. He sees himself standing on that tomb and saying, with a break in his voice, 'You're goin t'look on HUR (meaning Ellen) for the last time'.

I feel as if I had been stealing a child's coral. He intimated just once that a gentleman with a generous nature would take 8 per cent, but that he knew it was no use appealing to Shylock. I intimated in return that I would willingly let him have the play for nothing had I not promised Klaw not to give anybody better terms that I gave him. So he agreed to my terms; and we parted warm friends.

Oh, these men of business! I have not yet met one of them who had any notion of business. They are all stage-struck dreamers: that is what makes them so dangerous & destructive when they are allowed their own way.

Ellen's tour is only a three months business – a rush round the big cities. She will not exhaust Brassbound: my plays are not for a run but for all time.

Is your sister a good press agent? If she is, tell her to make public the fact that you have seen Ellen Terry play in Brassbound and have insisted that she shall play it in America on her jubilee tour, waiving your own right to create the part of Lady Cicely in the United States. This will do Ellen a good turn; and it will, unlike most press paragraphs, be true, as you know very well that I would have held it for you if you had as much as held up your little finger. I wish it had been possible for you to do so & still be Ada Rehan.

On Monday I go off to Cornwall – Pentillie, Mevagissey, is the address – for some sea air. When you come back to London, see You Never Can Tell: it is one of the best performances we have had at the Court. Why not spend the winter here for a change? It will console me for Brassbound if I can see you occasionally.

yours ever
G. Bernard Shaw

Ellen Terry's American **tour** was extended to four months. From late January to early May 1907 she visited 15 cities (including Toronto and Montreal), performing Shaw's play 71 times. *You Never Can Tell* was added to the Royal Court bill for its third engagement on 9 July, for a run of ten weeks, with Louis Calvert as the Waiter and Lillah McCarthy as Gloria. The play became one of Shaw's most enduring money-makers.

48 / To J.E. Vedrenne   10 Adelphi Terrace WC
17th October 1906

[ALS: Theatre Museum]
Shaw was determined to costume Lillah McCarthy ravishingly for Jennifer's appearances in the Act II Star and Garter terrace scene and the Act V Bond Street picture-gallery scene in The Doctor's Dilemma, *scheduled for eight matinees at the Royal Court from 20 November. Madame Hayward was a leading theatre costumier in Bond Street.*

My dear V.D.

The bolt has fallen: Madame Hayward wants £170 for the dresses. Possibly this means only £150; but the difference is of no account.

I foresaw that it would come to something like this; but if you consider that there is only one woman to dress instead of, as usual, half a dozen, you will see that I have saved on the swings what you will have to spend on the roundabouts. I am deliberately spoiling Lillah to get the best out of her for this play; for it will depend on her getting as much enchantment into it as possible. The alternative is Mrs Patrick Campbell; and just think what it would cost to dress *her*, not to mention her salary.

So cheer up: it might be worse.

The exasperating thing about these first rate people is that they charge you ten guineas for ten shillings worth of extra quality; but the extra is there & Lillah knows it. She must not feel cheap, whatever it costs – I mean, you will say, whatever it costs *you* – but you know I dont throw money about as recklessly as you do yourself. This will not be wasted.

disinterestedly

G.B.S.

49 / To Ralph D. Blumenfeld   [10 Adelphi Terrace WC
14 November 1906]

[HD: BL 50734, ff 2v–4v]

Ralph D. Blumenfeld (1864–1948), an American journalist, was editor of the Daily Express, *whose theatre critic Archibald Haddon (1872–1942) had published in his 'Green Room Gossip' column on 14 November a complete, detailed synopsis of* The Doctor's Dilemma, *containing portions of the dialogue from the Epilogue to the play.*

Dear Sir

Will you please look at the first two columns of Green Room Gossip in your issue of today. When I tell you that these paragraphs, which contain not only a complete disclosure of the action of an unperformed & unpublished play, but portions of the dialogue, are unauthorized by me, you will see that the writer has involved us all in a very serious difficulty. Somebody who has had access to the rehearsals has sold his information. This, I need not tell you, is the grossest breach of confidence that can be committed in a theatre; and I cannot believe that your contributor would have taken advantage of it had he not been led to believe that it was authorized. The information appears also in The Standard; but there it has been more cautiously used, actual quotations from the dialogue being avoided, and the story told in more general terms.

Knowing as I do how much an editor is in the hands of his contributors on points of good sense, good faith, & copyright law I am anxious not to take any unfriendly step. May I therefore ask you to answer me a question & to do me a service.

1. The Question. Do you claim a right to reproduce the dialogue & disclose the plot of a play without the owner's sanction before the first performance?

2. The Service. Will you ascertain from your contributor, & communicate to me the name of the person who gave the information & the quotations?

yours faithfully
[*unsigned*]

Shaw learned from Blumenthal that Haddon had obtained the information from a freelance journalist and playwright Boyle Lawrence (1869–1951). The latter, however, declined to reveal his source (it was, in fact, strongly suspected that he himself had somehow gained illicit entry to the theatre). Shaw, much concerned about the possibility that a journalistic bribe of a theatre underling could, by anticipating first performance, result in a loss of copyright, requested Blumenfeld to publish, alongside of the review on 21 November, a disclaimer that Shaw drafted for him: 'In a recent issue of the Daily Express ... a premature disclosure was made of the plot of Mr Bernard Shaw's play The Doctor's Dilemma, and passages from the dialogue were quoted. The editor has since learnt that these disclosures were not authorized, and that they must have reached the press through an abuse of confidence. Under these circumstances we hasten to disclaim any right to make known the contents of an unpublished or unperformed copyright manuscript without the consent of the owners of the copyright, and to assure the author and the management of the Court Theatre that no countenance is given to the procuring of information by improper means for the columns of this paper' (c. 15–17 November 1906; BL 50734, ff 78–77). When the disclaimer did not appear, Shaw consulted with the Society of Authors, the attorneys Field & Roscoe, and the Association of West End Managers. Advised that legal action would involve nearly a year of litigation and a substantial bill of costs, Shaw eventually let the matter drop; but it was six years before he contributed so much as a letter to the columns of the Daily Express.

50 / To Judith Lytton 10 Adelphi Terrace WC

23rd November 1906

[TLS: BL 54155, unfoliated]

The Hon. Judith Lytton (1873–1957), later 16th Baroness Wentworth, wife of
the artist Neville Lytton (1879–1951) and friend of the Granville Barkers, gen-
erously offered to lend her jewelled tiara to Lillah McCarthy (who had married
Barker on 24 April) to wear in the Epilogue of The Doctor's Dilemma, *and*
brought it to the Court Theatre stage door just before the opening matinee on the
20th. As a result, however, of the probable journalistic intrusion a week earlier
and of the sudden invasion of the theatre by a mentally disturbed young man
(Shaw's comic description of this incident is wildly exaggerated), who had to be
ejected, the strictest security of all entrances to the theatre had been ordered, and
Mrs Lytton was turned away. At Shaw's urgence a letter was instantly des-
patched to her by the management to express the 'horror and remorse' of all prin-
cipal parties at the Court and to invite her to return – with the tiara, urgently
needed to replace the tinselly headdress supplied by the costumier.

My dear Mrs Lytton

I have seen the headdress this morning; and it is just what I wanted,
only it may be made much more so. It will bear many more magic jew-
els. The play is so moving in that moment that if she came in with ser-
pents hissing in her hair, ten feet high, and with a Greek tragic mask, it
would not seem exaggerated. She is wearing it today. I also want the
dress redesigned for the revival of the play in January. The present
thing is evidently made by Jay, and doesnt belong to Jennifer at all. This
modiste-made dressing is no use: we must build the character right up
from its stockings to its hairpins. Your headdress is a perfect sample:
you understand the thing. In fact, your own head began it: you were the
original inspiration.

Destiny has very fearfully avenged your treatment on that fatal Tuesday. I no longer sympathize with you. I wonder at the ways of Nemesis.
The Barkers are all but divorced. Vedrenne is hardly on speaking terms
with them. Relations are strained beyond endurance; and unless you
restore peace there will be an end of the Court Theatre.

Here is the true story of it all. Last week a lunatic, venerating me
beyond all deities, took it into his head that Barker's make-up in Man &

Superman was a blasphemous mockery of his Master, and resolved to slay him. He got past the stage doorkeeper, who fell downstairs in trying to overtake him. He got almost on to the stage when a sceneshifter seized him and carried him out, where his mother was found looking for him. He then tried a protest from the stalls and was ejected. The doorkeeper, lamed by his fall, was then given orders of Roman sternness. Nobody was to be admitted. Barker went forth guarded by carpenters. Discipline was to be inflexible on pain of instant dismissal for everybody.

The next thing, of course, was a visit to the theatre by poor innocent Mrs McCarthy, Mrs Barker's mother. She was denied access to her child; kept in the cold passage; shoved to the wall by everybody; and reduced to indignation and tears. Mrs Barker had to see her on the stairs, half clothed and in a draught.

I leave you to imagine the curtain lecture Barker got that night.

With the rashness of youth, Barker refused, as I gather, to be mother-in-lawed out of the rules of his theatre. So Mr[s] Barker bided her time. It came in the person of YOU.

I will not go so far as to say that Mrs Barker was delighted: she was really concerned and ashamed at your misadventure. Still, human nature being what it is, she must have blessed you for making a door-mat of Barker and his rules. He has not been the same man since; and she is flushed, perhaps with remorse on your account, but also, I think, a little with domestic triumph.

Vedrenne is totally demoralized. He wants me to cut the death scene out of my play; has torn up Miss McCarthy's two best photographs as Jennifer; wants to sack the doorkeeper (a low spirited but most honest veteran); and wishes he had never been born.

Please forgive. If you only knew what a foolish place a theatre is, especially when it tries to be orderly and disciplined, you would think of us more in pity than in anger. You were much too nice, I suspect. If you had said, 'I am Mrs Lytton, a lady of considerable consequence. Go and tell your dog of a master to come down to me at once and lead me to his own office whilst I wait for Miss McCarthy,' you would have been treated becomingly.

As for me, when I think of the letters I wrote that day —!!!!

yours faithfully

(this typewriter always writes

yours faithfully)

G. Bernard Shaw

Jay was a London department store with its own dressmaking department. Although it sounds like a theatrical term, a **curtain lecture** – made famous by Douglas Jerrold (1803–57) through his *Mrs Caudle's Curtain Lectures* (1846), first published in *Punch* – is a nocturnal tirade by a spouse addressed to her cowed husband within the confines of their curtain-enclosed bed.

51 / To Cyril Maude   The Rectory
                                          Ayot St Lawrence, Welwyn
                                              27th November 1906

[Behind the Scenes with Cyril Maude, 1927]
Cyril Maude had 'ardently begged' Shaw to write him a play.

My difficulty about writing plays is that I have to keep the Court going, and I have hardly time for that alone. This Doctor play was produced by a *tour de force*. Last summer not a line of it was on paper or in my head. By the time I get a moment to start again, the Court will be howling for another play. This system of putting up plays for six weeks is certainly a wonderful success pecuniarily, for the plays dont die and the business doesnt slack; but it is the very devil in point of rehearsal. I spend months every year producing when I ought to be writing; and though Barker would take the odd plays off my hands, he too wants a respite to write his own plays, which are much better than mine in some ways. And I am heaped up with other work. Nothing would please me better than to do a comedy for you, a fantastic masterpiece for Tree, a problem play for Alexander, and another *You Never Can Tell* for Harrison, not to mention a romantic melodrama for Waller and a musical comedy for Edwardes. But even if I executed one of these orders, Vedrenne would jump to and seize the script on the unanswerable ground that you and all can do without me and he cant. And then failure is impossible at the Court and the play is not run to death. On the whole I think my best plan is to wait until you are all ruined and then give you engagements at the Court (£10 double star salary – to *you*) and have magnificently acted performances.

yours ever

G.B.S.

The **Doctor play** was *The Doctor's Dilemma*, begun on 11 August and completed on 12 September. The Royal Court opening was on 20 November. Lewis **Waller** (1860–1915), a matinee idol, was noted for romantic costume roles: D'Artagnan in *The Three Musketeers* (1898) and *Monsieur Beaucaire* (1902). George **Edwardes** (1852–1915) inaugurated musical comedy in London at his immensely popular Gaiety Theatre in the Strand.

52 / To Carl Hentschel   10 Adelphi Terrace WC

17th January 1907

[ALS: Universal City Public Library]

Carl Hentschel (1865–1930), head of a firm of photo-etchers and lithographers, was founder of the Playgoers' Club and, later, the 'O.P.' Club (from the stage direction 'Opposite Prompt,' meaning stage right, the prompter's position in English theatres always being at stage left). On several occasions Shaw addressed the clubs or took the chair for other speakers. The play to be discussed on the next day was The Doctor's Dilemma.

Private

Dear Mr Hentschl

As Friday is seldom a free night with me, I cannot attend the meeting on the 18th, nor have I any communication to make to you in your official capacity as chairman.

However, I will tell you one or two things that may help you in discussing the play. It is much more closely founded on fact than most of the critics realize. For instance, the newspaper man may be taken as a simple adaptation to the stage of the gentleman who called on Mrs Patrick Campbell the moment the news of her husband's death was wired from South Africa & wanted to interview her – obviously on 'how it feels to be a widow,' as he had no other possible business with her. The editor mentioned the fact, and expressed a reserved surprise at Mrs Campbell's refusal to see the interviewer. This passed without a word of public comment. I think the paper was the Chronicle; but I may be wrong as to that.

Again, a youth named Rankin was sentenced last year to six months imprisonment for attempting to blackmail his father, a schoolmaster. In the dock he told the judge that he acted as he did because he was a disciple of Bernard Shaw. In Wormwood Scrubbs he refused the ministrations of the chaplain, and asked that I should be sent for. As I was not in the country, Mr Stewart Headlam visited him in gaol. It was quite clear that he was under the impression that my teaching was simply an advocacy of reckless and shameless disregard of all social and moral obligations, an error which he owes, I should say, not to reading my works unsophisticatedly, but to reading the follies which the press utters about me, and then perhaps reading me in the false light of those follies. It was as a reductio-ad-absurdum of this error, and partly as a warning against it, that I made Dubedat in the play use Rankin's defence. The fact that several critics concluded that I was formally giving my sanction to Dubedat's moral imbecility proves that, in spite of all my experience, I underrated the intellectual imbecility of the attitude in which many otherwise sensible critics approach my plays.

The medical part of the play is all true to actual scientific circumstances. The dilemma actually existed last year at St Mary's, Paddington, where Sir Almroth Wright, the discoverer of opsonin, always had more cases to treat than he and his little trained band of assistants could cope with. Under such circumstances there is no question of whether a doctor ought to choose or not: he MUST either choose or draw lots; and no man draws lots where an intelligent choice is possible.

Almost all the critics blundered over opsonin. They thought it something which the doctor injected. It is nothing of the kind. It is a natural product of the body, like blood or bile. The inoculation of the vaccine provokes the body to produce it to resist the attack. This is not dramatically interesting; but it bears on the failure of the critics to understand the real nature of the mysterious advantage I possess over the romantic playwrights. By going to actual life and science for my materials, and accepting even the most (dramatically) irrelevant conditions of accuracy, I discover unsuspected veins of irony and pathos, and unused situations. I am able to give away situations which would make an ordinary romantic play apiece, at the rate of about a dozen per page. The result is that I am said not to produce situations at all, just as Wagner, when he went in for continuous melody, was accused of having no melody at all. It is not a cheap way of working; but it is irresistibly effective. As you know, The Doctor's Dilemma, like John Bull's Other Island & Man & Superman, has been denounced as undramatic, disagreeable, blasphemous, as a sign of the exhaustion of my talent, as, in short, my Waterloo. But it is succeeding to the utmost possibilities of the Court Theatre. When it went into the evening bill, the critics had weakened perceptibly in the face of the public interest in it. When it is revived for the first time, they will cover it with compliments. The second time, they will proclaim it a masterpiece. Then I will write another; and, untaught by experience, they will announce that my Waterloo has really come at last, and that the qualities which made my doctors so delightful and my dying artist so moving and impressive have been swallowed up by my bad taste, my untimely ribaldry, and so on and so forth. That is the invariable routine.

I have marked this letter Private because I have not written it for publication nor for reading to the meeting. If, however, you wish to state its facts in your own way, you are very welcome to say that your private relations with me are sufficiently friendly to enable you to speak with authority as one knowing my own account of the play. I owe you that much for your interest in the theatre, and the work you have done in interesting others in playgoing.

yours faithfully `

G. Bernard Shaw

George Valler **Rankin**, a 26-year-old clerk, found guilty in Central Criminal Court of 'writing and publishing a false and defamatory libel of and concerning' his father, was sentenced to six months' imprisonment (*The Times*, 2 May 1906). **Wormwood Scrubbs** (popularly misspelled, the correct spelling being Scrubs), in West London, was the largest male prison in Britain; young prisoners in the London area generally were confined there. Sir Almroth **Wright** (1861–1947), eminent bacteriologist, had advised Shaw on technical medical aspects of the play.

53 / To Lillah McCarthy   10 Adelphi Terrace WC

27th April 1907

[ALS: HRC]

Lillah McCarthy was engaged for the restored Man and Superman *in the Royal Court repertory, but only after Shaw craftily had convinced her to refrain from*

*making an unacceptable salary demand, bribing her instead with an expensive
gown for the Act IV scene in the villa garden in Granada. The Barkers had
leased a retreat in Fernhurst, Surrey. Over the next few years the Shaws and the
Barkers made frequent weekend or Sunday country visits to each other's homes.*

My dear Lillah

I have stolen the enclosed agreements from Vedrenne. As I am insisting
on your playing, you have him too completely at a disadvantage to
indulge in a victory. I think it would be wiser to play for nothing than to
force him to surrender just now. If you want a £25 dress for the garden
scene, let me pay for it; and I can easily get Vedrenne later on to repay
me spontaneously. Besides, if you took the money now, you could not
give him a piece of your mind, whereas by letting the rope go when he
is pulling his hardest, you will place him on his back in a favorable attitude for receiving a ton of it right on his chest.

There is no fun in getting one's way by mere brute force at a cost of
humiliation and bad blood. I enclose a draft of the sort of letter you
might write when sending back the agreements signed. I could give you
lots of other important reasons if I had time; but the train is just starting, so to speak.

My Lord Harley has telephoned to ask whether we are coming down
as arranged with you. Charlotte declares she never heard of it. Is that
my fault? have I forgotten anything in your letters? If so, forgive & pity

yrs ever
G.B.S.

Shaw's draft letter for Lillah was enclosed.

My dear Mr Vedrenne

You are very unkind and obstinate about the dresses; and I have a great
mind to take away my husband and my author and shut up the Court
Theatre. Only, as I could not take you as well, and the two gentlemen
would be unhappy without you, and nobody cares how dowdy I look on
the stage, and you have stolen all the sympathy from me by letting your
eyes get bad again, and I have had an illness and am cheap in consequence, and I have spoiled you by my weakness in the past in taking a

walking lady's salary from you, and I cannot force you to give me my £25 willingly and wont take it if you grudge it, and am not going to let you quarrel with me no matter how hard you try, and Mr Shaw tells me that you are an angel and that I am only worth thirty shillings a week and find my own stockings and laces, I will indulge you just this once more, and then go for ever to some theatre where they really appreciate hard work & good temper.

I shall buy my own dresses, and only ask you to put a line in the program – 'Miss McCarthy's dresses have been supplied by Messrs Brown & Wilkins, 789 Old Kent Road – 23/11¾ the skirt and blouse – the hat a real bargain at six shillings.'

I return the agreements, signed. After all, I am just as glad that the Superman one gives me control of my dresses. I hope you will like them.

And I *really* hope you are better, and that I have not worried you too much.

54 / To Charles Hughes   10 Adelphi Terrace WC
                                                2nd November 1907

[TLS: Theatre Museum]

Charles Hughes (1851–1917), textile merchant, scholar and theatre enthusiast, was the founder of the Manchester branch of the Independent Theatre. He later sponsored a number of local productions with the Charringtons. In 1907 Annie Horniman bought Manchester's Gaiety Theatre to house a permanent repertory company; between 1908 and 1917 she mounted over 200 plays there. Her enterprise created a serious competitive situation, for the Vedrenne-Barker touring companies would be affected if Shaw licensed to Horniman's theatre plays that were in the Royal Court repertory. Shaw's statement that the Court Theatre 'campaign' required no backing (an afterthought he inserted into the margin) was technically correct, though misleading. There was no outside backing, for Shaw had supplied the needed financing on a loan basis rather than as an investment, and eventually waived some of his royalties, a fact he apparently did not wish to divulge to Hughes.

My dear Hughes

I have made an appointment to see Miss Horniman on Monday. I am sorry to say that this theatrical business is much more complicated financially than it seems on the surface. The campaign in London which has set the whole thing on its legs, could not have been faced for a moment but for the calculation that the provincial tours would repay the money lost in London. I may tell you in strict confidence that I have had to put down three thousand pounds myself to enable the business to go on (This refers only to the Savoy: the Court's campaign scraped through without backing.); and my sole chance of getting that money back lies with the Vedrenne-Barker Companies in the provinces. Now you see the situation. Manchester is what is called a number-one town: that is, one of the prizes of the provincial circuit. It would break the back of any tour to have Manchester knocked out of it; and if I break the back of the number-one tours, I break the back of Vedrenne-Barker and my own back as well. How then can I hand over Manchester to Miss Horniman? She will not find it any easier to make both ends meet than Vedrenne and Barker. She will have to send out tours; and then the clash will be worse than ever. I do not see any way out of this difficulty except by making London and Manchester independent of one another; and that seems impossible without a municipal endowment. Under the existing system it looks as if the new theatres would spend a few years work and a good deal of money in ruining one another.

Of course I am entirely friendly to the Manchester enterprise, and have already given it the run of the plays Vedrenne and Barker have not yet touched. But you can see, as a man of business, that I am rather in a cleft stick.

yours ever
G. Bernard Shaw

55 / To Henry Mapleson 10 Adelphi Terrace WC
4th December 1907

[*Pall Mall Gazette*, 13 December 1907]

Henry Mapleson (1851–1927), an opera impresario in London, offered Shaw a commission to provide an opera libretto for Camille Saint-Saëns (1835–1921). Shaw was frequently solicited for opera or operetta librettos, for Richard Strauss

(1864–1949), Arthur Sullivan (1842–1900), André Messager (1853–1929), and Oscar Straus (1870–1954), among others; he rejected all offers. Edward Elgar (1857–1934) was Shaw's favourite English composer, whose music he championed for nearly four decades.

My dear Colonel Mapleson

Unfortunately I have a prior engagement with Richard Strauss, which is at present rather hung up by the fact that I want to write the music and he wants to write the libretto, and we both get along very slowly for want of practice.

I wonder whether Elgar would turn his hand to opera. I have always played a little with the idea of writing a libretto; but though I have had several offers, nothing has come of it. When one is past fifty, and is several years in arrears with one's own natural work, the chances of beginning a new job are rather slender.

yours faithfully
G. Bernard Shaw

56 / To Lillah McCarthy

10 Adelphi Terrace WC
30th December 1907

[TLS: HRC]

Lillah McCarthy had been rehearsing Arms and the Man, *to be revived by Vedrenne-Barker at the Savoy Theatre on 30 December, while performing concurrently in a farce,* Angela, *at the Comedy Theatre through the 28th. Contrary to standard practice among theatre directors not to burden actors with last-minute advice or instructions, Shaw had no compunction about bombarding performers with extended notes shortly before an opening performance.*

My dear Lillah

I made a few notes on Saturday which you did not get as you had to rush off to your matinee.

I am now quite convinced that it is a mistake to say 'You look ever so much nicer' (in the third act) before you come down to the table. You can take as much time as you like strolling down and looking at him: the more the better in fact.

When Bluntschli sits down and says 'My dear young lady, dont let this worry you,' you are so full of the business you have just before you, that you do not listen to him. When he says 'One is hearing people tell lies,' you do not play to it.

In the melodramatic bit immediately after – 'that is how men think of women' and 'Captain Bluntschli!!!' – you have got the idea perfectly; but you have not yet carried your dramatic indignation to the point of totally forgetting your clothes. You still do not sweep with a sufficiently majestic unconsciousness of them.

You now say 'How did you find me out?' in the act of sitting down. This is quite fatal to the effect. You must sit down, look at him, and then speak.

Be careful not to let down 'Oh, how could you be so stupid.' That whole speech should come out with the most intense vexation.

Dont make a pause between 'You have a low shop-keeping mind' and 'You think of things that never come into a gentleman's head.' The two sentences should tumble out on top of one another.

You now always miss the cue 'first-rate stables.' Fix it hard in your head: we must not have a hitch in the finale.

You are quite right about the line in the book being 'Some soldiers, I know, are afraid of death'; but the book, as usual, is wrong. Better say 'afraid to die.'

The part makes such enormous demands on your presence of mind, that I feel quite apologetic about it. The transitions are very sudden, and come one after the other with fearful rapidity. But on the other hand, when once they become mechanical, their effect is certain. To get the maximum of effect you must feed Bluntschli very carefully. Your high horse will not amuse the audience unless he knocks you off it; and you must take care to caracole very proudly indeed every time a fall is coming. However, these are only counsels of perfection. You must now let yourself go and enjoy yourself: even if you miss a few points, you have enough in hand for a handsome success. So go in and win.

In haste,

yours ever
G. Bernard Shaw

57 / To J.E. Vedrenne Ayot St Lawrence. Welwyn. Herts.
19th April 1908

[ALS: HRC]

Following the failure of the Vedrenne-Barker season at the Savoy Theatre in 1907, the management joined forces briefly with Frederick Harrison at the Haymarket Theatre. J.J.M. (John James Moore) Davis (1862–1916) was the scene designer for the production of Shaw's Getting Married, *scheduled to open at the Haymarket on 12 May. He had earlier designed* The Devil's Disciple *for Vedrenne-Barker at the Savoy Theatre, 1907. The 'dresses' were executed by G.M. Redfern & Co.*

My dear VD

. . . Tell Davis to go and look through the Tower [of London] on a sunny morning. There must be NO PANELLING: that Haymarket stage will look like a smoking room if any compromise is attempted. It must be clean Norman stone work, supposed to be lit by big windows in the proscenium opening – big oak doors (not painted, but axe-cut raw oak doors with big latches – clean & splendid). Nothing stands looking at so long: nothing is more cheerful: nothing shews up dresses better: nothing like it has ever been done on the stage. Davis will tumble to it.

In haste – post hour
GBS

58 / To Henry Arthur Jones Banhof Bayreuth. Bayreuth
28th July 1908

[ALS: HRC]

Henry Arthur Jones, one of the most successful of the London dramatists at the end of the 19th century, maintained a friendly, mutually respectful relationship with Shaw from the mid-1880s until 1914, when Shaw's polemical Common Sense *about the War caused a permanent rupture. Shaw detoured to Sweden before visiting the Bayreuth Festival in order to meet the dramatist August Strindberg (1849–1912).*

My dear H.A.J.

Your letter did not reach me until I arrived here, after wandering through Sweden and down the Baltic & Germany without an address.

My European reputation was engineered systematically on a heroic scale; and I dont know how the trick can be done on a reasonable one. I always steadily refused offers of sums (from £150 downwards) for the foreign rights of separate plays, also all sporadic applications for authorizations to translate. I calculated that the only way to make the job really worth doing was to catch some man in each country who would undertake *all* my work, and thus get something like an income out of half the fees. At last I succeeded everywhere except in Portugal. Sometimes the men came of their own accord as devoted disciples. Sometimes I picked a man who had never dreamt of the job & hypnotized & subsidised him into it. Whenever possible, I got a man with an English or American wife. To keep him alive whilst the grass was growing I advanced him £16 for every play he translated except the one-acters, which were half price. The results have been very varied. At best, as in Germany, the translator took no advances & sent me £500 a year in half fees & half prices for translated essays, articles &c &c. Sweden has also been a great success. The opposite extreme is France, where I have had to extricate my translator (an Anarchist) from debt, build a large house for him on mortgage, and lend him the money to pay me the interest, besides advancing him more than he is ever likely to repay. This explains the seriousness of his article in the XIX Century. Another had to have a photographic studio financed as stand-by pending the catch-on, which has not yet occurred. The others have had their £16 per play and no more. Printing operations to save lapse of copyright have also been costly; and, on the whole, I have perhaps consulted my own peace of mind in not making out the total profit & loss account. The trouble, including occasional lawsuits, is sometimes so devilish that I curse the day when international copyright was invented, and wish the whole world were like Holland & Russia, out of the Berne Convention. Still, when I get the pirates thoroughly intimidated by reckless litigation and my men trained, there will be much less bother.

If you cannot go in for the job in this colossal manner, be very guarded about the rights you give your translator. It is safer to refuse to deal with anyone but a manager (who gets the play translated for seven & sixpence or so); but the managers dont come along without a translator to worry them. So deal with the translator thus. Say that you will promise him to let him do what he can with the play for one year. If within that time he can get its performance contracted for, then so much the better for him, he taking half tantièmes. If not, you must keep yourself free for other arrangements.

Here I am peremptorily interrupted by the hour of performance at the Wagner Theatre & must break off hastily. If I find on referring to your letter that I have forgotten anything I will resume later.

GBS

The July 1908 **article in the** *Nineteenth Century* was 'Un nouveau Molière' by Augustin Hamon (1862–1945), radical author and editor, who (with his wife Henriette, 1870–1964) had become Shaw's French translator in 1904.

59 / To Marion Chappell   10 Adelphi Terrace WC
                                12th October 1908

[TLS: Cornell]

Marion (Mary Ann) Chappell (1851–1942) of Dipley, Hants, a frequent Shaw correspondent, was a gardening specialist and dog fancier. An avid musicologist, she sought for years to persuade Shaw to write opera or operetta librettos. '[Y]our pertinacity is so magnificent that it almost shakes my recognition of manifest facts,' Shaw wrote to her on 28 August 1919. 'If you had found an Offenbach for me thirty years ago, something might have happened. But Providence evidently had other views' (ALS: Cornell).

Dear Miss Chappell

It would of course be impossible for me to refuse to allow Richard Strauss to make use of any work of mine which appealed to him. My impression is, however, that he is looking out for material of a more tragic cast.

Besides, there is a business difficulty in the way. Music is an international language; but my plays are translated into seven or eight languages by men who have exclusive rights of translation for their own language. I do not see how that difficulty is to be got over unless the authorized version is used in every case; and, as you know, this is technically impossible.

Another difficulty. If any man is going to set my play to music, he must take it as it stands. If a character in my play says 'Open the window, dear,' I am not going to have some idiot changing that line into 'Ope, ope thy casement, dearest,' or in any other way turning my poetic prose into bad verse. As a matter of fact, my plays are already in a sense set to music: that is to say, to their own music; and if the composer cannot add *his* music to them unless they are first turned into illiterate balderdash for the purpose, then he had better leave them alone. There would be no interest at all in giving Strauss what is called a libretto. It would be very interesting indeed to see whether he could tackle Beaumarchais without the impertinent interference of Da Ponte.

I doubt whether the enterprise is possible on these terms, except as a *tour de force*. The reasonable thing would be for me to write a play for the express purpose of being set to music; and this would be absurd, as I could not write a play in German.

> yours faithfully
> G. Bernard Shaw

Lorenzo **Da Ponte** (1749–1838) was Mozart's librettist for *Le Nozze di Figaro* (1786), based on Pierre Beaumarchais's comedy *Le Mariage de Figaro* (first performed 1784).

60 / To J.E. Vedrenne   10 Adelphi Terrace WC
                                              15th October 1908

[TLS: Theatre Museum]
A Vedrenne-Barker touring company of John Bull's Other Island played Dublin 18–23 November 1907, to critical approval and strong box office. On a fall 1909 tour it again performed in Dublin, for a week in November.

My dear V.D.

The difficulty about a Spring tour is the cast. The one you pencilled for John Bull is beyond description impossible. Unless we can get the old cast or something very near it, the play will be a ghastly disappointment in Dublin, and a failure in most other places.

I went to the Coronet last night. I should like some days to elapse before trusting myself to express a calm opinion of that infamy. The recollection came back to me twice while I was trying to drive a motor car this morning; and on both occasions I came within an inch of suicide and murder. I need not go into such specific points as that most of the characters are hopelessly wrong – that Ann Whitefield has to say in the last act that Violet gets her way without practising on men's instincts when the audience have seen Violet ogling everybody the whole evening for all she's worth – that Mrs Whitefield is a hollow-voiced, grief-stricken old anomaly who does not quite know whether she is the Duchess of York in Richard III or the Old Woman in a harlequinade – that Straker begins the 2nd act by being simply insolent instead of amusing – that Ann Whitefield looks like a dowdy Brixton widow of forty in the first act and does not even pretend to think her part worth a tinker's oath until the love scene in the last act, for which she puts on a new make-up – that with the exception of Lloyd, Hearn and Sherbrooke, nobody makes an attempt to present a human being, much less a definite character, or to regard the play as anything else but an intolerable deluge of clever talky-talky. What is infinitely worse from the general business point of view is that the production is not a Vedrenne-Barker production. It is the ordinary touring company business without a ray of distinction or style or beauty or grace or any of the other qualities that distinguish a really artistic production from commercial ragbagging. Barker saves it from being merely contemptible and unsuccessful by bursts of desperate extravagance, and by pulling off the love scene in the last act, which, you will observe, is a purely human scene which might occur between any man and any woman, and is quite independent of any realization of the Whitefield family, and the Robinson family, and the contrast and interplay of individual character, on which nine-tenths of the play depend. It is perfectly awful to think that the Vedrenne-Barker Man and Superman has been introduced to the provinces so villainously. If we cannot do better than that, we must simply give up the whole thing, or else confine ourselves to the sort of plays that can be done in this way.

I suppose I shall have to go to Arms and the Man; but I shudder at the prospect.

Oblige me by communicating the contents of this letter to your partner with my solemn curse. A more outrageous impostor, whether as actor or producer, has never disgraced the stage.

I feel no further disposition to pursue the heart-breaking trade of playwright, and shall henceforth devote myself to the advancement of the human race as a politician and essayist.

yours ever

G. Bernard Shaw

Shaw was taking driving lessons, having just purchased a 28–30 h.p. De Dietrich **motor car.** The **Coronet** Theatre, Notting Hill Gate, was a fringe operation, in which Vedrenne-Barker's new touring production of *Man and Superman* was then playing, the cast including Frances Dillon (1872–1947) as **Ann Whitefield,** Auriol Lee (1881–1941) as **Violet,** Helen Rous (c. 1862–1934) as **Mrs Whitefield,** Richard Haigh as **Straker,** Frederick Lloyd (1880?–1949) as Hector Malone, James Hearn (1873–1913) as Mr Malone Sr, and Michael **Sherbrooke** (1874–1957) as Roebuck Ramsden. *Arms and the Man,* also touring, followed at the Coronet the week of 19 October.

61 / To Margot Asquith   Ayot St Lawrence. Welwyn. Herts.

29th October 1908

[ALS: present source unknown]

Margot Asquith (1864–1945) was the wife of the Liberal leader Sir Herbert Asquith, who became prime minister in April 1907. Shaw first broached the subject of a knighthood for Arthur Pinero at Mrs Asquith's garden party on 2 July 1908, after ascertaining from Pinero that he would accept the honour if it were bestowed on him. Mrs Asquith responded that she could do nothing until November. Shaw's letter was intended as a timely reminder. Pinero received his knighthood in the June birthday honours list, 1909.

My dear Mrs Asquith

Will you be so good as to remind the King (either the uncrowned one or the crowned one will do) that Pinero ought to be knighted next month. On that National Theatre Committee there are peers, professors, and actor-knights by the dozen, and not a single dramatist with an official dignity of any sort. It really is a scandal. Gilbert is a knight; but he is not a representative dramatist, and not on the committee. Most people consider him a literary Bab Ballad and libretto writer, not a dramatist in the single & serious sense. Pinero is exclusively a dramatist: a knighthood for him is an unquestionable unambiguous theatre knighthood. And he would take it seriously and do it as well as Leighton did the presidency of the R.A. The honor would, besides, be thoroughly popular: it would be felt as the right thing.

If a high-literary knight or baronet, or even baron is wanted, Gilbert Murray, now Regius Professor of Greek at Oxford and son-in-law to that extremely Liberal peer Lord Carlisle and his formidable and even more Liberal wife, is the very man. His translations of Euripides are magnificent.

However, that is of no immediate consequence. Sir Arthur Pinero, however, is quite indispensable & most urgent. Singlehanded you must do it; for I have no one else to help me in the matter.

yours sincerely

G. Bernard Shaw

W.S. **Gilbert** (1836–1911), collaborator of Sir Arthur Sullivan and author of *Bab Ballads* (1869, 1873), became Sir William in 1907. The artist Sir Frederick **Leighton** (1830–96) was president of the Royal Academy 1878–96. Gilbert **Murray** (1866–1957), English classical scholar, noted for verse translations of Euripides (three of which were staged by Granville Barker at the Royal Court), eventually was offered and declined a knighthood (as did Shaw, twice), but accepted the Order of Merit in 1941.

62 / To Charles Hughes

10 Adelphi Terrace WC

4th November 1908

[TLS: Theatre Museum]

My dear Hughes

I have really no business reasons for sending my plays to the Syndicate Theatres in preference to Miss Horniman's – quite the contrary. What I intended to convey in our previous correspondence was that I could not refuse to allow Messrs Vedrenne and Barker to take my plays round the provinces when they had borne the brunt of their production in London. I could only give Miss Horniman those plays which Messrs Vedrenne and Barker said definitely they did not want: namely, Widowers' Houses and Candida. But all this had nothing whatever to do with the question of the selection of theatres. Nothing seems to me to be more exasperating than the appearance of my plays at the ordinary commercial theatres in Manchester when Miss Horniman's theatre is available. Of course it is not always available; and you must remember that as, from the point of view of the people who book tours, Miss Horniman's enterprise and Vedrenne and Barker's are simply rival competitive speculations, they may quite possibly, now one comes to think of it, have purposely avoided the Gaiety. However that may be, the avoidance, if avoidance there were, was made without my knowledge, and was altogether against, not only my wishes, but my interest. In my relations with Miss Horniman I have never had to make any sacrifices for her sake: the only sacrifices have been on her side. I am not sure that I do not morally owe her a good many thousand pounds. In future, when tours are in question, I shall take care to ask whether the dates are to be booked at the Gaiety, and, if not, why not.

I am sorry to say that the touring business is that worst kind of business [from] which neither loses enough money to make you drop it, nor gains enough to make it worth while to go ahead hopefully. I have just vetoed a Spring tour of John Bull and You Never Can Tell with Calvert as the star. I even turned over in my mind the possibility of trying a few weeks of it in Manchester and in Dublin. But the truth is I cannot afford to lose any more money just now. The net result of following up the Court Theatre campaign with an experiment at the Savoy, Queen's, and Haymarket Theatres, at which the production of new plays by new men was one of the conditions attached to the performance of my own plays, was that I had to find not only a new play, but about £6000 hard cash to enable the enterprise to retire in due solvency and decency. I need hardly say that if I had to bear such losses every year I should soon be a ruined man.

yours faithfully
G. Bernard Shaw

63 / To Charles Hughes 10 Adelphi Terrace WC
12th November 1908

[TLS: Theatre Museum]
Although Vedrenne and Barker were no longer producing in London, and had gone their separate ways in new business ventures, they continued to send out touring companies to the provinces in plays from the Vedrenne-Barker repertory, for which they owned sets and costumes. Hughes, who apparently suggested that

Shaw withdraw these touring rights and allow his plays to be freshly mounted in Manchester, was specifically seeking rights to Major Barbara *and* The Doctor's Dilemma *for Annie Horniman.*

Dear Hughes

The matter is not quite so simple as all that. If I let Vedrenne and Barker drop, I abandon not only the money I have myself sunk in it, but also the relatively considerable sums sunk in it by Barker, who practically pawned his shirt more than once to save the situation. Vedrenne's interest, though not so much, is still not negligible. Under these circumstances, I cannot take any such decisive steps as you suggest without very careful consideration – certainly not before the net result of the present V.-B. tour is before us.

. It is no light matter to cast either Major Barbara or The Doctor's Dilemma. Some of my London people could not be replaced; and their engagement would be no joke financially.

yours faithfully
G. Bernard Shaw

64 / To William Poel   10 Adelphi Terrace WC
                                              19th June 1909

[TLS: Folger Library]

William Poel (1852–1934), stage director and actor, who succeeded Barker in 1906 as Peter Keegan in John Bull's Other Island, *was founder of the Elizabethan Stage Society (1894), which revolutionized modern stage concepts of Shakespeare's plays, performing on an Elizabethan platform stage with Elizabethan costuming. His* Macbeth, *in which the Lady Macduff scene (IV: ii) was restored for the first time since the early 17th century, was presented at the Fulham Theatre 22–26 June 1909, with Hubert Carter (1868–1934) as Macbeth and Lillah McCarthy and Evelyn Weeden (1874–1961) alternating as Lady Macbeth. Shaw's allusion to refereeing suggests Poel had applied to the Shakespeare Memorial Committee or the London Shakespeare League for a subvention for his production.*

My dear Poel

I did not hear about the Macbeth rehearsal until late on Thursday, when I had already fixed up a luncheon party here for Friday at half-past one. Under these circumstances, though I rushed away from my table as soon as I could without being downright uncivil, the first line I heard on entering the theatre was 'Wake Duncan with thy knocking.' However, I was not very anxious about the matter, as this quaint dramatic refereeship is in your case a very empty form.

I found the production, as I expected, very interesting. I was particularly struck by the Macduff scene. I never before saw it played in such a way as to make you feel with absolute certainty that Macbeth was a doomed man if he ever let Macduff catch him. There is just one final touch needed. When your rather happily invented priest offers consolation to Macduff, Macduff accepts it in the conventional way which in real life is the sure sign of the absence of genuine feeling. Try the effect of making Macduff walk *through* the priest as it were – too completely preoccupied with his vengeance to be conscious of any external thing.

There were one or two little hitches which you have probably noticed yourself, but I may as well mention them in case any of them should escape you. It is almost always a mistake to repeat any bit of business on the stage. In the Macduff scene the business of Malcolm giving people permission to sit down becomes a nuisance after the first time, and has a very bad effect after the bad news has swept all mere ceremonial considerations out of Malcolm's head. Also, Lady Macbeth's second faint is a mistake, solely, I think, because she has already done a faint on hearing of the murder of Duncan. Anyhow, the effect is not good; and this is a great pity, because the whole handling of the scene, especially 'You lack the season of all natures' seems to me quite beautiful. Of course it would be better if Carter could only be induced to discriminate between the way an actor rants at the public and the way a man goes on when he is alone with his wife, even when he is frightening her.

In the sleep walking scene the doctor [*Roland Hope*] is impossible. That is not his fault; and I cannot honestly say it is his misfortune, because the congenital and ineradicable comicality in his voice will be probably worth at least £15 a week to him when he becomes better known. But such a voice must not be heard in the sleep walking scene. He positively did something that I had never dreamt of as conceivable or possible: he contrived to suggest that his relations with the lady-in-waiting were of an improper character.

Your porter [*Fred Dobell*] has such an overwhelming personality that I think it extremely dangerous to let him reappear as the murderer. The porter always makes an impression out of all proportion to the length of his part. I have actually seen it played as the star part – by Ben Greet. Your man, by the way, has not got the good old trick, which I believe to have been invented by Shakespear, of repeating 'Knock, knock, knock' more and more sleepily and slowly as the knocking gets more urgent, until finally he speaks through a terrific yawn.

In the banqueting scene, I think it might be worth while to get rid of Miss McCarthy's white table cloth, and substitute a colored one. As she sits there at the back apart behind the white table cloth, there is an irresistible suggestion of the lady from Lyons's, refreshments sixpence, which I believe could be avoided completely by sticking to the colors one associates with an enthroned madonna. It is a small matter; but it is worth considering; for the arrangement is otherwise very effective and happily conceived.

I was sitting in the front row of the balcony – probably the best place in the house for hearing; and there was a good deal that I did not hear. Making all allowance for the way in which voices rattle in an empty house, your exhortations to them to make themselves heard were badly needed. The apparitions were almost the worst. It is very difficult to get people to speak in an inhuman, unearthly way (which I take to be your notion) without making them speak in a meaningless way, which is quite another pair of shoes. The apparitions were unintelligible. You must also watch the mechanical part of the business from the balcony. None of the heads came up far enough to be visible to me.

Carter sometimes makes such a noise with his voice that you cannot hear what he says; but I suppose that cannot be helped.

I should let the sound of a man falling come from behind the traverses when Banquo is murdered. It was very effective with Mercutio.

The only thing I really missed was the procession of kings. Barry Sullivan used to make the banquet scene very effective by having no ghosts and simply playing at the empty chair; but the kings require seeing: Carter's attempt to make the audience imagine them walking past Putney station is not successful.

Your notion of putting up Duncan's ghost at the banquet is audacious; but the effect justifies you. Also the Lady Macduff scene is very good indeed; though, in the absence of properties, I did not quite catch how they were supposed to kill her. Apparently the man chloroformed her.

I hope you are religiously keeping prompt copies with all your business set out in detail. They ought to be left to the Museum, or to the library of the Garrick Club, or whatever better depository may hereafter be created.

yours ever

G. Bernard Shaw

Ben **Greet** (1857–1936) formed a Shakespeare company that toured Britain and the United States for many years. He created the Old Vic tradition as a classic house by his 1915–18 seasons of Shakespeare, staging 24 of the plays including his legendary uncut *Hamlet*. **The lady from Lyons's** is a quip that links Edward Bulwer-Lytton's romantic melodrama *The Lady of Lyons* (1838) with the image of a server in one of London's ubiquitous Lyons Corner Houses. The reference to **Mercutio** is to Poel's 1905 production of *Romeo and Juliet*. Shaw is suggesting that Poel's prompt copies be left to the British **Museum**. The **Garrick Club**, founded in 1831, was created as a gentlemen's private club for theatrical professionals, limited to 700 members, named in honour of David Garrick (1717–79), the great actor-manager at Drury Lane.

65 / To Winifred Emery

Ayot St Lawrence. Welwyn. Herts.

10th August 1909

[ALS: Honnold Library]

The job Winifred Emery had thrust upon Shaw was a commission for a variety theatre sketch, The Fascinating Foundling, *subtitled 'A Disgrace to the Author.' It was drafted, as Shaw noted, at odd moments during early August; the eleven-page manuscript (BL 50643.I), in shorthand, identified only by a caption 'Winifred,' is dated 10 August 1909 on the final leaf. In 1926, when publishing the playlet in* Translations and Tomfooleries, *Shaw miscredited the motivation for its composition as a request from Elizabeth Asquith, daughter of the prime minister, for a play to perform for charity with a group of amateurs. It was first performed at the Arts Theatre Club in 1928 with Peggy Ashcroft (1907–91) as the foundling.*

My dear Winifred Emery

You really have no conscience. Of all the nonsensical & ridiculous jobs ever thrust on an unfortunate man of genius at the busiest moment of his life, this is the very absurdest.

This Select Committee on the Censorship has almost killed me with overwork. To keep myself from crying I have jotted down in shorthand, at all sorts of odd moments, a string of hysterical bosh such as might be hurled at the head of a variety theatre audience for 20 minutes if they would stand it. I have just sent these notes up to be typed; and I expect to find them ready when I go up to London on Thursday . . . What they will be like, heaven knows: all I can tell you is that there is a leading lady, a smart & beautiful youth, and two comedians – a *père noble* & a low. And I dont believe any human being over 10 years old could learn the parts. Will you be at home any time between 4.30 and 7 on Thursday, or anywhere within reach of Adelphi Terrace or the Playhouse; so that I could call on you or you on me, whichever suits you better?

You must keep this the deadest of dead secrets from everybody. At the variety theatres, there are, thank goodness, no authors. Nobody expects an author's name in the bill; and nobody cares twopence whether it is there or not. If my name came out, your debut would be utterly spoiled. All the paragraphs would be ill natured ones about me instead of goodnatured ones about you. The press would come determined to dislike the show; and all the censor's friends would accuse the sketch of imaginary nastinesses to prove what I was capable of when there was no Redford to keep me in order. I should not draw with you as much as you would draw without me, as there are a thousand sane people who adore you for every crank that affects the Shavianismus.

I havnt mentioned it even to Cyril.

Probably by this time your fancy for appearing at the Hippodrome is over, or I am too late, or something of that sort. If so, it doesnt matter: I am accustomed to the wastepaper basket. But dont say I didnt try.

yours sincerely
G. Bernard Shaw

A Joint **Select Committee** of the House of Lords and House of Commons convened in July 1909 to examine the question of stage censorship, following prolonged dissent by dramatists, organized and fomented by Shaw, who stage-managed the playwrights' efforts to sway the Committee. For an extended examination of the censorship issue and parliamentary proceedings, see Shaw, *Collected Letters 1898–1910* (1972) and Shaw, *Agitations* (1985). A **père noble** is a 'serious' or 'tragic' parent. In Shaw's playlet he is treated comically as a pompous Lord Chamberlain, 'father of all the orphans in Chancery' (shades of Gilbert and Sullivan!). George A. **Redford** (1846–1916) was Examiner of Plays for the Lord Chamberlain, whose office had the responsibility of licensing plays for stage performance (but not for variety theatres). **Cyril** Maude was Emery's husband.

66 / To Mona Limerick

10 Adelphi Terrace WC
24th November 1909

[TLS: Harvard]

Irish-born Mona Limerick (1882 ?–1968), leading lady of the Annie Horniman Players, was the wife of Ben Iden Payne (1881–1976), Horniman's manager at the Manchester Gaiety. Shaw's choice for Hypatia in Misalliance, *she had accepted the offer, then been obliged to withdraw when Manchester commitments intervened. After the play opened on 23 February 1910 in Charles Frohman's repertory at the Duke of York's Theatre, she came to the rescue for the final few performances when Miriam Lewes, who had replaced her, was obliged to leave the cast.*

Mona Limerick, my feelings are beyond expression. You have ruined my play. You have ruined Frohman's enterprises. You have ruined yourself. You have ruined your infants. You have condemned your children to the workhouse. You have broken my heart.

I solemnly curse Iden Payne. I curse Miss Horniman. I curse the Gaiety Theatre. I curse Manchester. I curse destiny. I lay a blight on every theatrical enterprise in England until you do your duty and come and play for me.

You had no business to let me see you again if you were not going to accept the part. You left me more than ever convinced that – but there is no use talking about it: you have trampled on my grey hairs; and there's an end.

Much Ado will be a ghastly and ridiculous failure. Serve you right. You are a bad actress. Iden Payne is a bad actor. Miss Horniman is a bad manager.

To think that *my* arrangements – MINE – are to be upset because of this trumpery Manchester absurdity. Never speak to me again; never mention my name without a blush. I will give up writing for the stage. The caprice, the ingratitude, the folly, the selfishness, the domestic infatuations of its geniuses are unbearable.

Farewell. Heaven forgive you: I cannot.
My play is simply damned.
Damned!
DAMNED!!!
I am, Madam,

your obedient servant
G. Bernard Shaw

67 / To Irene Vanbrugh   [10 Adelphi Terrace WC
postmarked 11 January 1910]

[APCS: Princeton]
Shaw was about to read the full text of Misalliance *– a standard practice at first rehearsals of his plays – to Irene Vanbrugh's husband, Dion Boucicault, and the cast. She would be an auditor.*

Go back to the theatre immediately after!!! He little knows, poor man. My plays, read *fast*, last three hours; and the strongest men are no good for days & days after enduring them. You can have no idea how fatiguing it is. However, he shall do as he likes. You will not be able to act for at least a week; but it will be delightfully cruel to read the play to you. I'm afraid it really is dreadfully long, though I have cut mountains out of it.

G.B.S.

68 / To James Waters   Ayot St Lawrence. Welwyn. Herts.
5th January [February] 1910

[ALS: Cornell]
James Waters (1860–1923) was a journalist who provided dramatic notes for the Daily Mail. *Charles Frohman early in 1910 unsuccessfully attempted to establish a repertory system at the Duke of York's Theatre, which included Shaw's* Misalliance, *Granville Barker's* The Madras House, *and a triple bill featuring Barrie's one-acter* The Twelve Pound Look, *a revival of Pinero's* Trelawny of the 'Wells,' *and Galsworthy's* Justice. *Only the last two drew substantial attendance.*

Dear Waters

It is arranged that nothing is to come out about the repertory scheme at the Duke of Yorks until Monday, when the arrangements for the opening weeks will be sent to the press. No doubt you will get them along with this.

You may remember that the campaign of the press against my plays culminated last year in an unprecedented outburst of denunciation when my Getting Married was produced at the Haymarket. One London daily (the Morning Post, but dont specify it) described the curtain as falling amid a storm of hisses: the bald fact being that there were six curtain calls and no hisses. The effect was, for the moment, very serious. The booking at the Haymarket went down to the lowest point ever reached in the recorded history of the theatre. I immediately released all the managers who had undertaken to produce the play elsewhere. The pressure which has been put on me for some years past in Germany to produce my plays there in the first instance, and so avoid the reports of disastrous failure which invariably follow my London productions, was redoubled. It seemed for the moment impossible to expect any newspaper reader to go to a play so furiously denounced as intolerable. Fortunately, a curious thing happened. All the people who saw the first performance kept coming again and again until the word passed round that I had fooled the press again – though I protest I had no intention of doing it. The situation was saved; and the play pulled through handsomely.

I now wish it to be known as widely as possible that Misalliance is just like Getting Married, only much more so. I have carefully cherished, repeated & exaggerated every feature that the critics denounced. I have again gone back to the classic form, preserving all the unities – no division into acts, no change of scene, no silly plot, not a scrap of what the critics call action, nothing but Shaw and some very good acting. I shall be sorry to see my old colleagues leaving the theatre angry, weeping, broken men; but it does them good; and as they will spend the rest of the year sedulously advertising me as the most brilliant of beings, I bear no malice.

I see that in spite of early and authentic information published in the Daily Mail, The Chocolate Soldier is being announced as a setting of my Arms & the Man. In justice to the composer & librettist I contradict this for the fiftieth time. I have read the libretto . . . & can certify that it amused me quite genuinely, and that it is much more to the taste of the general public than my comedy. It will not contain a single line of mine; and I have no more to do with it than I have to do with Our Miss Gibbs or The Belle of New York, except that Mr Jacobson, the librettist, has obtained my cheerfully accorded permission to state that the notion of his first act was suggested to him by Arms & the Man.

In haste

yours ever

G. Bernard Shaw

PS. I rely on you, in using the above stuff, not to say 'Mr B.S. writes to the D.M. as follows' or anything of that sort. This is a private letter to you, and not a communication to the press; but you may use it as your own stuff or as part of a *casual* conversation with me. You understand, dont you?

Shaw's **old colleagues** are the drama critics. Oscar Straus's *Der tapfere Soldat* [*The Valiant Soldier*], with a libretto by Rudolf Bernauer (1880–1953) and Leopold Jacobson (1878–1949), was produced in Vienna on 15 November 1908. Translated as *The Chocolate Soldier* it became one of the most popular musicals of the decade both in New York and in London (where it ran for 500 performances). *The Belle of New York* (1898) and *Our Miss Gibbs* (1909) also enjoyed enormous popularity in London.

69 / To Mona Limerick   10 Adelphi Terrace WC

3rd June 1910

[TLS: Harvard]

Dear Miss Limerick

What on earth is going to become of Miss Horniman? Every member of her company seems to me to be starting a tour and asking me for plays. How can they all get dates, and all make fortunes?

I need hardly say that a tour which boasted you for its leading lady would have very special claims on me. In particular, I should like very much to see you try your hand at the part of Ann Whitefield; but the difficulty about Man and Superman is that you require a quite out of the way interesting and fascinating man for Tanner, not to mention one with exceptional powers of physical endurance. Of course Iden would tackle it like a bird if he got the chance, just as he would tackle anything else; and he would make a sort of kind of species of manner of show in it; but he would not be the right thing. The part requires the vivacity of Wyndham and the mere brute physical endurance of half a dozen prizefighters.

Charteris in The Philanderer requires the same sort of man; but it does not put anything like the same physical strain on him. In fact, as far as physical staying power is concerned, Charteris is child's play compared to Tanner; but the interest and fascination are even more important, because Man and Superman will carry through a second rate Tanner without absolute disaster; but The Philanderer goes to smash unless Charteris has what Barrie calls charrum. And this is all the more important in your case, because you are rather strong on charrum; and you must have a correspondingly fascinating antagonist for the duel of sex which runs through both plays. How do you propose to get over this difficulty? If you could discover a fascinating beginner with the necessary talent and hard work in him, you might pick him up cheap; but any man of established reputation of the requisite calibre would add a good deal to your salary list.

Iden had better discuss the matter with me when we come up to town.

yours sincerely
G. Bernard Shaw

70 / To J.E. Vedrenne   10 Adelphi Terrace WC
                                                     19th July 1910

[TLS: Theatre Museum]
*F.C. Whitney (1865–1930), American manager who was bringing The Choco-
late Soldier to London in September, submitted a script to J.E. Vedrenne for
Shaw's perusal to determine if there was anything in it to which he might object.*

My dear VD

I return the wretched libretto, which is as much worse than the German as the German was worse than the original. It is a gross violation of the understanding on which I tolerated the German production. I am not sure that I shall not try to stop it in America. Had I had access to the libretto I should certainly have moved when the American run began. Mr Whitney might just as well have approached me and come to an understanding with me: you can see that I am much more reasonable than he has any right to expect me to be. He has behaved as if he were dodging a blackmailer instead of dealing with a decent man of letters.

I shall probably not be in London again until October.

yours ever
G. Bernard Shaw

71 / To Olga Nethersole   Parknasilla-on-Sea. Co. Kerry
18th September 1910

[ALS (p): Cornell]

Olga Nethersole (1866–1951), sultry English actress, gained notoriety – and popularity – in America when her performance in Sapho *(1900), a drama by Clyde Fitch (1865–1909), resulted in her arrest (and subsequent acquittal) for indecency.*

My dear Miss Nethersole

I shall *never* get this dreadful book out: I am still struggling with proofs.

Besides, the idea wont bear reflection. If you are going to star in America, they will want you on the stage all the time. In Getting Married, which is all in one scene with no division into acts, though the curtain can be taken down twice to relieve the audience, you would not enter until the third section; and then two thirds of your part would be low comedy – regular fried fish farce. You would need a cast of expensive people – no less than seven men with strong parts, only one of which could be pulled through by an ordinary actor. There is another woman's part which you ought to play yourself, and two fascinating young brides. In London I had Ainley & Loraine, Fulton, Farren, Hearn & Holman Clarke, Beryl Faber, Auriol Lee & Fanny Brough; and nothing cheaper would have a chance. Think of all the salaries – on the American scale too! It would be very nice if somebody would produce the play & give you a handsome engagement in it; but as a speculation for you, it is too hazardous. You will recognize this when I send you a copy, which will happen soon, I hope, but not, I fear, within the next few days: that is, not in time to found any plans for next season on it. If I felt that there was any serious chance of your being able to handle the wretched thing, I should make an effort; but I know very well it's all nonsense: I must have a regular Shaw theatre for those monstrosities of mine; and in the meantime you must live and work.

The Americans would not stand you as a coal merchant's wife with fits of inspiration; or, if they did, they would undo the work of your life-time, and make you play coal merchantesses to the end of the chapter.

Therefore forget that such a being exists as

G.B.S.

The book **proofs** Shaw was working on were for a volume of plays – *The Doctor's Dilemma*, *Getting Married*, and *The Shewing-up of Blanco Posnet* – published in February 1911. The expensive London cast of *Getting Married* in 1908 included popular leading men Henry **Ainley** (1879–1945) and Robert **Loraine** (1876–1935), William **Farren** (1853–1937), James **Hearn**, E. **Holman Clark** (1864–1925), Beryl **Faber** (d. 1912), Auriol **Lee**, and Fanny **Brough** (1854–1914), who created Shaw's Kitty Warren in 1902.

72 / To R.C. Carton   10 Adelphi Terrace WC
                                            3rd November 1910

[TLS: HRC]

Richard Claude Carton (1856–1928), a playwright who comically limned the aristocracy and society women, was immensely popular with London audiences. His wife Katherine Compton (1853–1928), one of seven theatrical offspring of the actor-manager Henry Compton (1805–77), rarely appeared in any but her husband's plays. Shaw was seeking her services for the benefit matinees for the Shakespeare Memorial National Theatre, which included, in addition to Shaw's The Dark Lady of the Sonnets, *two short plays by 'George Paston' (Emily Morse Symonds, d. 1936),* The Kiss *and* Stuffing, *and J.M. Barrie's* A Slice of Life. *When Compton declined to play Queen Elizabeth, Shaw gave the role to Suzanne Sheldon (1875–1924).*

Dear Carton

At the Haymarket Theatre on the afternoons of the 24th and 25th of this month the Shakespear Memorial National Theatre will give two matinées. The program will consist of two plays by George Paston, a little play by Barrie, and something by myself that I do not know how to describe, leading up to an exhortation to the audience to start a National Theatre. It is a scene with four characters: Shakespear, A Warder, Mary Fitton (The Dark Lady of the Sonnets), and Queen Elizabeth. It will last nearly half an hour, and end up with a dance led by Shakespear and Queen Elizabeth. Elizabeth and the Immortal have quite a good little ten minutes or so all to themselves on the stage after they clear out the other two! Now my object in writing to you is not to ask you to play Shakespear, though I may have to fall back on you for that if Barker, who has the refusal of the part, treacherously *does* refuse; but if you ask me who is to play Queen Elizabeth – mind, I do not say you *have* asked me: what I say is, IF you ask me who is to play Queen Elizabeth, well, I put it to you, who *is*? It is not exactly a Lady Algy kind of part, nor quite on the lines of Mr Preedy's Countess. But the fact is you go on sticking up these kind of things for the lady I am thinking of until people imagine she cannot do anything else.

Now believe me, my dear Carton, I do not want to break up your home. If you want Miss Compton all to yourself, well, I am a Socialist and abhor private monopoly; but I am a friend and can indulge a friend's weakness. Still, I have an idea in my head that Miss Compton as Queen Elizabeth would astonish London not only because it is just the very last part they would expect to see her in, but because my instinctive guess is that she would do it extraordinarily well. Raise yourself from the floor on which you have fallen, and think it over. Do you think you dare propose it?

It is the chance of a lifetime: stalls and first row of balcony two guineas; the author pays six guineas for his own box; no salaries; and probably unlimited mismanagement. There ought to be a Compton in the bill.

Still, the proposal is audacious. Be very amiable at breakfast; and break it gently through the keyhole of a strong door with the line of retreat open. If it is hopeless, send me a wire on the enclosed form; for time presses, as I have promised to have the cast complete for announcement in next Sunday's papers. But if you think there is [a] ghost of a chance I will hold it over to the last conceivable moment.

yours ever
G. Bernard Shaw

Carton's wife played the female lead in one of his biggest successes, *Lord and Lady Algy* (1898). *Mr Preedy and the Countess* was a 1909 farce by Carton.

73 / To J.E. Vedrenne

10 Adelphi Terrace WC
10th March 1911

[TLS: HRC]
Shaw's letter, to which he affixed a penny stamp at the end, crossed with his signature, served as a formal receipt for moneys received from liquidation of the Vedrenne-Barker partnership.

My dear Vedrenne

I have received from you a cheque for £84.3.10, being the amount of cash in bank to the credit of the firm of Vedrenne and Barker at the moment of remittance. I await a further payment of the amount to be realized by the sale of the firm's scenery and other assets. In the meantime, I undertake to accept these payments as a full discharge of the indebtedness of the firm of Vedrenne and Barker to me in respect of the sum of £5250 advanced by me to them; and in the event of my decease before a final settlement, you may treat this letter as such a discharge.

yours faithfully

74 / To Arnold Daly

[Ayot St Lawrence. Welwyn. Herts.
c. 14 May 1911]

[Shorthand: BL 50560, f 194]
Arnold Daly, ambitious young American actor, raised $1350 to mount a single showcase performance of Candida in New York on 8 December 1903. Enthusiastic press reaction the next day encouraged him to do some further borrowing and schedule additional matinees. Daly's production shuttled around to five venues, for a total of 132 performances; by the time it was withdrawn in April 1904 two

touring companies of the production were blanketing the United States and Canada for nearly another year. A second success, You Never Can Tell, *followed, before failures with* John Bull's Other Island *and* Mrs Warren's Profession *(shuttered by New York's police after a single performance, at the behest of the local vigilance society, but subsequently vindicated by the courts) slowed the Shavian boom. Daly now, against Shaw's advice, had come to London to perform* Arms and the Man, *on 15 May, under the aegis of F.C. Whitney. Shaw's new comedy* Fanny's First Play *had opened at the Little Theatre on 19 April. A tentatively scheduled production in May of* Man and Superman *with Robert Loraine, who had just completed his second American tour in the play, was postponed until the end of September.*

My dear Daly

I have just had a letter from an amateur who wants to give a performance of Peer Gynt at a little theatre. It is the biggest Ibsen chance that remains for an actor in London. What a pity Mansfield spoilt it for New York.

If Loraine shews up at the Comedy on Saturday, I may get on yet another Shaw season: three plays running simultaneously; and you on velvet with the safest of them.

Since you wont believe in me, I must submit to the humiliation of explaining that 3rd act to you. What will happen is this. You will have a great success in the first act, as you play the second half of it extremely well – better than it has ever been played, in fact – and I see no reason why the first half, which is already good enough for all practical purposes, should not presently be equally good, now that you have got that sleepy notion into its right place. But the third act requires stage management to make it a series of victories for Bluntschli instead of a mere set of smart sayings which any amateur could score in. You think that the act is only one wave, rushing to its end in a single sweep, with everything sacrificed to a rattling finish. Really it is a succession of waves, more or less tempestuous, and all breaking exhausted against the impenetrable Swiss. The calms which frighten you so much are far more important than the storms. They mark Bluntschli's victories, and they give the audience time to enjoy the play instead of gasping it out in bewilderment. The timetable is as follows.

1st victory = 'How did you find me out?'

2nd victory = 'What else can he do, dear lady? He must defend himself somehow.' If, after these words, you utter another sound until the enemy's collapse into utter prostration is signalized by the deadest, flattest calm, you ruin your part. Once grasp this point, and you will no longer dash in in a frenzy of anxiety to keep the scene going when I am taking such pains to let it drop and secure a moment of heavenly calm and complete victory for you before the fat is in the fire again with the discovery of Louka listening at the door.

A second dead calm begins with Petkoff's entrance. It is up to him to play that scene up from its long pauses and silences, to the row with Nicola, who again lets it all down to stupended awe with his exit.

The rest is obvious. The sitting down of Catherine is the same old trick: it means 'Keep your seats: there's lots more, funnier than ever.' But there is now really no need for this with a London audience; and there never has been any such need with my plays. When you have a play with nothing in it, keep it going so that the mechanical excitement may conceal its emptiness. In my plays, the whole difficulty is to keep both actors and audience self-possessed enough to follow it and grasp it.

If you still have any doubts, ask Loraine or ask Barker. They know the game; and they know how well it pays Bluntschli – how it enables him to reap all the effect of the raging of the rest instead of being played off the stage by it.

In short, believe implicitly in me; and do exactly what I tell you; and you will see what you will see.

yours ever
[*unsigned*]

Richard **Mansfield** had staged the first production in English of *Peer Gynt* in his final season, 1906–7.

75 / To Margaret Halstan   10 Adelphi Terrace WC
27th May 1911

[TLS: U. of North Carolina]
Although the critics had been remarkably kind to Daly he was an unknown

*quantity to London theatre-goers, and the box office became a lonely place.
Though Daly sought a hurried change of bill, to add* The Man of Destiny *and,
possibly,* How He Lied to Her Husband, *with which it had been coupled in New
York, with his Raïna (Halstan) as the Strange Lady, Shaw had written Daly off
as an actor insensitive to Shavian style and declined to license additional plays
to the luckless performer.*

My dear Margaret Halstan

I am very sorry about The Man of Destiny on your account; but there is
no use involving you in another failure. The last three returns from the
Criterion are disastrous: the play has gone back 17 years in point of
drawing power. I have had to tell Mr Whitney that in the face of such
figures I cannot hold him to our understanding that the play must run
six weeks at least. As to asking him to engage in a fresh production, at
the risk of all the good notices of Arms being upset by much less favorable ones of Destiny, how could I reasonably propose such a thing?

But even apart from the business side, I have quite made up my mind
that Mr Daly is neither the right actor nor the right producer for my
plays. Destiny, when it is not very brilliant and vivacious, and full of delicate and sparkling touches, is horribly long and horribly dull. I now
know precisely how Daly would do it; and how impossible it would be
for you to keep the play going in spite of him; for after all, you would
have to wait for your cues, and that waiting would be fatal.

I was furious about the alteration the other night, because it had the
most appalling effect on you. All the dignity and beauty and style were
gone; and you were like a comic opera soubrette without any music.
Did you notice that the line about the noble attitude and the thrilling
voice produced no effect whatever, though the audience is always
delighted with it when Raina's attitudes really have been noble and her
voice thrilling? The great difficulty about Raina is always to prevent her
from guying herself – to make her 'respect the dreams of her youth'
and play with sincerely lovely romance, as if she were playing Mary
Queen of Scots. This is more than ever important at present, because
Arms is no use unless the audience can fall in love with at least somebody on the stage; and Daly is not a hero of romance. He has no beauty
and no youth and no style; and unless you all push your youth and

beauty and style to the finest and most brilliant point, the play will simply put the audience asleep, in spite of the very deceptive ease with which laughs can be got from it – though you will find that even the laughs will stop the moment you begin to play for them. If you bear that in mind, and also make it a rule never to guy yourself, but always to play so that if there is a sensible manager in the house, he will give you an engagement on the strength of your performance, you cannot go far wrong.

As to Mr Daly's position, it is just the same as yours, except that he is a personal friend of Mr Whitney, [*balance of letter is handwritten*] who, however, knows his failings pretty well, and has backed my judgment all through (it happened, by the way, to coincide with his own).

In haste to catch the post (I am now in the country for the week end)

G.B.S.

76 / To Harley Granville Barker   Ayot St Lawrence. Welwyn. Herts.
13th February 1912

[TLS: HRC]

For some time Granville Barker had been flirting with a scheme to produce a series of unconventionally staged productions of Shakespeare, using simple draperies and imaginative costuming, aiming for poetic beauty visually and aurally. His initial production was The Winter's Tale, *staged at the Savoy Theatre on 21 September 1912, with Lillah McCarthy as Hermione. It was followed on 15 November by* Twelfth Night.

Here is a thing for you to consider.

All captures of the front rank of the profession are effected by a revival of Hamlet. The play revives sensationally every 15 years or so, with intermediate successes of esteem. Thus you have Irving & Forbes-Robertson, with Wilson Barrett or Tree in between. Neither W.B. nor Tree could touch I. & F.R. because they were personally incredible Hamlets.

Now F.R. was about 15 years ago. The hour has come for a new credible Hamlet; and, in my opinion, a feature of the new one will be (as in Poel's Juliet) youthfulness. Having digested this, turn your eyes now to Moscow, where Teddy Craig has staged Hamlet (or induced the papers

to say so). Why not collar Craig's production – whatever there may be
of it – or devise a Craigesque production yourself with Wilkinson, Ricketts, or another, and play Hamlet yourself! If Teddy would play the
ghost with the voice of a lost soul (he *could*), all the better. Lillah, who
is too big & strong for Ophelia, could make a new thing of the queen,
who has never had a chance so far. The cast should be carefully kept
free of any flavor of the legitimate: for instance, if Lauzette could learn
English, he would be right for the king.

Post here. Think it over.

G.B.S.

Dorothy Minto (1888?–?), the memorable **Juliet** of William Poel's 1905 production, was
one of Shaw's favourite performers. During the Vedrenne-Barker seasons at the Royal
Court he cast her as Jenny Hill in *Major Barbara*, Dolly Clandon in *You Never Can Tell*, and
Sylvia Craven in *The Philanderer*. She also created the role of Dora Delaney in *Fanny's First
Play*, 1911. Edward Gordon **Craig** (1872–1966), innovative theatre designer and director,
son of Ellen Terry, staged a Russian *Hamlet* at the Moscow Arts Theatre in December 1911.
Norman **Wilkinson** (1882–1934) was chosen by Barker to design the Savoy productions.
Charles **Ricketts** (1866–1931), who was noted both for costume and for book designs, pro-
vided stunning costuming for Vedrenne-Barker's *Don Juan in Hell* (1907) and later
designed costumes for *Saint Joan* (1924). Raymond **Lauzette**, who played Lt. Duvallet in
Fanny's First Play, vanished from the London scene in 1914.

77 / To Edwin A. Alderman   10 Adelphi Terrace WC
8th March 1912

[TLS: U. of Virginia]
*Dr Edwin A. Alderman (1861–1931), American educator, became president of
the University of Virginia in 1904.*

Dear Sir

My American agent, Miss Elizabeth Marbury, has applied to me on
behalf of your University for permission to perform a play of mine for
the benefit of the University's hospital without charging the usual fees. I
have had to refuse this application; but I do not like to leave the matter
without a word of explanation. My refusal is not a personal one: it is
really a matter of professional etiquette. All professions, as you know, are
Trade Unions: that is, they are conspiracies against the public to defend
the livelihood of their members, who have to agree not to cheapen their

services either by individual competition or individual benevolence. Now it happens in my profession that an appreciable part of a successful playwright's income is derived from amateur performances. These amateur performances are practically all given for charities, and the author is appealed to in nine cases out of ten to remit his fees for the sake of the charity. But you will see that if the author were to do so, he would be spending perhaps a thousand dollars a year and upwards on charities not selected by himself, in addition to his private and direct charities. What is more, he would have no guarantee whatever that the charities would benefit, as these performances are organized really to gratify the desire of the performers to act, and the business management is so careless and inexperienced, that there is very often nothing left for the charity. Under these circumstances, it was inevitable that the societies of dramatic authors would make it a rule that fees were never to be remitted. Indeed, it would be hard to induce agents to undertake the collection of amateur fees on any other conditions.

I need not labor my explanation: you will take it in at a glance. It will, I hope, clear me of any suspicion of churlishness in the matter, or of insular ignorance of the claims of the University of Virginia to any service which a man of letters is permitted to render to it. '

yours faithfully
G. Bernard Shaw

78 / To Ellen O'Malley 10 Adelphi Terrace WC
26th December 1912

[APCS: HRC]
Shaw had just returned from the first performance of a revival of John Bull's Other Island *at the Kingsway Theatre, in which Ellen O'Malley recreated her original role of Nora Reilly.*

My dear Ellen O'Malley

A most beautiful, lovely, noble, divine performance. Oh, if I could only get it all like that! I kiss your hands a thousand times.

yours, grateful & delighted
G. Bernard Shaw

79 / To William Armstrong   Ayot St Lawrence. Welwyn. Herts.

27th May 1913

[APCS: Mary Hyde]

William Armstrong (1882–1952), who served his apprenticeship with the Shakes-
peare company of Frank Benson (1858–1939) and with the Birmingham and
Glasgow repertory companies, later became director of the Liverpool Repertory Com-
pany. Shaw's 'sketch' was The Music-Cure, *which Armstrong performed in Janu-*
ary 1914 with Madge McIntosh (1870–1950), the actress who created Vivie
Warren in Mrs Warren's Profession *(1902). Mrs Patrick Campbell never performed*
the playlet, but Armstrong toured as her leading man in Ibsen's Ghosts *in 1922.*

I have actually been inquiring for your address, as I was writing a sketch
for you and Mrs Patrick Campbell, your musical accomplishments
being indispensable. But the lady is terrified at appearing as a pianist,
and cannot be brought up to the scratch yet; so the sketch remains
unfinished; but we may quite likely bring it off someday; and in the
meantime, if you can find a lovely actress who can play a bit, you might
try it on the dog in some obscure corner.

Why did you not warn me about Candida? I should have gone to see
you, as Eugenes are scarce.

G.B.S.

80 / To William Armstrong   10 Adelphi Terrace WC

27th March 1914

[ALS: Mary Hyde]

After an initial seven-performance run of The Music-Cure *in January, as a*
curtain raiser to Magic *by G.K. Chesterton (1874–1936) at the Little Theatre,*
Armstrong contracted with Alfred Butt (1878–1962) to perform it with McIntosh
in a variety bill at the Palace Theatre.

Dear Armstrong

The explanation is very simple. The first half, which goes quite well, is
my sketch. The second half is wearisome tomfoolery. Now the Palace
audience, presented at 10 o'clock [with] a piece by a star author and
real actors & actresses from a high class theatre, expects something very

dignified and superior, whereas the intellectual persons at the Little rather enjoy a silly lark. That is why the tomfoolery is indulged at the Little and resented at the Palace.

I have written to Butt apologizing for the infamy of the performance, and telling him to sweep you out into the dustbin if you dont do better tomorrow.

Cut out *all* the gags – every one of them. Tell Madge to be tragically dignified, and to keep every scrap of style she has at its most impressive all through. Make the concertina piece a musical success by playing it as beautifully as you can: the audience tonight *wanted* to hear it and was quite savage because it was worried and murdered by silly interruptions. What on earth do you suppose they know about *smorzando* and *rallentando?* and if they did, how much repetition do you think the joke would bear before it became irritating? You cannot compete with Wilkie Bard in comic patter: you *can* compete with him in being distinguished and gentlemanlike & ladylike and classical. *That* is what the audience wants. Keep up the characters, and be ten times more on your good behaviors than you are at the Little. Be imposing; and dont be afraid of being dull: they expect high class acting & drama to be dull. And make the music enjoyable as music. Let Madge remember that there is no fun whatever in her being tempted to dance ragtimes unless she begins as a very dignified person.

It requires a good deal of judgment to know exactly how far it is safe to gag; and as you and Madge have evidently no judgment at all, stick to your author.

Now try again and see whether you do any better. The latter half of the piece as you gave it tonight was simply unbearable. The audience didnt want more politics: they wanted you to be serious, as you were in the first half.

yours, frightfully disgusted
G. Bernard Shaw

PS. Note that the doctor, who keeps his style, is quite successful. I was not ashamed of *him.*

Smorzando means 'dying away' and *rallentando* 'with gradually reduced speed.' Wilkie **Bard** (1870–1944), a music-hall comic who specialized in tongue-twisters like 'She sells seashells on the seashore,' shared the Palace bill with *The Music-Cure* from 23 March to 4 April.

81 / To Lee Shubert   10 Adelphi Terrace WC
9th April 1914

[TLS: Shubert Archive]

Lee Shubert (1875?–1953), following the death of his brother Sam in 1905, became head of the Shubert Organization. Before the opening of Pygmalion *at His Majesty's Theatre (on 11 April) with Sir Herbert Tree as Higgins and Mrs Patrick Campbell as Eliza Doolittle, Shubert negotiated with Shaw for American management of a tour. When he would not accede to the terms set down by Shaw and Mrs Campbell (who held the American rights), they opted for management by George C. Tyler of Liebler & Company. Ironically, Liebler's filed for bankruptcy several weeks after the 12 October opening in New York, which cost Shaw his November royalties, amounting to some £600.*

Dear Mr Lee Shubert

In the course of a conversation with Sir Herbert Tree he mentioned that if his part in Pygmalion should turn out as well as he expects, he would like to revisit America with it. I told him that I would keep it open for him until he had time to consider it in the light of the result of next Saturday's performance. It certainly would save a good deal of trouble if he would take the English production out; and although of course he would want a pretty big share of the plunder, he would be a very sure attraction. Anyhow, it might be worth your while, if you think well of the idea, to let him know your mind on the subject, as you can no doubt do as well for him in the way of theatres as anyone else.

I am not committed in any way; and Tree is not committed in any way; so everything is entirely open to discussion.

yours faithfully
G. Bernard Shaw

82 / To Lee Shubert   Ayot St Lawrence. Welwyn. Herts.
12th April 1914

[ALS: Shubert Archive]

Shaw became so irate over Tree's performance as Higgins at the previous night's opening performance that he abruptly departed from His Majesty's Theatre before the final curtain. 'For the last two acts,' he informed his wife, who was en route to America, 'I writhed in hell. The raving absurdity of Tree's acting was quite beyond description' (Collected Letters 1911–1925, 1985, p. 227).

Private

Dear Mr Lee Shubert

After last night you may leave Sir Herbert Tree out of your plans as far as they concern *Pygmalion* in America. I must have Mrs Campbell for Eliza, and any of the others I can get; but it would clearly be a mistake for Sir Herbert to stake his next visit to the States on a part so ill adapted to his personality and his methods. Consequently you may consider my last letter unwritten.

This is of course between ourselves.

yours faithfully
G. Bernard Shaw

83 / To Madge McIntosh
The Hydro. Torquay
25th August 1915

[ALS: present source unknown]

In October 1914 Madge McIntosh was appointed director of the Liverpool Repertory Theatre, an appointment that was short-lived. During her brief reign she performed Candida and Jennifer (in The Doctor's Dilemma). *Following the outbreak of war in August 1914 Britain issued war loans in November and in June 1915. Shaw contributed £20,000 (a staggering sum) to the second loan.*

My dear Madge McIntosh

Fifty pounds! Hang it all! Fifty pounds!! How much loose pocket money do you suppose I carry now that I have put my last farthing into the War Loan, and am looking forward to double income tax, forced loans, and destitution among all the people who have kindly elected me their Earthly Providence?

What is to be the nature of the transaction? It is the business of the Repertory Theatre to advance sufficient capital for the opening. That is what they are to get their 50% for, is it not? Or have you to find the capital? Are you sharing just as a touring company shares? Were they responsible for the London adventure?

You see, if I lend money to you I have no security. You throw every-thing you make away on London seasons. And I cant sell you up, though I could extract the [board of] directors' last drop of blood with-out a twinge of remorse. You know this very well; and therefore you will not be able to pay me *ever*. You cannot pretend to yourself that you *must* pay me: you can only make good resolutions knowing very well that you need not keep them. Result: you wont keep them. I shouldnt myself, under such circumstances. Your conscience would tell you that you had worked frightfully hard and earned every penny of the money, and that I had done nothing and would never miss it.

Will the directors advance you £50 if I guarantee that you will repay it by next Easter? In that form I should perhaps consider it; for it is not my interest that the Repertory Theatre should relapse in commerce and varieties. I want to make them parties to the transaction: there is no use in leaving them under the impression that you can do impossi-ble things. They need educating.

What do you say to *that*?

always

G. Bernard Shaw

84 / To W.B. Yeats   Ayot St Lawrence. Welwyn. Herts.
8th November 1915

[ALS: National Library of Ireland]

Shaw had written a one-act war play O'Flaherty V.C. *for the Irish National Theatre, of which Yeats was a founder and director, waiving royalties for all per-formances in Ireland. Arthur Sinclair (1883–1951) and J.M. Kerrigan (1887–1964) were leading members of the company. Shaw intended the role of O'Flaherty for Sinclair, and would accept no substitute. Eventually the produc-tion was 'postponed' – and later quietly cancelled – by the management, with Shaw's assent, after receiving intimations from the government and the military that it might foment riotous demonstrations in the theatre by the Abbey's volatile audience, which could cause damage to the Irish war-recruitment program that Shaw was seeking to assist. Sinclair didn't get to play O'Flaherty until 1920 – in London.*

My dear Yeats

I wrote to Ervine on Sunday, explaining why I committed myself to Sinclair subject to his rejoining the company. Kerrigan is really the only male member of the company who has charm; and if O'F were a romance of illusion, instead of a comedy of disillusion, and ended with the hero's union to a colleen bawn, he would be perfect in it; for he has not only charm but youth. I think his Fenian in The Rising of the Moon one of the best things in repertory. But he lacks variety, and is not a real comedian. People want a happy ending for him; but for Sinclair, who *is* a comedian, they want confusion, disillusion & bathos. It is Kerrigan's tragedy that there is so little romance in the repertory: he is always character-acting, which is a mechanical business; and Sinclair gets all the fat. Writing for Kerrigan, I should have done quite another sort of part. By the way, I'll turn this postcard into a letter, because I want to say that I think Ervine is wrong in clearing the idle members out of the green room. The alternative is the public house; and he will curse the day he drives them there if he carries his plan out. I think the theatre ought to be a club for the company if there is room for them. You have a lot of building next door that you have taken in, havnt you? If a room could be furnished as a reading room & library, with books & papers and cheap teas &c, it would not only avoid the demoralization of loose ends of time in the streets, but act as a substantial addition to the salaries, which are devilish small. Ulster discipline will never do: Ervine will be the first to kick through it himself; and a Utopia that breaks down is ten times worse than an Alsatia that evolves law & order. . . .

G.B.S.

Irish playwright St John **Ervine** (1883–1971), an Ulsterman from Belfast, was a recent and unpopular appointment as manager of the I.N.T.'s Abbey Theatre. A **colleen bawn** is Irish for a fair-haired girl, title of a play by the Irish-American dramatist Dion Boucicault (1820–90). **The Rising of the Moon** was one of the Abbey's most frequently performed plays of Augusta Lady Gregory (1852–1932), another founder and director of the I.N.T. Shaw's reference to Ervine 'clearing the idle members out of the **green room**' (until modern times a backstage gathering place for the social mingling of performers and guests before and after performances) is a criticism of Ervine's attempt to bring discipline to a theatre that had in the decade since its 1903 founding operated quite informally as a home away from home for its peasant-like company. **Alsatia**, in London's Whitefriars district, was a 17th-century haven for criminals resisting arrest, which could be accomplished only under a writ from the Lord Chief Justice, until an act of 1697 put an end to the 'safety' zone.

85 / To Louis Calvert

10 Adelphi Terrace WC
12th November 1915

[TLS: Sotheby Parke-Bernet; sold 6 May 1981]

Louis Calvert, who settled in New York, persuaded the New York manager William A. Brady (1863–1950) to seek rights for the first American production of Major Barbara, *to star Brady's wife Grace George (1879–1961). When Shaw responded unfavourably to the request, Calvert cabled to urge him to relent.*

My dear Calvert

Nothing short of my personal regard for you, and my sense of your achievements in my plays, would induce me to submit to the infamous conspiracy of which you have made me the victim. Brady has been bombarding me for months to let him have Major Barbara for Mrs Brady. On the other hand there has been Granville Barker. He also has a wife who is keen on the part; and, as you know, Brady's claim on me compared to Barker's is as dust in the balance; and if Barker were really going ahead I should have had to hold the play for him, leaving you to get out of your agreement with Brady as best you could. I hope you were not mad enough to engage yourself unconditionally to bring the play with you. I guessed from your cablegrams what was up, as you must have guessed from my reference to Miss Grace George; and the way you tried to land me after this was – well, no matter. I forgive you; only, as the result will be that you will certainly try to do it again, do remember that you will run a considerable risk of coming up against some contract or engagement of mine which will make it impossible for me to see you through. Your luck on this occasion is due to the very unexpected fact that Barker has suddenly made up his mind to abandon theatrical management and devote himself to writing plays; and I am so mortally afraid that Mrs Barker will ask me to allow her to start on her own account in New York with Major Barbara, and ruin herself trying to manage a theatre by herself, and eventually drag Barker into that Maelstrom, that I have suddenly made up my mind to give you and Miss George a chance. For Heaven's sake dont let Cusins play the breezy young naval Lieutenant. He must be the spectacled professor. I forget whether you ever met Gilbert Murray; but he was the original of the character and Barker's Cusins was a fairly close imitation of him. You cant do better for Bill than Oswald Yorke, if you can get him.

As I have stipulated in the contract that you are to play Undershaft, you had better read it through, as your own contract with Brady will be to some extent governed by it. I therefore send the contracts to you. Will you please present the counterpart to Brady for his signature, and then give him in exchange for it the copy signed by me. Get him to initial the corrections in Clause 5; and fill in the dates at the beginning & end of both copies. Then send me my copy, and the trick is done. Under ordinary circumstances I should have submitted a draft contract to him for discussion; but as he has jumped the claim he must produce on my terms, subject only to the scale of fees which I mentioned to you in my cablegram, and which I have modified a little in his favor so as to make it easier for him to hold on if business is very second rate.

If there is any hitch cable to me at once. I am writing to Brady by this mail. I am mentioning to him among other things that I have no objection to the limited run system. There can be no doubt that – backed by your Broadbent – it was the secret of the Barker-Vedrenne success at the Court. By the way, why dont you make Brady put up John Bull's Other Island? Daly's disastrous muddle of it is forgotten by this time; and as America is full of character actors you ought to be able to stick up quite a good performance.

yours ever
G. Bernard Shaw

Oswald **Yorke** (1867–1943), now resident in the United States, played Bill Walker in the London production (1905).

86 / To Louis Calvert   10 Adelphi Terrace WC
17th December 1915

[TLS: Sotheby Parke-Bernet; sold 6 May 1981]

My dear Calvert

If I had made the agreement with you you would have become responsible for my fees and for all the proceedings of the management as far as they affected my rights. There would have been no sense in such a course even if I had had any authority from you for it. Besides, I

shouldnt have done it in any case, as you are not a manager; you have
no theatre; and you have an unquenchable appetite for ruining yourself which I desire to starve rather than to gratify. By making it a condition of the agreement that you should play Undershaft, I put Brady in
your hands sufficiently for all reasonable purposes. All the risk was his;
and you were made independent of the strong possibility of his losing
by the adventure. If the agreement had been with you, he could, and,
unless he is a nincompoop, *would* have simply compelled you to sub-let
it to him, leaving the responsibility to me on your shoulders.

You are not my agent: if any agent had treated me as you did I would
have his life. Brady was pressing me to let him have the play for months;
and what you did was to jump the claim for him. You acted as *his* agent
– almost his bravo [*desperado*]; and if you have not stipulated for a percentage from him accordingly, that is not my fault: I gave you the necessary pull, although no other author alive would have stood being
bounced so unscrupulously. But here again I could not in any case, as a
matter of professional etiquette, enter on this business of giving or taking commissions. If authors started that game, they could blackmail
every cast for commissions on their salaries, because it is the author
who selects the cast and has the power to insist. What would you think
of me if I demanded a commission on your salary? Well, if the authors
are to keep their hands off the actors salaries, the actors must keep
their hands off the authors fees. The practice of giving an actor a percentage is an established one; but it is always the manager who pays the
percentage. I named my terms on that understanding. I am not free to
do as I please in these matters: I am, like yourself, bound not to do anything that would be regarded as an unprofessional practice; and to pay
an actor a percentage out of my fees would certainly be regarded in my
trade union as the act of an unparalleled sweep [*blackguard*]. Trade
union or not, I am an author and not an agent, and you are an actor
and not an agent; and we will both feel much better if we stick to our
respective roles. I dont know why I tell you all this; but I cannot make
out whether you are a man of business or a great baby.

I am not at all grateful to you for the production of Major Barbara. I
am grateful to Providence for sending you along to play Undershaft
and look after the production, just as you should be grateful to it for
sending along me and my wonderful plays, without which you would be

playing Sardanapalus and Wolsey instead of relegating poor Charles Calvert to the minor part of 'father of the celebrated Louis Calvert, q.v.'

Brady cables that the play is a huge success. I hope it will last more than a fortnight. At any rate it will pay in Kudos for everybody concerned. And now I wish you would turn your attention to Misalliance. I tried to get you for that at the Duke of Yorks here; but you were fooling over that millionaires theatre in New York instead of minding your proper business of playing Shaw. The part of Tarleton, a comic Undershaft, is the best monumental comic part written since Falstaff. If you can play both Undershaft and Tarleton, you are the Nonpareil.

You were quite right about Tearle. I felt sure he would play the fool with Cusins by refusing to give himself away as a spectacled professor. What you said in your last letter but one about Bill is all right. Barbara is like a Beethoven symphony in one way. It comes all right when you really know all the tunes by heart; but no matter how skilful a player you are you can do comparatively little with it when you are only reading the parts at sight. We were all in that stage more or less at the Court; and now that you have fully caught on, there is no end to what you can do.

I write in great haste and without the least regard for your feelings. Your letters are always interesting except when you discuss business, when you always make me fear that you have let yourself be done, and make me feel like a Shylock.

yours ever
G. Bernard Shaw

Major Barbara ran for 91 performances. **Charles Calvert** (1828–79) and his wife Adelaide (1837–1921), parents of Louis Calvert, were managers and leading players of a stock company at the Prince's Theatre, Manchester, considered to be one of the finest in 19th-century Britain. The senior Calvert gave memorable performances in 1877, at the Theatre Royal, Manchester, as Cardinal **Wolsey** in Shakespeare's *Henry VIII*, and at the Alexandria Theatre, Liverpool, in Byron's *Sardanapalus*. Shaw had seen Calvert in an earlier production of *Sardanapalus* in Dublin, 25 October 1875. A number of New York **millionaire** speculators undertook to build 'a true repertory theatre,' the New Theatre, which opened in 1907. Granville Barker, wooed for its managing directorship, declined the offer, insisting the mammoth house, seating 2500, might be ideal for opera and spectacle, but was too large for drama. The enterprise failed within two years. Conway **Tearle** (1878–1938), American-born film actor, was cast by Brady as Bill Walker after initially being considered for Cusins.

87 / To St John Ervine   10 Adelphi Terrace WC
                                                   [5 February 1916]

[Text from typed transcript: BL, LCP(C) *Blanco* 1916/91]

*On 1 Februrary 1916 St John Ervine applied to the Lord Chamberlain for per-
mission to present performances of* The Shewing-up of Blanco Posnet *in April
at the Liverpool Repertory Theatre, presumably by the Irish Players on tour. The
chief clerk, responding on the 3rd, returned the script and reading fee, informing
Ervine that the play 'was licensed for performance at the Gaiety Theatre,
Manchester on the 21st September 1909, subject to the excisions noted on the
accompanying memorandum' (BL: LCP(C),* Blanco *1916/91). Ervine posted
the letter to Shaw.*

Dear Mr St John Ervine

Thank you for sending me the communication from the office of the
Lord Chamberlain in reply to your application for a licence for the
Shewing-up of Blanco Posnet. The licence issued in 1909 was in effect a
refusal to license. To omit the forbidden passages would be like printing the book of Job without Job's reproaches to the Almighty; and it
must have been evident to any competent reader of plays that the offer
to allow me to put forward as a 'crook melodrama' a play which was so
patently a religious work that it became the subject for several sermons
on its production by the Abbey Players, was a polite device for suppress-
ing it and at the same time making it possible to deny officially that the
licence had been refused. Since then important changes have taken
place in the department; and it is possible that the communication you
have received is not meant as a refusal to reconsider the play, but a
courteous return of the fee on the ground that the play is already
licensed. It was stated at the last public inquiry into the working of the
department that censored plays were always open to reconsideration
(presumably after a reasonable interval); and as Blanco Posnet has now
been played for years on the best Irish and American stages without the
slightest scandal, I have no doubt that if you explain the matter the fee
will be accepted and the play reread and reconsidered.

   If, however, the Lord Chamberlain should refuse to reopen the matter, or insist on the play being performed in accordance with the ideas
of his former reader of plays, you must not ask me to allow any such

performance; in fact I know that you would not desire me to. I have never made any secret of the fact that I felt very strongly on the subject of the construction put upon my play by the two gentlemen at whose mercy my reputation lay at that time; and I feel very strongly about it still. I should be very glad to learn that their views no longer govern the Lord Chamberlain's office; but if this is not so, I hope the situation will be made quite clear, and not obscured by offering a licence on conditions which I cannot accept.

yours faithfully
G. Bernard Shaw

Shaw's letter, designed to give the Lord Chamberlain an opportunity to 'save face' for his department by granting a licence, was forwarded at once by Ervine with a request for a fresh reading of the play. It was promptly denied. '[I]ts offence against taste might, like its doubtful moral, be passed,' the reader Ernest Bendall (1846–1924), joint-examiner of plays, commented, 'but for the fact that the latter is expressed in its perverted ingenuity with the truculence characteristic of its Author.' The passages he had marked 'must offend many by their outrageous blasphemy ...' (transcript: HRC). By a strange circumstance, however, it developed that the Lord Chamberlain's authority did not extend to Liverpool, and the public performances were offered. An official licence to permit a London production was not forthcoming until 1921.

88 / To Lord Sandhurst   Ayot St Lawrence. Welwyn. Herts.
8th October 1916

[TLS: BL, LCP(C) *Mrs Warren* 1924/5632]

When the Plymouth Repertory Theatre requested a licence for public performance of the long-proscribed Mrs Warren's Profession, *the Lord Chamberlain's joint-examiner of plays G.S. Street (1867–1936) submitted a memorandum to the Lord Chamberlain (J.W. Mansfield, 1857–1933, Lord Sandhurst), on 5 October: 'I do not think this play should have a licence for general performance. My opinion is based not on the dialogue or incidents – given the theme – but simply on the theme itself, which is the question of the advantages and disadvantages of prostitution as a profession for women, as compared with other professions, and which involves the presentment of a brothel-keeper as the chief character. Such a discussion and such a character are not fitted for casual audiences of various ages. I agree with Sir W. Raleigh [Professor Walter Raleigh (1861–1922), an Oxford don, who was a member of the Lord Chamberlain's advisory committee] that the author is entirely earnest, and no doubt the theme is important and can be rightly discussed in the press. But the theatre is not the place, except before an audience well knowing what it is to expect and of a special kind, as is the Stage Society.' The theatre's request was denied in a terse communication from the Comptroller, Col. Sir Douglas Dawson (1854–1933). Shaw, notified of this, wrote privately to Lord Sandhurst.*

Dear Lord Sandhurst

A point has just arisen with reference to a play of mine, as to which I have to take a mean advantage of our personal acquaintance because, being merely an author, I have no *locus standi* in your office, and I do not care to leave the matter to a manager. The point is quite a technical one; and as its settlement in the sense I think the right one will not help me personally in the least, and will bring additional reading fees to your office, you will perhaps forgive me for raising it in a way which will protect me from the mere official rebuff that I do not exist for the purposes of your department.

The facts are these. About twenty years ago I wrote a play with certain public objects that were then considered quite outside the scope of the theatre. I wanted to shew what was the real character of what is now called the White Slave Traffic, and how it was boldly defended morally by the people who profited by it. Also how its real root was in the refusal to secure higher wages for virtue than for vice. Incidentally also to shew the objection to what was called politely (by 'advanced' people) Group Marriage: namely, that when the children of such marriages grew up and fell in love with one another they were confronted with the impossibility of determining the questions of consanguinity raised by the marriage law.

As all this happened long before your time, you will not mind my saying that the play simply horrified the Reader of that day, just as he would have been horrified by the White Slave agitation, the Minimum Wage Board legislation, and the treatises of Westermarck and Havelock Ellis. He refused to license it, with very serious consequences to me, which I need not trouble you with. The play has now been worn out on the American and Continental stages, and is, besides, so old fashioned by this time, that at one of the so-called private performances which took place in London a few years ago, Mr Granville Barker and I could do nothing but laugh at its technique. I now take no personal interest in it, though the lesson it conveys is, I am sorry to say, as much needed as ever.

Now for my technical point. The other day a Plymouth manager, wishing to add the play to the Repertory of his theatre, which aims at doing work of a special class, sent in the play for licence, with the usual fee. The official reply was that you regret that you cannot see your way to alter your decision not to license Mrs Warren's Profession for public performance on the stage, and that the Office therefore returns the script *and the reading fee.* That underlined (by me) passage is the crux of the case. The statement that you do not see your way to alter a decision that you never made is only a form: Heaven forbid I should hold you responsible for the things that were done by your predecessors in those dark days! But the return of the fee, which brought the whole transaction to my knowledge because I promised to reimburse the management when I knew what it intended to do, implies a refusal to re-read the play.

I contend that your Reader should have read the play again; pocketed my two guineas; and, if he felt still in the eighteen-nineties about it, reported against licensing it exactly as if it were a new play. I quite recognize that the return of the fee was an act of consideration, outside the official routine, for which the manager should have felt obliged, as no doubt he did. And I appreciate it myself. But you will see the position it creates. If the Reader reads the play again he has no right to return the fee: the auditor, if you have an auditor, ought to surcharge him. If he refuses to read the play, he is putting your Office in the position of governing the stage by the Dead Hand, and giving me an excuse for agitating for a Statute of Mortmain against you. I need not elaborate the argument.

I should explain, by the way, that Mrs Warren's Profession *is* licensed in a form which could be played today if I were unscrupulous enough to allow it. In those old days I could save my American performing rights only by giving a public performance of the play here; and for this a licence was necessary. Accordingly, I had to go through the farce of changing Mrs Warren from a procuress to a trainer of thieves like Fagin in Oliver Twist. The play thus became a quite gratuitous Crook Drama, and was solemnly licensed and performed in that state. I think this has been forgotten at the Office, where – to be quite frank – I suspect them of making it a point of honor not to give in about this particular play because I did not take its fate lying down.

By the way, I of course do not contend that it would be reasonable to send the play in every month – though for the life of me I do not see why the Reader should object at two guineas a time – but a reasonable interval has passed in this instance since the last attempt, which, if I recollect aright, was made some years ago by Miss Gertrude Kingston. Probably some other enthusiast will return to the charge later on, and will consult me on the subject. I always say 'You can try if you like'; but I have not said that the play will not be read again. Only the other day a play of mine was reconsidered and licenced after seven years of suppression. Why is Mrs Warren beyond reconsideration? Please do not misunderstand me: I am not pleading for a licence for Mrs Warren: it would rather embarrass me nowadays, except in its old capacity as a stick to beat your department with. What I do want to know is whether there is any provision in the office rules for reconsidering a decision which was arrived at in view of the state of public opinion on matters subject to change. One play of mine licensed for performance here has been forbidden for long periods of time in Austria, and caused the wrecking of a theatre in Rome. The same play has been performed at other times without causing the slightest perturbation. I have myself stopped performances of my plays at moments when I thought they might be publicly mischievous. At such moments your department might reasonably have stopped them. But such cases only prove that anything like a rule of Once stopped always stopped would be outrageous. If the principal of a Convent School asked me for an authorization to perform Mrs Warren's Profession I should refuse it. But I still regard it as nothing short of a crime that suitable legislation on the White Slave Traffic was burked, and a miserable Act for the flogging of *souteneurs* and the protection of Mrs Warren substituted because I was not allowed to educate public opinion as to the real nature of that traffic. Some day you will have a Reader of Plays with some knowledge of the subject and some conscience as to the guilt of the nation in the business. We shall both be dead by that time, probably. But is it not desirable, in the interest of the public if not in mine, that he (or perhaps she) should earn an honest two guineas by reading the play again?

I am not keeping a copy of this letter, and would suggest, if I could do so without impertinence, that you should not answer it directly, because it is extraordinarily difficult to treat any reference to such a controversial matter as private; and the advantage of a betrayal of the sanctity of a private correspondence would be all on my side. In leaving a letter unanswered at my own request you will not feel that you are treating me discourteously; and yet I shall, I hope, have succeeded in bringing to your notice a point of some importance, and possibly inducing you to make a regulation that plays may be sent in for reconsideration after a certain interval on payment of a fresh reading fee. Such a regulation, or one in the contrary sense if you should decide against it, would come to my notice sooner or later without being made the subject of a personal communication to me.

Forgive the inordinate length of this letter. Our conversation at Sassoon's encourages me to depend on your indulgent reception of it.

yours sincerely

G. Bernard Shaw

The original **reader** of plays, to whom Shaw makes reference, was E.F.S. Pigott (1824–95). Edward **Westermarck** (1862–1939), Finnish philosopher, was the author of *The History of Human Marriage* (1891). Havelock **Ellis** (1859–1939), English physician, was the author of *Studies in the Psychology of Sex* (7 vols, 1897–1928). The **private performance** in London was that of Edith Craig's Pioneer Players on 16 and 18 June 1912. In legal terms the **Dead Hand** (Mortmain) means posthumous control exercised by a testator over the uses of a property. Gertrude **Kingston** (1866–1937) was an actress-manager, who built the Little Theatre, in which *Fanny's First Play* was initially performed (1911). Shaw's play suppressed for **seven years** was *The Shewing-up of Blanco Posnet. Arms and the Man* had been forbidden in **Austria**. The **theatre in Rome** is the Argentine (1909); but Shaw is exaggerating. *The Devil's Disciple* was withheld ('**stopped**') by Shaw during the Great War. The Criminal Law Amendment Act (1885; revised 1912) called for the **flogging** of procurers. Two generations of Sassoons were at this time merchant bankers of the firm of E.D. Sassoon & Co., India, China and London. Shaw may be referring to Sir Jacob **Sassoon** (1844–1916), 2nd Bt., who died that month.

89 / To Lord Sandhurst   10 Adelphi Terrace WC

20th October 1916

[TLS: BL, LCP(C) *Mrs Warren* 1924/5632]

Shaw's letter of 8 October led to a memorandum by Ernest Bendall: '[I]t might, I think, be replied that the 'point' which [Shaw] says has arisen with reference to his play ... has arisen only in his imagination. The Lord Chamberlain returned the Reading-fee for that play when it was again submitted for license simply because his Readers could not accept a fee for work which he did not require them to perform. They are both of them familiar with the play in question, and they could serve no useful purpose by re-reading, for another fee, a work as to which they – like the Lord Chamberlain himself and his Advisory Board – have already made up their minds. I may add as regards my personal views on the subject that, even apart from the question of incest raised by the plot, I should always regard the play as unfit for performance before a general audience, because one of its acts consists of a long and serious discussion between a mother and her daughter as to the desirability of prostitution as an alternative occupation for girls whose respectable labour is underpaid. The more cleverly Mrs Warren defends prostitution the more objectionable does it seem to me that she should be allowed to do so on the public stage.' On 19 October Lord Sandhurst sent Shaw a short, formal reply: 'With regard to the specific point you raise, the reason why the reading fee was returned was because both my present Examiners of Plays had read the play. I was thoroughly well acquainted with it and I did not require it to be read again before giving a decision. Therefore it would have been unfair to have retained the Reading Fee.' (The Bendal and Sandhurst texts are in BL, LCP(C) Mrs Warren 1924/5632.)

Dear Lord Sandhurst

... The reason you give me for the return of the reading fee is exactly the reason I assumed. It happens that in order to write the preface to [*Androcles and the Lion* in] my last volume of plays I had to read the New Testament through very carefully. Of course I had read it before; and I thought myself – to use your phrase – 'thoroughly acquainted with it.' I will not say that I discovered that I knew nothing about it; but I was amazed to find the number of things I had formerly read into it that were not there, and the number of things I had not noticed and that were there. In future I shall have to read it once a year to keep myself up to date; for though the New Testament will not change, my perception of it will change, just as the public perception of it will change. My contention is that Mrs Warren's Profession should be read carefully through every year by your whole staff, including Col. Sir Douglas Dawson; and I repeat my offer to pay an annual reader's fee as an additional inducement to this exercise. My only fear is that it may end in the play being licensed, and my finding myself, as a respectable elderly gentleman over sixty, credited with the recent production of a play written with a brutality extremely unbecoming to my age and serenity.

The play, like the gospels, will never change; but the old rule of your department 'We dont object to vice, as long as you dont make it horrifying' is what I really want to have reconsidered. The stern moralist was muzzled whilst Mr Arthur Roberts was let loose; and I really think that this result was a *reductio ad absurdum* of the rule. However, Mrs Warren is having the time of her life with our men in training and on leave from the front; and as the older I grow the more inclined I am to believe that all plays whatsoever should be prohibited, I have nothing more to say, and am unaffectedly apologetic for having said so much.

yours sincerely

G. Bernard Shaw

Across the top of Shaw's letter Lord Sandhurst wrote: 'This letter not ack^d as I look on it as closing the correspondence. S.'

Arthur **Roberts** (1852–1933) was a popular performer, a 'Veteran of Variety,' famed for risqué innuendo.

90 / To Cecil Gray   10 Adelphi Terrace WC

15th January 1917

[TLS: BL, 57786, f 44]

Cecil Gray (1895–1951), young Scottish composer, journalist, and musicologist, later to become music critic of The Nation *and author of several books, including* Sibelius *(1934), suggested that Shaw undertake a modern adaptation of Mozart's one-act comic opera* Der Schauspieldirektor *(*The Impresario*) (1786).*

Dear Mr Cecil Gray

I find that a letter of yours which required a prompt reply is dated the 20th November last. You mustnt mind: that is the sort of thing that happens to my correspondents every day.

As to the Schauspieldirektor there are two difficulties. First, I am not at all well acquainted with the contemporary theatre. I hardly ever go. I am twenty years out of date. Second, there is no such thing as a play done 'in a day or two as a kind of recreation.' The most trifling sketch, if it is seen right through to the rise of the curtain by the author, means at least a month's work. This is a young man's job. If I were under forty, I should be extremely tempted to do it for a lark; but as it is I must put the temptation behind me. If you have a copy of the libretto and will lend it to me I might suggest something or somebody; but perhaps you have already made arrangements.

yours sincerely
G. Bernard Shaw

91 / To William Faversham   10 Adelphi Terrace WC2
                                                          19th April 1917

[TLS: HRC]

William Faversham (1868–1940), English-born matinee idol and one of America's finest actors, was then touring with Getting Married *after 112 performances in New York. He had made a request for American rights to* Misalliance *and* The Devil's Disciple *(the latter eventually vetoed by Shaw for reasons given in a letter to the* Boston Evening Transcript *on 9 June 1917, which follows).*

Dear Mr Faversham

. . . A broken down Corsican brother is no use for Soames. Nothing less than a great success as Richelieu or Louis XI will move me. I am old enough to have seen T.C. King star in the C.B. Besides, you dont say which brother he played. You bet it was the ghost.

Clearly Misalliance is Wise's play, so you must get him for me. He will make it possible for you to keep out of the bill if Getting Married has still any life in it. Bryant, Nazimova's husband, was the original aviator, and quite good in it. He knows the business.

Irving was echoing Talma when he said that it takes twenty years to make an actor. The last time I tried a perfectly acted play without an actor in the cast who had not been less than twenty years on the stage it drew $150 a night. The same play, badly acted by really young people, had two roaringly successful tours in the States. Irving created a furore in London when he was quite the worst actor in the world technically. The last time I went to see him in his old theatre the man in the Box Office nearly fainted when I put down half a guinea for my stall. He had not seen money for years, poor fellow! The most successful performance of Candida I ever saw was given in a provincial theatre by ridiculous novices with hardly a week's experience. The audience laughed and cried like mad. My wisdom and skill were confounded.

The uniforms in The Devil's Disciple dont matter. If you want to be historically accurate, you will find Burgoyne's regiments mentioned in the book of the play. There is no choice: if they are right and not too shabby, there is nothing more to be said. Any costumier ought to be able to provide them. The play is a melodrama, and needs, besides Dick, a very good and genial heavy man for Anderson, a fine comedian for Burgoyne, a good disagreeable man for Swindon, and a regular melodramatic heroine for Judith. By a regular melodramatic heroine I mean a woman who has the trick of exciting pity and nothing else. I have seen most accomplished actresses struggling with Judith without much effect. On the other hand I have seen a hack provincial heroine who could come in with snow on her cloak to slow music to her heartbroken parents in the last act, and didnt know the difference between Eschylus and East Lynne, pull it off to perfection.

Float lighting and top lighting may toss up as to which is the worst. The proper way to light is from the front of the house. A couple of arcs in the middle of the circle at about the level of the top of the proscenium arch – or lower, perhaps, in your flat-staged straight-up American theatres, should be the main, though not the only, source of illumination. Barker is much the best lighter of a theatre I know, because he always makes the stage the glory of the theatre: you can see nothing else in fact, whereas the ordinary manager often takes more trouble to display the front of the house and brag of his audience, as it were, than to take care of the stage. When Getting Married was produced, Barker was not in London. I think he was in America considering the offer of the management of the then new millionaires' theatre, which he turned down on seeing the plans. He is thrown away on my plays, because he is at his best in work that requires subtlety and delicacy. To set him to produce me is like setting Debussy to conduct a very brassy Italian opera: he can do it; but he'd rather not. By comparison with him I am a vulgar old duffer. What my plays need is not only great accomplishment in mere physical speaking, clear articulation, fine tone, and swiftness and clearness of articulation, which every actor should have as a matter of routine, but energy, vivacity, impetuosity of delivery, brightness and high spirits. The man I dread is the actor who thinks that Shaw is 'intellectual drama,' and that he must play it as if there were a sick person in the house, the result being that the whole audience presently consists of sick persons. There is absolutely nothing subtle in my plays. Unless I know exactly what I mean I dont say it; and when I do know, I give it straight in the face. I dont care whether the actor understands it or not, provided he says it as if he meant it. *Conviction* is the alpha & omega of Shaw playing.

I will do nothing with Misalliance or The Devil's Disciple without letting you know, unless I change my mind about them; and there is no likelihood of that.

yours ever

G. Bernard Shaw

The Corsican Brothers (1880) was a costume melodrama by Dion Boucicault, one of Irving's most popular successes, as was Lord Lytton's *Richelieu* (1839) for William Macready and Boucicault's *Louis XI* (1855) for Charles Kean (1811–68). Thomas C. **King** (1818–93), a graceful tragedian with a rich bass voice, was long a favourite with Dublin play-goers. Thomas A. **Wise** (1865–1928), a much-respected American actor born in England, was a burly, Falstaffian character player whom Shaw conceived as Tarleton. Charles **Bryant** (1879–1948) and Alla **Nazimova** (1879–1945), exotic Russian-born actress, performed together 1912–23; they may have lived together as man and wife, but were not married. François **Talma** (1763–1826), French declamatory actor, was long a major support of the Comédie Française. The **perfectly acted play** was *Fanny's First Play*; though Shaw's comment was somewhat exaggerated, the young generation *was* depicted by rather mature actors. *East Lynne*, based on the novel (1861) by Mrs Henry Wood (1814–87), was one of the most popular melodramas in the stock repertory of the day; there were numerous adaptations, the earliest dating to 1864. **Float lighting** would later be called footlights. **Top lighting**, or floodlighting, was supplied from overhead battens, known in the United States as borders.

92 / To Editor of the *Boston Evening Transcript*

10 Adelphi Terrace WC2

9th June 1917

[TLS: HRC]

The Copley Theatre, Boston, had recently been leased to Henry Jewett, Australian-born American actor, who played Sergius in Richard Mansfield's 1894 production of Arms and the Man. Jewett's repertory company at the Copley spanned nearly eight seasons, during which he offered nineteen of Shaw's plays. The Devil's Disciple was not released to Jewett until April 1924, following a major revival in New York and on tour by the Theatre Guild the preceding year. Shaw's letter was published on 28 June.

Sir

In your issue of the fifteenth May it is stated that the production of my plays in the United States 'is much hampered by the pre-emption of this or that piece by managers who do not mount it themselves, yet are unwilling that others should represent it. The Devil's Disciple for example – to cite a play of Mr Shaw long unacted and long desired in the American theatre – is thus denied to the Copley, though the holder of those precious rights to performance in the United States shews no disposition to exercise them.'

Will you allow me, whilst thanking your critic for a comment so entirely friendly and serviceable in intention, to say that the rights of my plays are in my own hands; that only three of my plays are at present subject to contracts in the United States; and that in no case does the contract give the manager power to retain his licence to perform without making the fullest practicable use of it. If obstacles have been encountered they must have been raised by myself: the managers are blameless.

The Devil's Disciple will not be performed during the war. The demand for it to which your critic alludes is a real one; but it set in so markedly at the end of 1914 that I had to conclude that the attraction was less in the merit of the play than in its liability to political exploitation in anti-British interests. I therefore withdrew the play from the stage pending a change in the European situation. But for this a project for its revival by Mr William Faversham would have been carried out. The project is, I hope, only in abeyance until Mr Faversham and myself are released from the public considerations restraining us at present from a commercial test of a play which began my conquest of the American stage, and completed that of the late Richard Mansfield twenty years ago.

May I add that as Mr Jewett, an old colleague of Mansfield, was one of my earliest exponents on the New York stage, the Jewett Players at the Copley Theatre can always count on the theatrical equivalent of a 'most favored nation clause' when dealing with

yours truly

G. Bernard Shaw

In stating that *The Devil's Disciple* **completed** Mansfield's supremacy on the American stage Shaw is conveniently overlooking his subsequent productions of *Cyrano de Bergerac* and *Peer Gynt*!

93 / To Gertrude Kingston

10 Adelphi Terrace WC2

6th July 1917

[ALS: King's College, Cambridge]

A play by Henry James (1843–1916), The Outcry, which had been written for Granville Barker but not produced by him, was presented by the Stage Society on 1 and 3 July 1917.

Little Devil

I saw you on the stage after the performance, but your expression was evil and menacing; so I fled past.

It was clear that somebody not mentioned in the bill had produced The Outcry; and if, as now appears, it was you, I congratulate Henry James on being more fortunate than I in gaining your veneration.

But nothing can make H.J. intelligible on the stage. The difficulty is not in the least that his dialogue is artificial and affected and involved: it is not more so than Congreve's now appears, or than Shakespear's was even in the spacious times of g. E. [*great Elizabeth*]. It is simply that he uses sounds that are not intelligible to the ear, though they are quite lucid on paper. On Tuesday I repeated to half a dozen people the phrase 'Sought asylum is perhaps excessive'; and not one of them could catch the words, though I uttered them quite fairly: they sound like simple gibberish. I did not, with all my literary expertness and knowledge of James's style, catch more than two thirds of the dialogue as it was spoken, though I could have read it without difficulty.

Your American expedition will fail; but no doubt it will amuse you. Is R. to be your leading man? You may have noticed that your receipts, bludgeoned down to nothing as they were by your stellar idiocy, were struggling to rise and actually succeeding slowly. You had the materials for a success for the program: you used them to make one for yourself – and who shall blame you? But no single success can keep up a theatre unless it be that of a man who can play the big Hamlet Macbeth repertory which has no female equivalent. It has been tried again and again; and the only apparent solid result is Sarah [*Bernhardt*], who always built herself in with the prettiest women and strongest men she could lay hands on.

No doubt The Wrong Box failed, as it was bound to do at such a moment. But Getting Married didnt.

GBS

R probably was Walter Ringham, who played Lucius Septimius in the New York (1906) and London (1907) productions of *Cæsar and Cleopatra* and Achillas in the 1913 production, and performed opposite Gertrude Kingston in a repertory of Shaw one-act plays (*Overruled, The Inca of Perusalem*, and *Great Catherine*) in the United States 1916–17. *The Wrong Box*, a farce by Granville Barker based on the novel by Lloyd Osbourne (1868–1947) and Robert Louis Stevenson (1850–94), was produced by Winthrop Ames (1870–1937) under the title *The Morris Dance*, in New York on 12 February 1917. Its timing was unfortunate, for the United States had broken diplomatic ties with Germany on 3 February and declared war on 6 April.

94 / To Beulah Jay   10 Adelphi Terrace WC2
17th November 1917

[ALS: HRC]

*Beulah E. Jay, a stage-struck dabbler in theatre, studied for grand opera in Boston, then enrolled in a New York acting school. Eventually, her husband Edward G. Jay, Jr, a mechanical engineer, indulged her (after she had established a Philadelphia school of acting), by building for her in 1912–13 a 330-seat playhouse on DeLancey Street. Mrs Jay, announcing that she would make the Little Theatre 'a sincere and original effort in dramatic expression' (*New York Times, 22 June 1913, V, 13:1*), attempted to operate a professional company. By 1915, however, spiralling costs compelled her to revamp the operation by establishing a society of amateur actors in her theatre. Kenneth MacGowan (1888–1963), dramatic and literary editor of the Philadelphia* Evening Ledger, *appealed to Shaw (through Gertrude Kingston, then touring in America), to let the theatre have the rights to his plays, though admitting that at an admission of 50¢ a ticket 'if we have to pay even such a ridiculous fee to authors as $5 a performance (nobody else gets* *anything, of course), the [management] will go into bankruptcy' (TLS to Kingston: BL 50539, ff 97–8).*

On 22 January 1917 Mrs Jay presented Misalliance *for a four-week run, sans authorization, defending herself subsequently by claiming she had written to Shaw, and when she received no response took his silence for assent (oblivious to the fact that vast quantities of mail were being delivered to the bottom of the Atlantic with an average of three million tons of commercial shipping a year being destroyed by enemy action on the seas). Shaw, obliged to notify William Faversham on 17 November that his 'first American production' had been anticipated, and that he would have to delete Philadelphia from his touring schedule, grumbled, 'These little artistic theatres are very useful in an educative way; but they are pestilent pirates, because they are so often managed by enthusiasts without a notion of business or legal responsibility' (TLS: HRC). There is no record in Shaw's account book of payment eventually being made to replace Mrs Jay's lost cheques, nor were royalties for the Philadelphia production of* Misalliance *ever paid.*

Dear Miss Beulah Jay

I have received your letter of the 30th October enclosing copies of letters dated December 19th 1916, and January 12th, May 5th, and July 2nd 1917. These letters do not seem to have arrived. Those of December 19th, January 16th and May 5th, enclosing cheques for $52.43, $56.42, and $208.58 respectively, and proposing to do Misalliance, certainly did not. Presumably they have been torpedoed along with their cheques; and incidentally they exposed you to a risk of an action for damages for at least $25,000.

The difficulty in dealing with you is that you have not had sufficient business training to understand the legal importance of the things you do. You have probably heard that Misalliance has now been produced by Mr William Faversham. That means that I entered into a contract with Mr Faversham by which he acquired the right to the first production of the play as an absolute novelty in all the leading cities of the United States. Now you calmly inform me that you have performed Misalliance for 4 weeks in Philadelphia, and that I have defrauded Mr Faversham by selling him the right to the first performance there. If this had come to Mr Faversham's ears before he was committed to his undertaking, he would probably have thrown the play back on my hands, as any other commercial management certainly would; and my only remedy would have been to take an action against you for the damage caused me by your making my play unsaleable, and probably to sell up your theatre if you were not in a position to find the money. Fortunately, I got wind of your piratical exploit before the agreement was signed, though I had no idea that you had run the play for 4 weeks; and I was just able to avoid putting myself in the position of being compelled by Mr Faversham to sue you for the damages you have inflicted on him by knocking an important city out of his circuit. How is it possible to do business with a woman who does things of this kind and imagines that they are only romantic adventures? In all conscience the hazards of running a theatre in a businesslike manner are bad enough to deter anybody but a confirmed gambler. But to run it on reckless piratical lines is to ask for ruin. It is not a question of going to prison. As you have never been there (though you really ought to be), you probably think that a few months of it would be amply repaid by having your fancy about somebody else's play. But that is not what happens. You find the Courts making orders that you must pay immense sums of money; and for one single little lark you find your private means gone, your theatre sold up, and your ambitions laid waste. Do not do it again, Beulah: you will not find Jewish theatrical syndicates as easy to play with as I am.

Now, as to your lost cheques. What were they? Did you go to your banker, and obtain from him a draft on London, payable to me there in pounds shillings and pence at the current rate of exchange? That is what you ought to have done. Cheques on your own bank payable in Philadelphia are no use to me: my banker charges me too much for collecting them. Anyhow you must find out whether these cheques have been presented and paid. If so, they have been stolen. If not, they have been torpedoed, and you must get a fresh draft for me.

Also, will you check your percentages. As the returns have been lost with the cheques I cannot tell how many performances your statement of gross represents. I enclose a memorandum of my scale of fees to remind you of my terms.

To conclude the business part of my letter, I give you notice that if I have not only to provide you with plays, but to train you in business as well, my terms will have to be doubled.

I did not receive the picture of your theatre: it was lost with the cheques. You say that it seats 330, that it is simple and dignified in design, and that you think it really beautiful. You had better send me another picture, and tell me how much money it holds. You should never think of anything else but money: I never do. The number of people a theatre holds is of no consequence compared to the quantity of money it holds. What are the prices of the seats; and how many are there of each denomination? What you say about the State Attorney and the Legislature would be very interesting if only you would be angelic enough to explain what it all means. You speak of a law and an interpretation. You dont tell me what the law is; but you carefully tell me that the interpretation is 'splendid.' That is the sort of thing that makes me thankful that you are not within reach of my hands and of the poker; for you would certainly drive me to the most unchivalrous extremes. Do people with whom you do business ever assault you?

This letter to you has already taken up nearly all my morning. I wish you had never been born.

yours faithfully
G. Bernard Shaw

95 / To W. Lee-Mathews

10 Adelphi Terrace WC2
4th July 1918

[TLS: HRC]

William Lee-Mathews (1862–1931), a business executive, was from 1905 (succeeding Shaw) chairman of the Incorporated Stage Society producing committee.

My dear William

That is interesting, but in my opinion unsound. I hold that an unknown author is either in a stronger position than a known one or else in no position at all. Suppose you are a manager, obliged to keep your theatre going or perish. You want a play badly. Naturally you dont want one by an unknown man. You try Barrie: he hasnt one written. You try Pinero: he can let you have one in six months. You try Carton, Maugham, even Shaw. None of them have anything ready. You are forced back on an experiment with an unknown man. The unknown man looks darkly at you (if he is a good man of business), and says 'You must be in a devil of a hole if you come to me. I am nobody. I want the same terms as Barrie.' 'Monstrous,' you reply. 'You, an obscure scallywag, ask what Barrie would give me a play for!' 'Well, my friend, go and ask him for one.'

Hankin acted on this principle when he was unacted; and V & B never forgave him; but they had to pay. I think he got an advance of £200 on a first class contract.

Moral: the beginner should be modest enough to know that his play will not be produced if anything better is on the market. And there his modesty should stop.

ever

G. Bernard Shaw

PS. I cant come tomorrow . . . as I have a lunch engagement. But the reaction against Be Careful, Baby, and Twin Beds is becoming so acute that I believe Sturge Moore is ripe for a delirious success; and the more sturgid the better. His little play about the accursed sword and the Viking corpse is excellent of its kind, though Hertz will not appreciate it.

W. Somerset **Maugham** (1874–1965) was a prolific dramatist, novelist, and short-story writer, who in 1908 had four West End productions running simultaneously; yet in 1918 his best dramatic work was still to come. St John **Hankin** (1869–1909), a suicide, was one of the most accomplished comic dramatists of his generation. The play for which Vedrenne and Barker 'had to pay' was *The Return of the Prodigal,* 1905.

The initial reference in the **PS** is to a meeting of the producing committee. *Be Careful, Baby,* a crude farce by Salisbury Field and Margaret Mayo, running since 17 April, and *Twin Beds* were the same play. The latter was the original title of the American version, produced in 1914. T. Sturge **Moore** (1870–1944), artist and playwright, wrote plays that for the most part had biblical themes. Henry A. **Hertz** (c. 1845–1923), a tea merchant who became a member of the stock exchange, was a founder of London's German Theatre (1899) and a longtime member of the executive committee of the Stage Society. Margaret Halstan was his daughter.

96 / To Lillah McCarthy   Presteign. Radnorshire
                                         (until Thursday morning)
                                              12th August 1918

[ALS: HRC]

Shaw's new play Heartbreak House, *completed in 1917, was his first full-length dramatic work in five years. At her request he supplied a copy to Lillah in rough proof, though he considered her too old for Ellie Dunn, the role she desired. Then, ironically, he cast Ellen O'Malley, who was the same age as Lillah, as 'the ingenue of eighteen.'*

My dear Lillah

You are incorrigible. I told you from the first that H.H. was of no use to you. How can you, at your age and with your reputation as a Siddonian 'heavy,' play an ingenue of eighteen against two women of forty playing off their sexual fascinations for all they are worth? You could do it perfectly well against Mrs Gilbey and Mrs Knox, but not against Hesione and Ariadne.

And are you quite insensible to the certainty that if you produced the play this winter, the raid at the end of it would become a real one every time the moon and the weather gave the Germans their chance?

Your suggestion of Fred and Julia is a brilliant one; and with you as Ariadne, and Ellen O'Malley as Ellie, might be a practical one if the bombardment difficulty could be got over. But that would not suit your plans, though it would suit mine fairly well. I want a much better actress for Ariadne than the part will attract: a hard working devil, and yet a handsome and authoritative person.

If I could call into existence by a wave of my hand a star play like Pygmalion, all would be better than well. Unfortunately I can't. What you need is a star play. Mind: I dont mean that you demand a star part: I mean that your situation makes it necessary. You see what has happened to Marie Lohr. Nothing was any use (£8000 lost) until she got her Nurse Benson. There is really nothing between the star system, much as I dislike it, and an endowed theatre. You will have to star; and I must fall back on my old plan of simply publishing my plays, and waiting for the endowed theatre to come along. I am not deserting you: I am only facing the facts. I have as much reason to grab at a production as you or Drinkwater, but it will not pay any of us in the long run to throw away H.H. on a failure – least of all on a half failure.

The theatre just now is impossible. . . . I really dont know what is to be done. I am too old.

ever

G.B.S.

Mrs Gilbey and Mrs Knox are the mothers in *Fanny's First Play*. Lillah McCarthy, now 42, had played the daughter Margaret Knox in the 1911 production. **Julia** and **Fred** were the wife-and-husband team of Neilson and Terry (see letter 12). Marie **Löhr** (1890–1975), much admired Australian actress, played Leo in *Getting Married* (1908); she had just gone into management at the Globe Theatre. **Nurse Benson,** by R.C. Carton and Justin Huntly M'Carthy (1861–1936), ran for 324 performances. John **Drinkwater** (1882–1937), dramatic author of historical subjects like *Abraham Lincoln* (1918), was for a number of years an actor and general manager of the Birmingham Repertory Theatre.

97 / To Rutland Boughton

10 Adelphi Terrace WC2
15th January 1919

[TLS: BL 52365, f 14]

Rutland Boughton (1878–1960), composer of musical dramas based on Arthurian legend and founder (1914) of the Glastonbury Festival, had expressed interest in the lion costume created for Androcles and the Lion *(1912).*

. . . The head mask is the only thing the lion wears that presents any difficulty. The skin is no worse than a suit of khaki; and the paws are necessary to jump about on. The man who played it for me sweated so frightfully in the skin that he swore he lost seven pounds weight at every performance. He must be a bit of an acrobat. He cannot go downstairs step by step: he has to spring clean from one landing to the other. But you could not do Androcles in Glastonbury: it takes no end of people and a revolving stage. The expense is damnable.

Blanco, of course, is quite easy.

ever
G.B.S.

Boughton was still in military uniform, at Blandford, hence the reference to **khaki**. The role of the Lion was created in 1913 by Edward Sillward (d. 1930), a professional animal impersonator.

98 / To Edith Lyttelton

Ayot St Lawrence. Welwyn. Herts.
16th April 1919

[ALS: Churchill Archives Centre]

Edith Lyttelton (1865–1948), nicknamed 'D.D.,' theatre enthusiast and occasional playwright, was, like Shaw, a member of the executive committee of the

Shakespeare Memorial National Theatre scheme. The committee at this time was contemplating financial support for the Stratford-on-Avon Festival Theatre, whose New Shakespeare Company had just been created, with the director W. Bridges-Adams (1889–1965) at its helm. A principal issue here was the cutting of the plays: Shaw was firmly against any but the most judicious trimming, and threatened to resign if the question of reasonable trimming were not made part of the agreement.

Oh Lord D.D., this is worse and worse and worse. Dont you know that the acts in Shakespeare's plays are not his at all, but only modern interruptions for selling drink at the bars? Only a few of them have any authority for the act divisions. The clause (which wasnt in the agreement when I read it) should bind B.A. *not* to observe the act divisions. 'Telescoping' is just what is wanted. If you play in acts you *must* cut. If you dont cut, you cannot play in acts.

As to experimenting, that has been done already as far as the points at issue are concerned. Poel and Barker have demonstrated once for all that the plays *can* be done in Shakespear's way. What I object to is going back on that.

I know B.A. and am biassed in his favor. His Bolshevist mother is an old acquaintance of mine. She did not even prevent me from becoming faintly aware of his comparatively invisible father. But he is after stage pictures first and Shakespear second; and I am after Shakespear first and everyone else nowhere.

Your committee of scholars (meaning Gollancz: you and I being ignoramuses) will do nothing but mischief. If the play is to be cut the producer must cut it.

I violently deny all your accusations about the hut; for though I forget all about it I am sure that whatever I did was the right thing to do, and if you opposed me you totally misunderstood the issue – whatever it was.

Lytton promises to stand by me: we are to have another meeting and see what can be done.

I return your affection with ardor; but the credit for our mutual flame is all on your side, as you are so much younger and better looking.

ever & ever

G.B.S.

Bridges-Adams's **Bolshevist mother** was Mary (Daltry) Bridges-Adams (1856–1939). Israel **Gollancz** (1863–1930), leading Shakespeare scholar and London University professor, was honorary secretary of the Memorial. The committee, some years before the war, acquired a site in Bloomsbury for the National Theatre, intending to build and open it in time for the Shakespeare Tercentenary (of his death) in 1916. As a result of the war the sole building on the site in 1916 was a 'Shakespeare **Hut**' operated for the military by the YMCA. Victor **Lytton** (1876–1947), 2nd Earl of Lytton, was a fellow member of the committee.

99 / To William Armstrong

10 Adelphi Terrace WC2
13th June 1919

[APCS: present source unknown]

I am dead beat, and must be off to Ireland presently to recuperate. I am in London for as short a moment as possible, once a week for public meetings, committees, and such like remnants of the season's junk.

There is nothing doing in my line at present. Theatre rents and expenses have risen far above what the highbrow drama can draw; and its only refuge, the Lyric, Hammersmith, is blocked up with Lincoln. Under these circumstances we are two tramps, asking one another to note that we are 'at liberty.' I note accordingly.

G.B.S.

John Drinkwater's *Abraham Lincoln*, which had been running at the Lyric, Hammersmith, since February, continued for a total of 466 performances.

100 / To William Poel

10 Adelphi Terrace WC2
27th June 1919

[TLS: HRC]

At a Council meeting of the Academy of Dramatic Art on 19 June, Pinero, who had been much impressed by reports of Poel's Elizabethan Players' production of 3 June of the anonymous play The Return from Parnassus *(1606), with Edith Evans as Sir Randell, suggested he be invited to join the teaching staff as an expert in Shakespearean delivery. Shaw agreed to sound him out, which he did on 20 June. Poel had now replied.*

My dear Poel

Dont make any conditions. Just take your hour and your class and go your own way. If you find that you cannot do good under the existing conditions, you can retire at any moment or ask for changes which your experience proves to be needed. You can then act with some knowledge of the school, and of what can be done there and what can't. For we none of us like all the conditions that are imposed on us.

For instance, there is the money difficulty. We only scraped through the war by posturing in a cinema film that began with an exhibition of the celebrities of the Council, and ended with Masks & Faces. And we have a theatre five sixths complete in the back garden, which we cannot afford to finish. Under such circumstances we are forced to exploit the folly and vanity and stage struckness of a certain people who have no earthly qualification for the stage and no chance of ever getting an engagement, who come and study hopelessly at the Academy. They are not encouraged. They get the broadest hints as to their chances; and the teachers suffer their presence in the classes without wasting time on them. But there are two obstacles to frankly shewing them the door as you suggest. One is that we cant afford to. Their fees enable us to keep going and to take poorer students at half fees. And, what is far more important, we soon find that except in the cases of women whose age and personality make all doubt impossible, it is not safe to condemn anyone; for it often happens that apparently hopeless novices end by being the most promising pupils.

Consequently it may be your fate to have one or two duds in your class, whom you will allow to listen to your lessons because their fees make the school possible.

As to attendance, the discipline of the school is not as lax as it might be if the students were all adult artists. Lots of them are children; and though they always seem to me uproariously free, and much more cubbish and footballplayerish in their manners than they should be, I do not think it would be possible to allow them to play fast and loose with attendance. As they cannot be punished in the usual way, they must go through regularly with the course of study or leave the school. They are by temperament inclined to be casual young devils; and you yourself would soon be obliged to insist that if they once go in for your course they must stick to it.

One suggestion of yours is wildly impossible. The whole object of engaging you is to get Shakespear's verse spoken on the stage as you teach it. It is an official admission that yours is the right way. The way it is commonly spoken is no way at all. To cry stinking fish by announcing to the students that your way is not the proper way (for they, poor lambs, of course think that the regular professional way is the right way) would bewilder, mislead and corrupt them. We do not intend that there shall be other teachers working at Shakespear. You must take on all the Shakespearean work, and give us not only scenes from Shakespear (or any other Elizabethan you like occasionally) at the little private school performances that go on for a week or so at the end of the terms, but take on a scene for the annual public performance. Without this you could not keep up your position in the school as a classical teacher: you would simply be announcing yourself as a crank; and not only would the proposal to engage you fall through; but if it succeeded, the children (for you must think of them as children and consider their parents) would refuse to disqualify themselves for their profession by learning in what they would consider (having been told so) a wrong and ridiculous way of speaking.

You see[,] the place is full of pitfalls; and the only safe and reasonable course is to accept the engagement as if it were an entirely normal one, as indeed it is, and take your place, not as a heretic, but as a pontiff.

I assure you the proposal was mooted quite spontaneously by Pinero without any prompting or suggestion from me, in consequence of what he had heard of your Parnassus performance. I backed it up, of course; but I did not lead up to it in any way; and as Pinero is one of the old school so far as that he absolutely abhors Barker's Shakespearean productions, you may count his conversion as a notable step in your progress towards general recognition.

ever
G.B.S.

The *Masks and Faces* film (1917), which opened with a meeting of the ADA Council, including Shaw, was adapted from the 1852 play by Tom Taylor (1812–80) and Charles Reade (1814–84). **Barker's Shakespearean productions** were influenced by Poel's stagings.

101 / To John Drinkwater

Great Southern Hotel
Parknasilla-on-Sea
Kenmare. Co. Kerry
11th August 1919

[ALS: Washington University Libraries]

The publishing agents Curtis Brown Ltd informed Shaw on 9 August that they had placed Drinkwater's Abraham Lincoln *in America, and would be grateful to Shaw for a few lines of praise to be used to introduce Drinkwater to the American public via the press. At the foot of the letter Shaw added a penned note: 'This is a wildly impossible game to start of dramatic authors puffing one another's plays. Abraham Lincoln, by John Drinkwater. "The noblest of modern plays" Shaw. Heartbreak House, by Bernard Shaw. "A sublime masterpiece" Drinkwater. Caw me; and I'll caw thee. In a few months the thing would become a putrefying scandal; and the authors would be sharing one another's royalties by way of commission. Tell J.D. to quote* critics, *and have nothing to do with testimonials from others.'*

My dear Drinkwater

When I got the enclosed I hastily scribbled the red ink insult on it, and was about to hurl it back at these idiots of agents when it occurred to me that I had better send it to you so that you might see what they are doing in your name.

I am depressed to learn that they have placed the play in America for you: an exceedingly superfluous service. I hope they got proper terms: at least 15% on houses exceeding £300 and so forth, with a limit date for production and a term of not more than two years. My experience is that agents live by procuring plays for managers and books for publishers at half or two thirds their market value.

I shall be here until the 20th, or so.

ever
G. Bernard Shaw

102 / To Karel Mušek

10 Adelphi Terrace WC2
28th August 1919

[ALS: U. of Delaware]

Karel Mušek (1867–1924) was a former actor and director of the Bohemian

National Theatre at Prague, who became Shaw's Czech translator.

Dear Mr Musek

Not until the end of last month did I ascertain from the Board of Trade here that I was free to enter into new arrangements with persons in Germany and Austria for the performance and publication of my works in those countries. Also, debts due to me before the war by persons, firms or companies *in Austria* (*not* in Germany) may be collected by me. I presume that you are still an Austrian in respect of money due to me before the revolution. And in respect of money due since then you can hardly be counted as an 'alien enemy'; so we may proceed as if the war had never happened.

However, I do not think that under existing circumstances any money should be sent from Bohemia to England if the English creditor can afford to wait for it as I can. Will you keep it for me until the rate of exchange shews that Bohemia can export to England without adding to her present privations? If your own personal position becomes difficult at any moment do not hesitate to draw on my share of the fees.

It is understood between us that our former agreement is to apply, *mutatis mutandis* [*necessary changes having been made*], as if Bohemia had occupied its present portion of independence at the date of its execution.

I hope soon to send you printed copies of the plays written during the war. They are not yet published here; but they are passed for press and are only waiting for a favorable moment in the book market. . . .

faithfully

G. Bernard Shaw

The **revolution** is the German social revolution of 1918–19. As a consequence of the disintegration of the Austro-Hungarian Empire, **Bohemia** was now part of the newly created republic of Czechoslovakia. The **plays written during the war** were the four 'Playlets of the War': *O'Flaherty V.C., The Inca of Perusalem, Augustus Does His Bit*, and *Annajanska the Wild Grand Duchess*, published with *Heartbreak House* in September.

103 / To Stella Beech   10 Adelphi Terrace WC2
                                             13th December 1919

[ALS: Patrick Beech]

Stella Beech (1886–1975), daughter of Mrs Patrick Campbell, was performing as Raïna opposite Robert Loraine's Bluntschli in a revival of Arms and the Man, *using the stage name Stella Mervyn Campbell. As Shaw was otherwise occupied on opening night, the 11th, he did not see the production until the 13th.*

My dear Stella

I have just seen the matinée; and before I catch my train I have a note or two for you.

You forgot to ask Bluntschli [*Act I*] what he was going to do when he gave you the cloak; and you did not make enough of the 'Oh, *thank you*' to prepare for the change of attitude towards him.

You did not scream Stop *through* the shooting.

In the third act you nearly made me faint by your place being empty when the curtain rose. The picture was spoiled.

Your next crime was the worst. When Petkoff & Catherine went off with 'You would only splutter at them,' you went on with the dialogue at exactly the same speed, precisely as if your scene were a continuation of the previous one. Now when B. & R. are left alone for the first time since their adventure six months before, the whole atmosphere should change; and this is done quite simply by waiting a little and then *commencing* (not continuing) in a new tone, at a new speed, in this case much slower and obviously provocative and mischievous. This is the sort of thing that matters more than lost cues or late entrances: it is how the fully accomplished leading lady prepares her effects and makes the audience listen to her and forget the low comedian. Whatever else you do or dont do, take care of this.

In the last act you should play a little to B's 'leave for home in an hour,' which is a dreadful blow. It explains the tragic tone of 'What does *he* care: what does *any* soldier care?'. By the way keep centre and time that exit so that you do not have to turn and wait for Louka to speak. You are not thinking of her.

I think Raïna, when B. is shutting the shutters after the soldiers have gone, should take a wrap – preferably a gold or silver one – from the chest of drawers, and slip it on before B. comes back. All the women I have consulted agree with me about this.

I am no longer very sanguine about a success. The experience of the first production is being repeated. At the first performance the company played the play, with sensational success. After that they played for the laughs; and the whole thing went to pieces. It is not your fault: you are doing very well, as far as it is possible for you under the circumstances; but the general effect is trivial and insincere: the audience longs for an earnest tone and doesnt get it. However, I shall write all that to Loraine and do my best to save the situation.

In great haste to catch my train
G.B.S.

104 / To Mrs Patrick Campbell   [10 Adelphi Terrace WC2

c. 5 February 1920]

[AL(u) (inc): Cornell]

Viola Tree (1844–1938), actress daughter of the late Beerbohm Tree, had gone into management at the Aldwych Theatre, opening with a revival of Pygmalion *on 10 February. Shaw undertook to stage the production, with Mrs Patrick Campbell recreating her role as Liza and C. Aubrey Smith (1863–1948) playing Higgins.*

[Act II]

On 'I'm going away. He's off his chump, he is. I want no balmies teaching me,' dont go down R.C. [*Right Center*] Swing round at him but keep C until he says 'Throw her out.' *Then* down R.C. This will avoid any repetition of the same movement.

Mrs Pearce went angry on 'Stop, Mr Higgins: I wont allow it'; but this was a slip. She will say it steadily and quietly; and there will be a little scene whilst they are all looking at Liza and asking her about her parents. She should be rather shy and naïve under their scrutiny and enquiries. You must study this, as it is one of my quick transitions of mood.

Be careful not to do anything to make Mrs Pearce forget her rather kindly but superior self-possession. It is invaluable to you as contrast.

Take the handkerchief from her with one quick snatch: it is impossible that this new Mrs Pearce should struggle with you for it.

All the rest is right; but you must not depend on *pushes* from the others for your acting. Aubrey cannot give you the cue-shoves you are accustomed to: they do not belong to the part as he plays it. You must *imagine* the cue, just as you would have to imagine a lovely Romeo if you were playing with an ugly one – or with me. . . .

Act V

You have lost some of the digs at Higgins in the conversation with Pickering. 'Oh, I didnt mean it either' should be 'Oh, *I* didnt mean it either.' If you get this right the next dig 'It was only my way' will make itself. And the slighting triviality of 'That is his profession' is underdone.

In the final grand duet with Higgins, you walk composedly & elegantly to the ottoman with 'The same to everybody,' and sit down on 'Like Father.' I must tell Aubrey not to fling away from you on 'You talk about me as if I were a motor bus.' He should look as if he were walking straight through you.

You are puzzled by his line 'you are a part of it that has come my way and been built into my house' because it is new; and you will see that it is too sincere and intimate a saying to bear the rhetorical gesture you wanted him to make.

On 'You wanted to get rid of me' 'Liar' 'Thank you' it is natural to sit at the R end of the ottoman; but as I am beaten by the problem of how to get you to the centre of it so that he can get his face on your right at 'for the fun of it,' you must get there on 'Thank you.'

You sat too soon after 'I'll talk as I like: youre not my teacher now.' There is a change there that is crucial. With 'He has a right to if he likes, poor lad' Liza stops being angry and becomes wistful and more and more distressed by his obtuseness, getting wretcheder and wretcheder until she collapses completely on 'That's not a proper answer to give me.' This is very important. It is the slow movement of the symphony, and gives the recoil for the final spring.

In the speech beginning 'It's all youll get until you stop being a common idiot' you have driven Higgins so far away that the audience cannot see you both at the same time; and your facial play is consequently lost: you might as well be off the stage. I took particular care to keep you in the picture until the last six lines so that it should be a duet; but now it is a baritone solo with a chorus girl in the corner. You have not yet mastered the art of using other people on the stage so as to get a share in their best work.

Now comes the most important point of all. When Eliza emancipates herself – when Galatea comes to life – she must not relapse. She must retain her pride and triumph to the end. When Higgins takes your arm on 'consort battleship' you must instantly throw him off with implacable pride; and this is the note until the final 'Buy them yourself.' He will go out on the balcony to watch your departure; come back triumphantly into the room; exclaim 'Galatea!' (meaning that the statue has come to life at last); and – curtain. Thus he gets the last word; and you get it too. . . .

The **Galatea** ending devised by Shaw differs from any printed text of the play. The letter, which is incomplete, consists of pp. 2–6 of seven or more pages.

105 / To Viola Tree   Ayot St Lawrence. Welwyn. Herts.
                                                            23rd March 1920

[ALS: HRC]
Pygmalion *was transferred to a smaller theatre, the Duke of York's, on 10 May, with Frank Cellier (1884–1948) taking over as Higgins.*

My dear Viola

I have influenza, diphtheria, sunstroke, and sleeping sickness. I can do nothing, care for nothing, feel nothing but a headache.

Highbrow drama is impossible. It is quite true that £1400 a week is about the level of expenses; and unless you could flood London with a very clever picture poster of Pygmalion, or induce Stella to play Higgins (which she could do really well) I dont see what is to be done, except let the theatre to a greenhorn from after Easter to the middle of September.

If you cant do this, you are caught in a cleft stick. No author with a good play on hand will let it be produced after Easter, because the run is limited by the close of the season to eight weeks or so. For the same reason no manager wants to incur production expenses with so little time to get them back. It therefore becomes a question, not of making money, but of losing as little as possible.

Once your father made a proposal to me for the off season. I convinced Dana that the result would be a loss of £800 a week. But he persisted in the proposal on the ground that closing the theatre would mean a *certain* loss of £800 a week, whereas by keeping open with my play there was at least a chance of doing better. And when the project fell through it was on some other ground.

Therefore, even if business does not improve after Passion Week, it *may* pay you to run Pygmalion to the end of the season in the ghastly sense that anything else you could do would cost you more. If you have taken this fully in, you will see that if you are going to change the bill, you cannot possibly do it too soon. Every week you wait shortens the possible run to the third week in June or so. Even if you start rehearsing a new piece this very blessed day, you could not (even if *I* produced it at lightning speed) get it on until the 19th April, which would leave time for 10 weeks run.

By the way, if the Afternoon Theatre is still contemplated, do not forget that Blanco Posnet (now fully licensed) was written for it, and has never been exploited in London, though it is an East Lynne in Dublin. It is right for an English company, which O'Flaherty is not.

I shall be in London (unless I die) on Thursday; and on Monday I shall probably go to Ireland and not return until about the 20th April.

ever

G.B.S.

Henry **Dana** (1855–1921) was Beerbohm Tree's general manager from 1897 until the latter's death in 1917. **After Noon Theatre** was a lunch-time scheme inaugurated at His Majesty's Theatre by Tree in 1909.

106 / To St John Ervine   Great Southern Hotel
Parknasilla-on-Sea
Kenmare. Co. Kerry
10th August 1920

[ALS: HRC]

The Theatre Guild, newly founded in 1919, was created as a subscription society for non-commercial plays, at the Garrick Theatre, in which in 1894 Richard Mansfield had introduced Shaw to New York with Arms and the Man. *Following a stunning success with St John Ervine's drama* John Ferguson *in May 1920, the Guild acquired rights to* Heartbreak House *for a world première. Shaw, however, declined to allow an opening until after the national elections in early November, taking a position that election fever invariably had a dire effect on box office. Despite pleas from the Guild he remained adamant: the first performance was postponed until 10 November.*

Dear St John Ervine

I am sorry for the poor Guild; but I have this fuss every four years. The theatre people know nothing about politics and are incapable of learning from experience. Besides, the Guild, being less than 4 years old, has no experience. The election, though it may not interfere much with an established running success, is fatal to a new production, because the candidates play authors and actors clean off the stage; and the papers will not devote an inch of space to them, nor would anybody read the inch if they did. Therefore never allow a piece of yours to be produced in election fall until a week after 'the Tuesday following the first Monday in November.' The management will protest, howl, implore, prove that the election is filling the theatres, that the play is topical and will be helped by the election, & all sorts of nonsense. Hold tight; and the management will admit that you were right afterwards, and then will forget all about it and make a fool of itself just the same four years later. I have been through it all.

I have cabled 'Inexorable' and written.

If they are determined to throw away a new play, they can have their £500 advance back (I never asked them for it) and keep Heartbreak House for later on; but dont let it be a play of yours.

I calculated that they could carry on with Jane. . . .

G.B.S.

Shaw's reference to '**Jane**' suggests he had confused Ervine's present play with an earlier one, *Jane Clegg* (1913).

107 / To Lawrence Langner   The Shakespeare Hotel
                                                  Stratford-on-Avon
                                                  3rd May 1921

[ALS: Yale]

Lawrence Langner (1890–1962), Welsh-born lawyer and occasional playwright, was principal organizer of the Theatre Guild, which he co-managed with Theresa Helburn (1887–1959). Back to Methuselah, Shaw's largest stage work, in five parts (he subtitled it 'A Metabiological Pentateuch'), had occupied the dramatist from March 1918 to completion in May 1920, followed by revisions, stage directions, and page-proofing for publication on 1 June 1921. The Guild's world-première production of Methuselah was staged in a three-week cycle of eight performances each: Parts I and II (despite Shaw's injunction) on 27 February 1922; Parts III and IV on 6 March; Part V on 13 March. For a second cycle Shaw reluctantly authorized cuts in the text allowing for more conventional curtain times. In all, 25 performances of the complete work were presented.

Dear Mr Langner

I have been travelling about for more than a month, delivering political orations; trying to recover from the too long spell of unbroken work that Methuselah brought on me; and writing nothing but the most urgently necessary letters on picture postcards. Hence my delay in replying to the letter you wrote on the Aquitania on the 18th March.

The second play will not mean Asquith and Lloyd George to your public; and [in] so far it will not produce the effect it will produce here on the few people who have any sense of political personalities. But in Fanny's First Play, the American public knew nothing about Walkley, Gilbert Cannan and E.A. Baughan (for that matter very few people outside a little ring in London were any better informed). Nevertheless Trotter, Gunn and Vaughan went down just as well in America as here. I therefore believe that if Joyce Burge and Lubin fail here, they will fail everywhere; and if they succeed here they will succeed just as well in America. However that may be, the thing must stay as it is now. The job did itself that way, and I cannot pull it to pieces and do it some other way.

As to the first play, it produced such an astonishing effect when I read it to an audience consisting mostly of women that I never ventured on the experiment again. I gather that it missed fire with you. It may do so with your public; but I assure you that it *can* explode with shattering consequences. To play it and the second play at the same performance is impossible. You will have to make up your mind to the three evenings and the two matinees. You must sell the tickets in batches of five, all five tickets on one sheet with perforated card divisions. If people buy them that way they will not throw them away. They may be bothered and disappointed by the first two plays as you expect; but their bewilderment will not take the form of throwing their tickets into the fire, especially if you charge enough for them. You can warn them that the prologue in the Garden of Eden will last only an hour (or perhaps 50 minutes; you can time it at rehearsal) and that no assumptions must be made as to the duration of each part of the play. Mark: each part of the play, not each play. The wording of your programmes and announcements must always rub in the fact that what the public is going to see is one play, with sections of various lengths.

Later on we can see about giving separate performances of the sections; but for the first ten performances (say) it must be impossible to take less than the whole dose.

The book will be published on the first of June or thereabouts. I note your calm suggestion that it should be held back until you are ready to produce. I told you you wanted the earth. If you want to produce simultaneously with the publication you must hurry up very smartly indeed.

I scrawl this in great haste in a hotel after a days driving.

faithfully

G. Bernard Shaw

David **Lloyd George** (1863–1945) succeeded Herbert **Asquith** as prime minister in 1916. Both were satirized in the second play in the cycle, *The Gospel of the Brothers Barnabas*. A.B. **Walkley** (1855–1926), Gilbert **Cannan** (1884–1955), and E.A. **Baughan** (1865–1938) were London drama critics satirized in *Fanny's First Play* (1911).

108 / To Ellen O'Malley   [10 Adelphi Terrace WC2
                                                    October 1921]

[6 APCs, sig. on last card: HRC]
Ellen O'Malley was performing in J.B. Fagan's revival of John Bull's Other Island *at the Royal Court Theatre: 'I am that most ridiculous of spectacles,' Shaw wrote*

to her after the first performance, 'an old author in love with his leading lady' (9 September 1921: TLS, HRC). Concurrently, she was rehearsing with Shaw for the opening of Heartbreak House *at the same theatre on 18 October. J.B. Fagan (1873–1933), Irish playwright and manager, was lessee of the Royal Court; he and Shaw co-directed the production. As was Shaw's fashion when working under pressure he submitted rehearsal notes to O'Malley on sets of postcards. Though in most instances the cards were posted individually, one or another occasionally going astray, on the present occasion the notes, which covered the entire obverse of each of six picture postcards, were posted collectively, in a single envelope.*

I

'You have not shewn me my room yet, Hesione.'

As this is an excuse for getting away from the odious Mangan, Ellie should move on it to R.C. where Hesione can come down to her.

II

When Ellie enters with Hector on the cue 'And you, Hesione, are just as bad,' she should come down R at once. She has met Lady U and need not bother about her.

III

'You little devil, youve done me.'

Today you walked straight up without giving the movement any sense: it was clearly a piece of stage business.

Try (a) a shrug of disdain.

(b) a nod at him meaning 'I *have.*'

The first was what you did before; but the second might be worth trying.

IV

When hypnotising him, get a little closer to him, so that your finger tips may meet easily on his forehead. They looked today as if you could hardly reach him. But this may have been an illusion.

V

You leaned against the doorpost when you entered and said 'Guinness said you wanted me, you and papa.'

This was all right; but you must get away with an interrogative movement when Hesione says 'so long that it almost came to– ???? Well,
never mind.'

VI
'what *I* think or dont think'

VII
'I promise you I wont do anything I dont want to do' should be very
firm. Leave the pathos to Mazzini.

VIII
'*You* have never known what it is to want money'

IX
The speech 'I suppose you think youre being sympathetic' and so on is
becoming pathetic. This is fatal: it must be brutal and fierce. I want you
to shew that you have this stop on your organ as well as the gentle ones.
Besides, that is where Ellie comes out as a stronger woman than
Hesione.

Pull in *completely* for 'I'm not angry: I'm not unfriendly': if you dont
you will have to overforce the 'but for God's sake &c.'

X
'He will be your owner, remember.'

You must listen to this. The secret is to make quite sure of your business in the next speech. You are still slightly bewildered about it; and
this puts Hesione clean out of your head.

XI
You lost the thoughtfulness in the beginning of the scene with the Captain (foot of p 74). Do not hurry it, even if you break Fagan's heart.
The effect vanishes unless you begin as if you had all eternity before
you. Haste will only remind the audience that the last train is starting.

XII
'Then why did YOU sell yourself to the devil in Zanzibar?' He has just

said 'All I can tell you is that if you sell yourself &c.' Your reply means 'Oh indeed! What price *you* and the devil in Zanzibar?'

XIII

The stage direction 'dreamily' on page 78, before 'I should have thought nothing else mattered' is misplaced. When you get him down on the sofa, speak quite prosaically and fairly brightly. The 'overflow' speech of the Captain drags the scene now: it must be vigorous. And 'But what can I do' must be impatient and keep the scene moving. The same with 'What could they do ashore but marry for money?' Let the Captain get back to the dreamy vein with his speech about drink and old age; and bathe yourself in it on 'You shall not drink. Dream &c.'

I think that will get the scene right.

XIV

The business with the book ('tales of adventure') was exquisitely right: you did it to perfection; but F. was thinking of the few stalls from which it was invisible; and he did not see how the effect depended on Ellie's aloofness.

Those are all my notes. Goodnight and bless you.

G.B.S.

109 / To Unidentified Correspondent   10 Adelphi Terrace WC2
                                            4th October 1921

[TLS: present source unknown; (p) RADA]
Theatre entrances to unassigned cheap seats (gallery and pit) opened earlier than doors to more expensive parts of the house in which seating was reserved.

Dear Sir

It is not clear that the institution of the early door is any more unjust than the reservation of all the more comfortable and favorably situated parts of the house for people who are willing to pay from half a crown to twelve shillings or a guinea for them. When I go to the theatre myself

I often have to put up with a back seat because all the better ones are booked. In this way the man who goes to the stalls suffers just as you do, though, unlike you, he pays as much for his back seat as the people who book do for their front ones. It is waste of time to agitate against a distinction that applies to every part of the house, and is inherent in the construction of our theatres and in the unequal distribution of income which is your real grievance.

Comfortable galleries with every seat commanding a full view of the stage are badly needed; and now that so many people who used to go to the stalls and boxes have to go to the gallery something might be done by writing letters to the press complaining of the existing accommodation.

faithfully
G. Bernard Shaw

110 / To W.S. Kennedy   10 Adelphi Terrace WC2
29th March 1922

[TLS: HRC]

William S. Kennedy (1878–1957) was treasurer of the Stage Society, for whose producing committee Shaw had been reading a play, Don Juan de Marana, *submitted by the playwright and novelist Arnold Bennett (1867–1931). Despite Shaw's recommendation it was rejected by the committee.*

My Dear Mr Kennedy

Don Juan is a queer affair, like most of the experiments of modern realists in Romanticism. I suggest that if we can get on our legs again sufficiently, we should do a Don Juan season, producing in succession Bataille's Homme de la Rose, Rostand's Dernier Nuit de Don Juan, and this play of Bennett's, possibly in the reverse order. That would be a stunt good enough to make us once more the most discussed Society in London.

B's play will require very splendid dressing; but in these days of fancy balls there are fairly gorgeous rags on hire. It will also need (and probably not get) very attractive casting. The Don would have to be interesting enough to hold the audience through a long series of duets. The other parts would not give as much trouble. It is rather a pity that the only man in the play who is really interesting gets disgraced and killed straight off; and the same holds good of the only woman from whom there is any hope of Don Juan getting what he deserves.

.The weakest part of the affair is the business of the ghosts at the end. The statue in the legend of Don Juan Tenorio (this Marana fellow is not the same) is so extraordinarily effective as a stroke of imagination that anything else must necessarily fall flat after it. This time Don Juan ought to defy God as of old; and God should not take the slightest notice of him. However, there it is.

We certainly ought to do the play: Bennett has that much call on the theatre; and I don't think our reputation would suffer: on the contrary, as the regular theatre has refused it, it is peculiarly our business 'to supply the want.' But only such a stunt as I have suggested above could carry it off really well.

The Pirandello was in my opinion almost our greatest score so far. Comisarjevsky certainly makes an enormous difference to us. Are there any more Pirandellos? And has Granville-Barker anything good in the Spanish line that he could give us?

I suppose I must fork out another twenty guineas, though my financial condition is deplorable. As to my wife, you must make an independent appeal to her. She has not attended the performances for a long time past, and rather resents my leaving her alone in the country on the Mondays.

ever

G. Bernard Shaw

One of the Stage Society's finest productions was the Luigi **Pirandello** (1867–1936) play *Six Characters in Search of an Author* (trans. Mrs W.A. Greene) the previous month. Theodore **Komisarjevsky** (1882–1954), Russian director and designer, who sought refuge in London during the revolution, also staged Tchekov's *Uncle Vanya* for the Society.

111 / To Lee Shubert   10 Adelphi Terrace WC2

27th October 1922

[TLS: Shubert Archive]

To assist the impoverished Siegfried Trebitsch, Shaw freely translated his domestic tragedy Frau Gittas Sühne *in 1920–1, giving its third act a comic twist. The*

Shuberts acquired American rights for a production with the Rumanian star Bertha Kalich (1874–1939), celebrated for her performances both in Yiddish and English. Jitta's Atonement, *following a break-in week in Washington, DC, opened in New York on 17 January 1923, lasting for only 37 performances.*

Dear Mr Shubert

It was a great relief to me to get your cabled message about Jitta, as it is much better both for Madame Kalich and for me that the play should be in your hands. The contract will have to go to Vienna to be signed by Herr Trebitsch before it goes to America. . . .

You know my contracts of old; but there are one or two novelties. I want an advance of $250 for Herr Trebitsch. He is accustomed to receive advances on his plays; and his situation, like that of all the other inhabitants of Vienna, is such that he cannot wait as easily as I can. I have tried to avoid troubling you with this advance payment by offering to make it myself; but Trebitsch is a Jew, very scrupulous on the point of honor when money is concerned; and he would not take it from me.

I do not want an advance for myself; but I want you to guarantee me $1250, not exactly win, lose or draw, but subject to the play doing a certain minimum of business. This is half my usual guarantee: the other half is in the form of the $250 to Trebitsch, which *is* win, lose or draw. My reason for asking this guarantee is that my plays, being highbrowed, cannot be depended on to play to capacity; and nowadays it may be good business for a manager to take them off when they are doing reasonably well to make room for something that will do better. In that case I want to have something for my labor; and considering what that labor is, I dont think $2500 exorbitant.

I am trying to get something about Trebitsch into the New York papers to work up the interest. After Methuselah any ordinary play by me would be an anti-climax; and in any case I am now so old that I have no longer the attraction of novelty. The novelty this time will be, 1, the new author, 2, my first appearance as a translator, 3, curiosity as to how I will treat a romantic love story that is against all my traditions, 4, how much of the play is the tragically romantic Trebitsch and how much the anti-romantic Shaw. See that your publicity people get hold of this properly; for their first impulse will be to suppress Trebitsch and try to pass the play off as a new play by me; and this would be the greatest possible mistake from the publicity point of view, to say nothing of the fact that I could not, without disloyalty to Trebitsch, leave such a report uncontradicted.

In casting the play you must be firm on one point. The parts of Lenkheim and Mrs Haldenstedt (Alfred and Agnes) are very important, and must be taken by good and popular comedians. I dont mean tomfool comedians, as they both have heavy work to do; but they must have good turn of comedy in them. In the original these parts have not a touch of comedy. The widow wallows in her bereavement all through; and the husband is the unforgiving outraged husband from first to last. The play begins with a tragedy and gets gloomier and gloomier from act to act. They like that sort of thing in Vienna; but New York and London will stand it only in the form of Italian opera. I have therefore contrived that the audience shall have a little amusement, and that the end shall not be too unhappy. And I have called the piece a tragi-comedy instead of a tragedy.

But Madame Kalich is a tragedienne, and would rather have the play as it stands in the German. She does not see anything amusing in these two characters; and she does not like my ending because it lets down Jitta's heroics. It is just possible that she might, by a *tour de force* of acting, pull the play through as an unrelieved tragedy. But in that case she ought to discard my version and get an exact translation. I should not oppose her doing so for a moment if Trebitsch consented. What I am afraid of her doing – and I have told her so frankly – is taking the fun out of my version by wrong casting and by cutting, and falling between the two stools in consequence. So get me for Lenkheim a man who can carry half the play on his shoulders, as ugly and prosaic as you like, but one who can amuse the audience and make them see that Jitta's contempt for him is romantic nonsense, and that, though no hero, he is quite a decent sort of chap.

The young woman must have plenty of fire, and be able to stand up to Madame Kalich.

I may say that I like Madame Kalich, and do not doubt her artistic good faith in the least. But an actress is never a good judge of anything in the play except her own part – and not always of that – to say nothing of the fact that people have to act in my plays for years before they come to understand my peculiar stage game.

I am sorry to trouble you with so long a letter; but it will be hit or miss with this play; and I do not want to leave anything to chance that can be foreseen.

All this, of course, is between ourselves.

It may amuse you to learn – if you dont know it already – that the Theatre Guild made $10,000 out of Methuselah, in the following way. They figured to lose $30,000; and they lost only $20,000: a clear gain of $10,000. I hope you wont have to keep the Jitta accounts on that system.

> faithfully
> G. Bernard Shaw

Shaw feels **great relief** that the play is not in Madame Kalich's hands. The **advance of $250** for Trebitsch is presumably an error for $1250 (£250), as indicated by Shaw's allusion to $2500 for the two.

112 / To Dorothy Massingham

Ayot St Lawrence. Welwyn. Herts.
27th May 1923

[APCS: HRC]

Dorothy Massingham (1889–1933), daughter of Shaw's longtime journalist colleague H.W. Massingham (1860–1924), played Barbara in two productions of Major Barbara *staged by Norman MacDermott (1889–1977) at his Everyman Theatre, Hampstead, in April 1921 and in May 1923. Her dubious claim to fame is that she was author of the play* The Lake (1933), *produced by the Theatre Guild, in which Katharine Hepburn (b 1907) suffered the most calamitous defeat of her theatrical career.*

I hoped to see you on Friday for a word about Barbara; but you gave me the slip.

Make Barbara much more trim and athletic than you did last time. There must be no snivel about her: she is her mother's daughter, bouncing and domineering quite unconsciously, amiably and sunnily. You were handicapped last time by relapsing into a long dress which might possibly have been worn by a very old maiden aunt of Barbara's in a cathedral town, but never by B. herself. It took frightfully from her energy, and aged her. Keep her young and bumptious and impetuous in general effect: the rest is all right. Mendelianly speaking, the lady is a dominant, not a recessive. Her voice is a bright voice; so let not the notes of the Maiden's Prayer be heard. Good luck!

G.B.S.

Gregor **Mendel** (1822–84) was an Austrian botanist and pioneer geneticist.

113 / To Cyril Phillips   Parknasilla. Kenmare. Co. Kerry

28th August 1923

[ALS: HRC]

Cyril Phillips (1894–?) was general manager for the Birmingham Repertory Company, which was rehearsing Back to Methuselah, *scheduled for 9 October. It was presented in five separate parts (four evenings and a matinee), as Shaw had desired, with four cycles performed. The management, concerned about the brevity of Part I,* In the Beginning, *contemplated inviting G.K. Chesterton to participate in a first-night pre- or post-curtain colloquium. Shaw declined to participate, insisting that 'the actors, whose show it properly is, will have a grievance' (ALS to Phillips, 17 August 1923: HRC). Under present consideration was a chamber-music concert.*

Dear Mr Phillips

I think the simplest plan is to announce that In the Beginning will begin at such and such an hour and conclude at such & such an hour. Then there can be no disappointment: the people will buy their tickets with their eyes open.

   Mozart quartets are all right for people who like chamber music; but they are not dramatic, and are out of place and ineffective in a theatre. You might as well sell tickets for a whist drive and offer the purchasers admission to a geological museum as an equivalent. If you decide to have music, it must not be between the two scenes of In The Beginning, as the interval should not be longer than ten minutes, and no fresh hare should be started in the course of it. If there is to be a concert it must come before or after; and the hour should be stated so that people need not come until the play begins if they dont care for music, or need not wait for it if it comes after the play.

If you have chamber music, it means that the players must be seated on the stage; and I should add three wind instruments to the quartet and play Beethoven's septet (a very pretty early work) after an opening with one of Bach's Brandenburg concertos. That would be a real attraction to musical people; but you would have to get your municipal orchestra man (I forget his name) to take over that part of the business. The program would then be a really good mouthful; but, I repeat, I do not think the public would complain of the play by itself if they were fully informed of its duration before they bought their tickets.

The dates seem to be all right inasmuch as all the matinée plays have an alternative evening. They involve a week end in Birmingham for every set except the first; but I suppose most of the visitors from afar will come to the first set.

The invitation idea was not that the public should be offered a sample performance before they took their tickets, but that purchasers of sets should have In The Beginning thrown in free. But there would be nothing in it really, as the prices for the other four performances would be 20% up, though it would give the purchasers of sets an advantage to that extent over purchasers of single tickets. Therefore there would be no interference with the opening of the box office beforehand as usual.

In haste to catch the precarious post here

G. Bernard Shaw

114 / To Harriet Cohen

Ayot St Lawrence. Welwyn. Herts.
22nd March 1924

[APCS: Harriet Cohen, *A Bundle of Time*, 1969]

Harriet Cohen (1895–1967) was a celebrated pianist, extolled for her Bach performances, and champion of modern British piano compositions. Shaw, who followed her career closely, became a firm friend. Saint Joan was in rehearsal for an opening on the 26th. Visitors invariably were barred from Shaw's rehearsals, which he looked upon as inviolable mystic rites, to be divulged to no one outside the performing company.

Rehearsal impossible, for reasons too many to explain – chiefly that there wont be anything that could be called a rehearsal, only·a scrimmage. I always try to prevent my people from acting all out – or indeed at all if they can help it – at the final rehearsal, because the chances are heavily against their doing so well next day if they do their best.

Say when you would like to come and I will send you tickets.

GBS

115 / To W. Nugent Monck
The Malvern Hotel. Gt Malvern
Until Monday morning
23rd April 1924

[APCS: Monck Estate]

W. Nugent Monck (1877–1958) was the founder (1911) and director of the Norwich Players, who performed in the Maddermarket Theatre, which Monck had converted into an Elizabethan-style playhouse. Many of Shaw's plays were staged there, including, in this instance, Getting Married, *written in one extended act that Shaw would have preferred be performed unbroken by intervals.*

Of course there is no artistic reason for an interval: quite the contrary.

But the sanitary limit for divers, railway passengers, and (presumably) playgoers, is two hours; and even the smartest delivery of the text will hardly get through G.M. in that time.

G. Bernard Shaw

The refreshment contractor also puts in his plea.

116 / To Edith Evans
Gleneagles Hotel
Gleneagles, Scotland
8th September 1924

[ALS: HRC]

In August 1924 Mrs Warren's Profession *was at last approved for performance, 'reluctantly,' by the Lord Chamberlain. Contemplating the mounting of a West End production, Shaw sought Edith Evans (1888–1976) for Kitty Warren. Evans, who was the Hesione in* Heartbreak House *(1921) and the Serpent and Oracle in* Back to Methuselah *(1924), was a rising star, whose personal successes as Mrs Millamant in Congreve's* The Way of the World *at the Lyric,*

Hammersmith, in February 1924, and as Daisy in the Elmer Rice (1892–1967)
expressionistic comedy The Adding Machine *for the Stage Society in March were*
bringing her an ever-increasing number of managerial offers. She demurred to
Shaw's suggestion that she take on the role of an aged frump, and he eventually
abandoned the notion of a major production, authorizing the Dublin-born
Charles Macdona (1860–1946) to add the play to the repertory of his Shaw
touring company. The first public performance in England occurred at the
Prince of Wales Theatre, Birmingham, 29 July 1925. Macdona, in association
with Arthur Bourchier, manager of the Strand Theatre, subsequently brought the
production to London in 1926 with an all-new utilitarian cast, headed by Edyth
Goodall (1882–1929) as Mrs Warren and Bourchier as Sir George Crofts.

My dear Edith

Your age has nothing to do with it. If you were a man you would play
Lear without waiting to be eighty: in fact if you were Lear's age you
couldnt play him. The same thing is true of Mrs Warren: a woman such
as Mrs Warren is supposed to be in the play couldnt play her. Poor
Fanny Brough, a wasted wrecked genius who had drunk herself all to
shreds, never could play her all through at the same performance. The
first time she pulled off the second act and made nothing of the finish.
The second time she was afraid of forgetting her lines in the second act
and made nothing of it; but pulled off the fourth act in a transport
(stimulated, I suppose) in which at one point she seized a chair and
whirled it round her head. There was no third time. Only a woman at
her physical best, as you are, could have the staying power – the second
wind – to come back after the first big scene and do another.

Consequently I shall have to give the part to a young woman anyhow;
and I think the young woman should be you, and not Edyth Goodall or
another. After Millamant it could not compromise you by classing you
as a matron. Of course you cannot make your neck join on at the back
as Mrs Warren's did; but the audience will not think of that.

Besides, Mrs Warren, who may be supposed to have become a
mother by her first escapade or thereabouts (it is a sterilizing profession), *cannot* be much over forty, and might be less. I have described
her as an old blackguard of a woman; but that was by Victorian reckon-
ing, which put women on the shelf in caps as matrons and called them

old the moment they were married and mothers. Victoria lived and reigned 7 years after Mrs Warren was created. You may make Mrs W. a battered old devil in point of experience; but she should be physically very far from being decrepit.

You are not too old to play Vivie; but you are too 'heavy' in the theatrical sense. You could play the part on your head; and nobody would find you too old for it, BUT – you would play Mrs W. off the stage and upset the balance of the play.

As likely as not, the Vivie will be older than you are. But she will not carry your guns.

I think you have a bit too much devil in you for Lady Cicely, who is a sentimental comedian; and you would be a terrible Ann. Tanner would be a trodden worm; but it is extremely difficult to guess what would happen. I should have said that you were too heavy for the girl in The Adding Machine; but it was perfect. When you have the true dramatic imagination, the most incredible transformations take place. You can act anything you really want to: the difficulty is to distinguish the fancies and interests that lure you into the wrong parts from the genuine response to it which overcomes every apparent unsuitability.

Think again about Mrs Warren. It is not the mere dread of the drudgery of looking for someone else that makes me hesitate to take No for an answer: it seems to me that you are capable of as great a success in it as the wretched old play will hold; and it will last all your life as one of your repertory parts.

ever
GBS

117 / To John Martin-Harvey   Ayot St Lawrence. Welwyn. Herts.
20th March 1925

[APCS: Harvard]
Sir John Martin-Harvey (knighted in 1921) licensed The Shewing-up of Blanco Posnet *for his next provincial tour. In October 1926 his company performed the play in London, in a variety bill at the Coliseum.*

The licence is quite sufficient as far as I am concerned. I can send a contract if you like – an appalling document tying both of us up into double knots to prevent us doing things that we neither of us have the smallest intention of or reason for doing, and to compel us to do what we are only too willing to do without any compulsion.

Why not leave yourself free? The stamp would cost you sixpence.

G.B.S.

118 / To John Martin-Harvey   Ayot St Lawrence. Welwyn. Herts.

15th April 1925

[APCS: Cornell]

Let the imagination play. There never was no such place nor no such people. On a basis of knee boots, breeches, Garibaldi shirts, cowboy hats, and a coat or two for the sheriff, Daniels, and Strapper as pillars of society, you can paint the picture as you please. Blanco should be an extraordinarily disreputable Buffalo Bill. The women wear print gowns (dry goods) and aprons, except Feemy, a rouged harlot in the cast-off clothes of Adelina Patti (circa 1860–70), and the Woman, in a white face and black shawl. Waggoner Jo is a stage joskin [*country bumpkin*], except that he does not sing that it's his delight on a shiny night in the season of the year. There are no pictures of any use. Invent it all, and have plenty of color in the shirts.

G.B.S.

Adelina **Patti** (1843–1919), one of the greatest of all coloraturas, reigned at Covent Garden 1861–84, her career lasting for 56 years. The refrain Waggoner Jo **does not sing** ('Oh, 'tis my delight of a shiny night, in the season of the year') is from an English folk song, 'The Lincolnshire Poacher.'

119 / To John Martin-Harvey   Ayot St Lawrence. Welwyn. Herts.

15th July 1925

[TLS: Harvard]

Dear Martin Harvey

In great haste – just off to Scotland – I have scribbled something for your press agent to use *as his own work* – not as mine.

In casting Blanco, remember that Elder Daniels goes to your first low comedian. He must intone all the time like a harmonium, rising to floods of organ melody in his climaxes of exhortation. He is the clown of the piece, and unless he is very funny as well as very convincing, the scene where you are alone with him will not go well.

The sheriff is dry and sardonic, never melodramatic but always masterful.

The others are pretty obvious. Dont let Feemy try to *act* her breakdown. She must say 'Oh God, he felt the little child's fingers on his neck' very quietly and distinctly, like a child trying not to cry. The rest she may pay out as she pleases; but without that little pathetic pause for contrast the effect will not come.

I shall miss the post if I go on.

ever

G.B.S.

120 / To Lord Cromer   10 Adelphi Terrace WC2
                                             27th February 1926

[ALS: BL, LCP(C) *Mrs Warren* 1924/5632]

An overzealous publicist for the recently licensed first West End production of Mrs Warren's Profession, opening at the Strand Theatre on 3 March, encouraged the director Arthur Bourchier to give an interview to the Daily Telegraph, published under the caption 'A Challenge to the Censor' on 27 February, intimating to its readers that first nighters would be hearing dialogue added in rehearsal. 'It is,' Bourchier is reported to have said, 'something in the nature of a challenge deliberately to insert words which have not hitherto been given the censor's approval.' Shaw sought to mitigate the blunder by writing instantly to the Lord Chamberlain – (since 1922) Rowland T. Baring (1877–1953), 2nd Earl of Cromer.

My dear Lord Chamberlain

I have just had my breakfast considerably upset by an insane statement in the papers about the forthcoming performance of Mrs Warren's Profession which you have no doubt seen. It is pure folly, quite unauthorized by me.

I will see that Mr Charles Macdona, the manager with whom I am concerned, sends in every word that will be spoken on the stage with my authority over and above what stands in the printed text as licensed, with the reader's fee. There is nothing but *remplissage* [*padding*] to fill up little gaps in the stage business, or to make preliminary murmurs of conversation off stage; but now that the question has been raised it seems clearly necessary that both your officials and myself should be in a position to state absolutely that nothing will be said on the stage on Wednesday next with our consent* that has not been licensed.

I wish your powers extended to the summary execution of theatre press agents. You could not license the epithets they deserve.

faithfully

G. Bernard Shaw

*PS I have no power to prevent an actor from gagging [*ad libbing*] if he is willing to take the risk of quarreling with me; but if he does so he defies the author, which may end in his being blacklisted. Authors are much more sensitive to liberties taken with their text than any public department can possibly be.

121 / To Lord Cromer   10 Adelphi Terrace WC

1st March 1926

[ALS: BL, LCP(C) *Mrs Warren* 1924/5632]

Lord Cromer, on 27 February, thanked Shaw for his 'most kind and considerate letter.' He indicated he would be present on opening night, and 'I naturally have every confidence in your insisting upon Mr. Macdona abiding by the text.' On 1 March he informed Shaw that he had seen 'the few additions' to the text 'inserted as remplissage . . . *which I take it were made with your authority,' and which had now been submitted for inclusion under the licence. He had only one reservation: 'I would prefer to see your original stage directions preserved where Crofts (black with rage) says "The old —" and "swallows the epithet," rather than his saying "The old bitch," as is now suggested' (BL, LCP(C) Mrs Warren 1924/5632).*

My dear Lord Chamberlain

Yes, most certainly. I did not alter that passage; but I suppose the prompter, hearing Mr Bourchier use the word (and many others) in his struggles to remember his part, wrote it into his copy. I will send him your letter, so that there may be no mistake.

Many thanks.

faithfully
G. Bernard Shaw

122 / To G. Herbert Thring   10 Adelphi Terrace WC
                                                    26th October 1926

[TLS: BL 56628, f 132]

G. Herbert Thring (1859–1941) was Secretary of the Society of Authors 1892–1930. During Norman MacDermott's incumbency at the Everyman Theatre, Hampstead, four seasons of Shaw repertory were presented, 1921–4, totalling 23 productions of 20 plays. Following Shaw's decision to make the successors of Mac-Dermott responsible for the royalty debts he incurred, only Overruled *(1927) and* Captain Brassbound's Conversion *(1929) were performed at the Everyman.*

My dear Thring

. . . I think the Everyman theatre must go on paying the extra percentage until its debt to me is cleared. I admit that it seems a bit hard on the present exploiters of that institution that they should have to pay 2½% more than anyone else. But then they are benefiting by a reputation which the theatre acquired by a revival of my plays at a moment when such a revival was very valuable, and when in letting it take place there I was making a considerable sacrifice. My fees were not paid; but the theatre became mildly famous and acquired its clientèle at my expense. That being so I hold that the theatre must pay its arrears to me, no matter who may be for the moment managing it. To treat it as a personal debt of the manager pro-tem would mean wiping it off as irrecoverable. If I asked Macdermott for it he would probably reply that he had put his livelihood into building up the Everyman, and had to give it up and leave it to others to reap the harvest he sowed, and that I might as well ask him for a million.

So, as the percentage as it stands is not highly excessive, I think we may without too much strain on our consciences go on making the theatre pay no matter who is renting it. However, as they seem to have given the performances of Widowers' Houses and Arms and the Man in July, August and September on the assumption that the fees would be at my normal rates, you may let it go at that; but you must warn them that for all future performances until the Everyman debt (which you may say is not specifically a Macdermott debt) is paid off, the fees will be 2½ per cent above the normal. This leaves them no grievance. If they produce any more of my plays they will do it with their eyes open. . . .

faithfully

G. Bernard Shaw

123 / To Theresa Helburn

4 Whitehall Court SW1

9th February 1928

[TLS: Yale]

The Theatre Guild in 1927 revived The Doctor's Dilemma *(which Granville Barker had staged in New York in 1915), with Lynn Fontanne (1887–1983) as Jennifer, Alfred Lunt (1892–1977) as Dubedat, and British actor Baliol Holloway (1883–1967) as Dr Ridgeon. A set of photos of the production by London-born photographer Florence Vandamm (1883?–1966) were sent to Shaw. The Act III stage direction calls for 'A lay figure, in a cardinal's robe and hat, with an hour-glass in one hand and a scythe slung on its back, [which] smiles with inane malice at Louis.' The Guild's director Dudley Digges (1879–1947) inserted into Act IV a death figure in the form of a life-size marionette, clad in black, seated on a regal chair on a dais, hour-glass in its lap, upstage right of the dying Dubedat. A photograph of the apparition is reproduced in Lawrence Langner's* G.B.S. and the Lunatic *(1963).*

Dear Miss Helburn

I have been for some time forgetting to make a criticism of The Doctor's Dilemma production. One of my directions is that there should be a lay figure on the stage. The effect aimed at is the contrast between this ludicrous and visibly unreal simulacrum of a human creature and the living figures on the stage: a contrast which becomes poignant and acquires a ghastly irony in the death scene, where Dubedat himself becomes a lay figure.

Now your producer has taken extraordinary pains to defeat this impression, and introduce a formidable and disastrous rival to the living actors by procuring, not a typical lay figure, but a marionette with all a marionette's intensity and persistence of expression; so that when I saw the photographs I immediately said 'Who on earth is that?', not only mistaking the simulacrum for a reality, but for a leading personality. It is as if I had prescribed a turnip ghost and you had given me the ghost in Hamlet instead.

A good marionette (and yours is a very good one) can play any real actor off the stage.

Sell him by auction with this letter attached for the benefit of the Guild; and make a note for reference in future productions.

faithfully

G. Bernard Shaw

124 / To Maurice Colbourne

4 Whitehall Court, SW1
14th February 1928

[TL: Theatre Museum]

Maurice Colbourne (1894–1970), who had played juvenile lead for Bridges-Adams in the Stratford-on-Avon Festival Company and created the role of Dunois in the Theatre Guild's première of Saint Joan *in New York, 1923, went into partnership in 1928 with fellow actor Barry Jones (1893–1981) to tour Canada with a primarily Shavian repertoire. After consultation with the Theatre Guild, Shaw licensed Colbourne to perform any of his already published plays in the Dominion of Canada provided that 'no performance shall be given . . . without the consent first obtained of the Theatre Guild'; and that the tour begin no later than 1 September 1928 'with a weekly repertory including at least two of my plays.' (The licence, dated 10 March 1928, is in the Theatre Museum.) Shaw's signature on the letter has been cut away.*

Dear Mr Colbourne

I am not at all illdisposed towards your scheme. I believe that a useful life and earnings not more desperately precarious than an actor's earnings always are anyhow are within the grasp of anyone enterprising and ambitious enough to exploit the places, some of them enormously populous, which do not exist for the conventional manager on circuit.

Without going to Canada I suspect that anyone with gumption enough to take an A.B.C. railway guide, and making a list of the places with more than 20,000 inhabitants where no theatre exists or ever has existed, could, by taking a tent on his back, do much better than on the old road.

You have also the advantage of having entertained me at Stratford in many parts.

However, I must confer with the Theatre Guild before I finally cut them out of Canada. When I hear from them I will write again.

I presume that what you want is a general licence to play as you go, choosing from a bunch of stable plays.

[*unsigned*]

125 / To Norman Veitch   Hotel Beau-Site
                                                              Cap d'Antibes
                                                              24th July 1928

[ALS: present source unknown]
Norman Veitch (d. 1938) was managing director of the People's Theatre, New-castle-on-Tyne. Shaw's early experiments with the British Broadcasting Corpora-tion had included his solo reading of O'Flaherty V.C. *on 20 November 1924, a broadcast of* Passion, Poison, and Petrifaction *on 13 January 1926, and a per-formance of* The Man of Destiny *by the Macdona Players, with Esmé Percy as Napoleon and Margaret Macdona as the Strange Lady, on the London Regional Service, 28 March 1928. Despite Shaw's statement that he was barring further broadcasts,* Saint Joan *was performed by the BBC in its entirety on two consecu-tive evenings in April 1929.*

Dear Norman Veitch

The broadcasting of plays raises the question of dialect. A broadcast of Methuselah in the Newcastle tongue would raise Somerset in arms and scandalize Oxford.

There is another difficulty. After considerable study I have told the B.B.C. & the gramophone people that I bar broadcasts and records by actors. The actor depends on visible as well as audible effects, and can-not get away from them. For wireless and gramophone I must have companies trained to work with the voice alone, and using inflexions that would not get across in the theatre.

I tried a broadcast of The Man of Destiny lately by the Macdona Players. It quite convinced me that the broadcasting of theatrical performance (except of an opera) is a mistake. It was very disagreeable to listen to; and the people who did not know the play could make neither head nor tail of it.

So I am afraid you must stick to the hard boards. . . .

faithfully

G. Bernard Shaw

126 / To Theresa Helburn   4 Whitehall Court SW1
                                            10th November 1928

[TLS: Yale]

A revival of Major Barbara *was offered to Theatre Guild subscribers in November 1928, with Winifred Lenihan (1898–1964), the Guild's original Saint Joan, as Barbara.*

My dear Terry

I do not suppose there is much danger of Winifred Lenihan making Barbara a low spirited person with large eyes, looking like a picture on the cover of The Maiden's Prayer, though that is the traditional stage view of a religious part.

Bear in mind that Lady Britomart has a most important part, and requires a first rate robust comedian and grande dame to play it; for the clue to a great deal of Barbara is that she is her mother's daughter, and that she bullies and bustles the Salvation Army about just as Lady Britomart bullies and bustles her family at home. Barbara is full of life and vigor, and unconsciously very imperious.

Cusins is easy for any clever actor who has ever seen the original (Professor Gilbert Murray). The next best model is perhaps Harold Lloyd.

Do not let Mr Waram make the mistake of making up like a Thug as Bill Walker. In appearance he is just an ordinary young workman excited by drink and a sense of injury, not in the least like a murderer in a nightmare or a melodrama. He should be clean and goodlooking enough to make the scene in which Barbara breaks down his brutality – which is a sort of very moving love scene – look natural, which it will not do if Bill is disgusting physically and sanitarily.

The most effective dress for Lady Britomart is a Queen Mary or Queen Alexandra dress, long and purposely a generation out of date.

I think these are the only points which my experience suggests as those of which there is most danger of going wrong.

There will probably be one more play if I live another year; but if you tell anyone this until I give you leave I will never tell you anything again.

faithfully

G. Bernard Shaw

Harold Lloyd (1894–1971) was a popular silent-screen comic, bespectacled, who specialized in shy, ingenuous, earnest young men. Percy Waram (1881–1961) was a character actor who graced many a Broadway production; at 48 he was too old for Bill Walker. The new play was *The Apple Cart*, begun five days earlier.

127 / To Thomas Hayes [4 Whitehall Court SW1
  c. 15 December 1928]

[Shorthand: Colgate]

The Society of Authors, hearing that St Bartholomew's Hospital was preparing to offer what appeared to be an unauthorized production of Arms and the Man for four performances in January 1929, wrote to the governors of the hospital for confirmation and explanation. Thomas Hayes, clerk to the governors, responded on 13 December, informing the secretary of the Society of Authors that admission to the performances would be by invitation only, limited to persons connected with the hospital, approximately five hundred of whom would be attending each of the four private performances. 'No money,' he wrote, 'is taken either by the sale of tickets or by voluntary collection. There is no subscription for Membership of the Medical Students Dramatic Society, by whom the performance is given, and all the expenses of production etc., are borne out of the Hospital funds. It has been the practice to give a Dramatic Entertainment of this kind at Christmas for some years and on no occasion previously has it been contended that this constituted a public performance nor has any fee been asked. Had it been thought that a fee would have been demanded in the case of "Arms and the Man" an alternative play would have been selected.' The gover-

nors, he concluded, hoped that Shaw would 'be disposed to waive his fee or . . .
to sanction the production of the play under these circumstances at a nominal
fee.'

Dear Sir

The secretary of the Society of Authors has sent me your letter dated
the 13th. From this it appears that the Governors of the hospital have
invited 2000 persons to be entertained by performances of my play
Arms and the Man. I do not know whether the Governors intend to
offer their guests any refreshments, and, if so, whether they are asking
the caterers to supply them gratuitously[;] but if so, they are treating
me worse than the caterers because the 2000 persons, being fed, will be
as hungry as ever next day, whereas their appetite for the play may be
so satisfied that the next manager who offers them a performance of it
on the usual terms will offer it in vain.

 My difficulty is that if I were to waive my fees I should be guilty of
'infamous professional conduct,' as it is a strict rule of the Society of
Authors that, whatever charities [the authors] may wish to support personally, they must do so in [the] usual way by paid subscriptions, and
not by allowing their plays to be performed without fees. Not only is
this necessary for the protection of the poorer authors against a
thoughtless generosity on the part of their more popular colleagues,
but even the most charitable author may reasonably claim the right to
select the charities to which he contributes.

 All I can say is this. If you claim a right to perform my plays without
my authority, then I must contest your claim legally. The incorporated
playwrights could not possibly admit a claim which might upset contracts involving large sums in which novelty or nonperformance for a
specified period was of the essence of the contract. But if, admitting liability, the Governors find after giving the performances that [they]
have no funds available for the payment, well 'Where there is nothing,
the King loses his rights.' But next year, please turn your attention to
Shakespear or the Restoration playwrights. They are no longer obliged
to live by their work, as the live playwrights are.

faithfully
[*unsigned*]

The quotation in the final paragraph derives from a legal aphorism *Inops audacia tuta est* cited by Petronius (d. 66 AD). In John Heywood's *Proverbs* (1562) it appears as 'Whereas **nothing** is, the kynge must lose his right.'

128 / To Maurice Colbourne · Ayot St Lawrence, Welwyn, Herts.
2 April 1929

[APCS: Theatre Museum]

The first Colbourne-Jones Canadian tour included Candida, You Never Can Tell, The Dark Lady of the Sonnets, *and* Fanny's First Play. *There was, however, some resistance to Shaw by Canadian diehards who had not forgotten Shaw's unpopular wartime utterances. To counteract this ill-feeling, in an effort to bolster his box-office intake, Colbourne startlingly announced in a talk he delivered in Toronto to the Young Men's Board of Trade Club on 18 February that, despite the unsavoury impression created by Shaw during the war, 'it is an established fact that he played a very valuable role as secret service agent to the British Foreign Office during the War,' obtaining, in his guise as a German friend, 'much useful information to the Allied Forces' (*The Globe, Toronto, 19 February 1929*). When the socialist journal* Forward *(Glasgow) passed on to Shaw the newspaper cuttings sent by Canadian readers, he responded: '"Secret Service" is about the last word that could be applied to my activities during the War. When I am employed I am employed for the sake of my publicity; in obscurity I should be of no use whatever. What Mr. Colbourne was thinking of was one or two occasions on which the Government, which understood well enough how to appeal to patriotic sentiment, found itself rather at a loss when it had to appeal to anti-English sentiment in Ireland and anti-French sentiment in North Africa ... I was able to give some hints as to the proper method of approach in such cases. It was easy to do this without deception or bad faith of any kind; and I did what I could. I did not share the silly illusions and disgusting rancours of the screaming patriots of that time; and they naturally thought I was a Defeatist. Some echoes of their vituperation may still linger in Canada; and no doubt it is to silence them that Mr. Colbourne, who is touring my plays there, took this method of asserting that the responsible authorities knew better' (*Forward, 16 March 1929*). There were two additional tours of Canada, the 1929–30 and 1930–1 seasons, with productions of* John Bull's Other Island, Man and Superman, The Philanderer, The Doctor's Dilemma, Arms and the Man, *and* The Apple Cart. *In 1932 there was a shorter tour with* The Apple Cart *and* Too True to be

Good. *In a final Canadian tour in 1939 (under the auspices of the British Council), just after the outbreak of war, the Colbourne-Jones Company offered the North American première of Geneva.*

Your remittances have arrived safely, thank you: my secretary will send formal receipts when she returns from her Easter holiday.

I am off, myself, for a month or so in Italy to recuperate after the flu.

The tour has been very satisfactory *to me*; and I have no mortal objection to your repeating it if you have not got cold feet.

But *dont* tell the Canadians that I was a British spy masquerading as a pro-German during the war. You started a serious heath fire with that. I hope to see you when I return.

G.B.S.

The tour had been **satisfactory** to Shaw to the tune of £775 in royalties to this date.

129 / To Floryan Sobieniowski   Hotel Danieli. Venice
31st May 1929

[APCS: HRC]
Floryan Sobieniowski (1881–1964), Shaw's Polish translator, at work on the Interlude in The Apple Cart, *had followed his custom of submitting a series of probing questions and suggestions.*

Smoking? No. It would vulgarize the whole play. The actors will need the whole of their mouths, and, as you say, the whole of their time, for the text.

The *regisseur* [*director*] may furnish Orinthia's room as his taste may direct. But he must not crowd up the stage with useless and obstructive furniture. Orinthia must have the space behind the settee and beside it clear so that she can tear and rage and sweep about in her boasting tirades as much as she feels she wants to. There must be no drawing-room comedy tricks with chairs and cigarettes: the scene is on the grand scale, not the cup-and-saucer one.

I shall be here for a week to come at least.

G.B.S.

130 / To H.K. Ayliff   4 Whitehall Court SW1
                                                                17th September 1929

[ALS: Hofstra]

Henry Kiell Ayliff (1872–1949) was principal stage director of the Birmingham
Repertory Company, whose London opening of The Apple Cart *was scheduled*
for that evening, following its August première at the Malvern Festival, with
Cedric Hardwicke (1893–1964) as King Magnus. Barry Jackson (1879–1961),
wealthy theatre amateur, founded the Pilgrim Players (1907), for which he built
and managed the Birmingham Repertory Theatre (1913). He remained director
and underwriter of the organization for more than two decades. The Malvern
Festival, created by Jackson in honour of Shaw and as a showcase for his plays,
old and new, was inaugurated in 1929 and renewed each summer through
1939, when it was interrupted by the outbreak of war. In Shaw's lifetime there
was only one postwar Festival season, in 1949.

My dear Ayliff

They mustnt wait for the laughs: they must kill them and get along with
it. And Cedric must get his business in on the lines, as in Shakespear,
and not between them. Every silence drags; and though a laugh may
finally be extracted by mugging the hour is far too late when the final
curtain comes.

Barry says the effect at the dress rehearsal was perfect. That was
because of the silence in front. My plays are nothing if not impetuous;
and that effect is produced not by hurrying or slurring, but by never
letting the current of speech (which is the action) halt for a moment.
The audience shouldnt have time to think and should never be kept
waiting.

Otherwise, all right.

                                        In haste to catch the midnight post
                                        G.B.S.

131 / To Alfred Sutro   Ayot St Lawrence. Welwyn. Herts.
                                                                7th October 1929

[Transcript from Winton Dean, 1988]

Alfred Sutro (1863–1933), prolific playwright and longtime friend of Shaw, wrote to him after viewing The Apple Cart *at the Queen's Theatre, where it ran for 258 performances. Sempronius is a character in the opening scene, whose father, he says, was 'a raging emotional Die Hard Ritualist right down to his boots ... [H]e couldnt imagine anything he didnt see; but he could imagine that what he did see was divine and holy and omniscient and omnipotent and eternal and everything that is impossible if only it looked splendid enough ...' Eventually he died of solitude: 'He couldnt bear to be alone for a moment: it was death to him.'*

Sempronius *père* was a false start. I began with a notion of two great parties: the Ritualists and the Quakers, and the King balancing them one against the other and finally defeating a combination of them. But I discarded this, as there wasnt room for it. However, I thought the opening would make a very good Mozartian overture to get the audience settled down and in the right attentive mood before the real fun began: hence its retention.

But the whole affair is a frightful bag of stage tricks as old as Sophocles. I blushed when I saw it.

G.B.S.

132 / To Baliol Holloway

4 Whitehall Court SW1
12th June 1930

[TLS: Donald Sinden]

Baliol Holloway was contemplating a production of Ibsen's Peer Gynt *that never came to fruition. Russell Thorndike (1885–1972) performed* Peer Gynt *in the first production of the William Archer translation, at the Old Vic for 26 performances, in March 1922.*

Dear Baliol Holloway

I have seen most of the truncated Peer Gynts; and though one of them did fairly well as a curiosity at the Old Vic for a while I am as sure as one can be of anything in the theatre that you had better either play it in its entirety or let it alone. This is not now the impossibility it once seemed. O'Neill's Strange Interlude, which occupied an afternoon and an evening with an interval for dinner, was such a success that the Theatre Guild begged me to write my next play in eight acts. The Macdona Players give Man and Superman in every town in its entirety because it crams the house to the last seat. People go for three successive days to see Back to Methuselah afternoon and evening. Hamlet in its entirety is a sure draw at the Old Vic. Colbourn found on his last tour that the theatres are being emptied by the picture houses in which people sit from two to eleven. It looks as if the Chinese theatre, where a play lasts a week, is what the public really wants. At Ober Ammergau, before the whole auditorium was roofed in, people used to sit from 10 to 6 in torrents of rain to see the Passion Play: I did it myself.

P.G. is therefore possible in its entirety. It is never satisfactory in selections, even to those who do not know what they are missing. So if you are determined to ruin yourself by taking a theatre, do it handsomely with two shows a day.

By the way, P.G. will kill you if you are not careful. An actor playing a part of such length and weight should be in perfect training and have nothing else to do: in fact he should be in bed all the time he is not on the stage. Combining it with the endless worry of running a theatre is an unnecessarily painful method of suicide in these days of lethal gas ovens.

Never mind Bishop: he was bound to get it running somehow; and I havent the least objection to being described as your bosom friend.

faithfully

G. Bernard Shaw

Strange Interlude (1928) by Eugene O'Neill (1888–1953) achieved a run of 426 performances in New York. It was Esmé Percy (1887–1957) who first successfully experimented with a full-length *Man and Superman* on his 1915 tour of Scotland, to include all of the *Don Juan in Hell* sequence. Shaw was astonished to discover that audiences were larger (generally at capacity) for the full version than for the shortened one. In 1925, when Percy became director of the touring Macdona Players, he added the full version to its Shaw repertory.

The **Oberammergau** Passion Play in Bavaria had been performed decennially since 1634. George W. **Bishop** (1886–1965) was a theatre correspondent for the *Observer* and freelance journalist, to whom Shaw frequently fed self-drafted interviews. No article linking Shaw and Holloway as bosom friends has, however, been found.

133 / To John Martin-Harvey   4 Whitehall Court SW1
9th October 1930

[TLS: Harvard Theatre Collection]

Although The Shewing-up of Blanco Posnet *in Martin-Harvey's repertory failed to draw provincial audiences and was quickly dropped, he risked adding* The Devil's Disciple, *with not very satisfactory results in its London engagement at the Savoy Theatre in September 1930.*

My dear Martin-Harvey

I am sorry this wretched old play has let you down, and that all my laborious abuse of you has been wasted. You may write it all off as mere Attaboy to stir up the performance. If I had looked at the returns and realized that £800 a week – a terrible symptom – had set in, I should have told you simply that the game was up, and that there was nothing to be done but keep up appearances and get the money back in the provinces on the London notices.

Whenever anything goes wrong in a play of mine I am told that it is in the book; and it generally is: I spend half my time at rehearsals in shouting 'Damn the book.' But there is something that I cannot give in the book, because there is no notation for it; and that is the voltage on the batteries. The voltage for melodrama has to be much higher than for cup and saucer comedy; and yet the stage directions may be the same. If I say you are to be angry or to be solemn you have still to ask whether you are to be angry at 50 volts or 250. Take my two D Ds: The Devil's Disciple and The Doctor's Dilemma. The first should be played violently. If you played the other violently the result would be ridiculous. Yet I have to use the same adjectives and adverbs in both, just as a composer has to write the same notes whether the movement is *adagio pianissimo* or *allegro feroce.* That is why I ought to have helped you with the rehearsals; but as Napoleon said when they told him about Trafalgar 'I cannot be everywhere.' I had to be at Malvern, where there were five plays of mine in hand. I had to let you down. You must not reproach yourself for the result. The play is one for large houses with low prices; and it is not politically sympathetic in England as it is in America. There was a chance, but not much more. And Gwenn looked so damnably young when so much depended on his being the older and more authoritative man. And then Mary: she gave such a wonderful representation of a perfectly wellbred civilized woman exiled among rapscallions, that all the sympathy went with her. She put you completely in the wrong. You must take care to get an elderly tall robust man and a hateful woman next time. Hang it all: give yourself a chance.

My stage direction in Act III is right if you hold Judith the right way for it. Your grip was wrong for it; and the remedy is to alter either the grip or the moment of release. As to the end, it is inevitable that when the reprieve comes the audience should reach for their hats. There is nothing for it but to play them out: after all, you have their money. But it was for this reason that I gave strong exits to Burgoyne, Swindon and the sergeant. If you do everything that is in the book, and do it hard, the audience may peter out but the play wont. Your omission of everything was an act of desperation: a surrender. That is never any use.

I think the old Irving game of being both leading actor and producer [director] is very dangerous. It was all very well for Irving, whose object was to extinguish everyone on the stage but himself, even at the cost of extinguishing the play. You should always have someone watching in front. If you produce you cannot give your own part undivided attention; and yet you have to give it so much attention that you cannot give full attention to the play.

I hope The Lyons Mail will retrieve the situation. It lacks a Lyons Female; but a good criminal trial is generally sure fire in the theatre. Dont make Tree's mistake of making the two men so outrageously unlike that they could not possibly have been mistaken for one another. I maintain that the parts should always be played by different actors.

faithfully
G.B.S.

Shaw had acquired the expression **Attaboy** at an exhibition baseball game by two American teams in London. 'Even those players,' he wrote, 'who had no gift of eloquence expressed their souls in dithyrambic cries . . . which sounded to me like "Attaboy." I confess that I am not enough of a Greek scholar to translate "Attaboy" but it is a very stimulating ejaculation' ('This Baseball Madness,' *Evening Standard*, 4 November 1924). Edmund **Gwenn** (1875–1959) had been a Shavian 'reliable' since he created Straker in *Man and Superman* at the Royal Court in 1905. In the Martin-Harvey production he played the Rev. Anthony Anderson, with **Mary** Rorke (1858–1938) giving support as Mrs Dudgeon. *The Lyons Mail* (originally *The Courier of Lyons*, 1854) was a tried-and-true Victorian melodrama by Charles Reade, one of Henry Irving's most reliable moneymakers, in five productions, from 1877 to 1901.

134 / To Shayle Gardner   4 Whitehall Court SW1
                                                                    14th May 1931

[TLS: HRC]

Shayle Gardner (1890–1945), a New Zealander who played the squire Robert de Baudricourt in Saint Joan *(1924), had followed a film career in recent years, appearing principally in* Disraeli *(1931) and later in* The Lodger *(1932). The latest incarnation of Sybil Thorndike (1882–1976) as Saint Joan manifested itself at His Majesty's Theatre on 6 April, with George Merritt in Gardner's former role. Lewis Casson (1875–1969), Thorndike's husband, doubled as director of* Saint Joan *and as a member of the cast, playing the chaplain De Stogumber.*

Dear Shayle Gardner

If you play a part to which your personality is not well fitted, and then go a filming and become associated in the public eye with a quite different and much more amiable type you cannot reasonably expect to turn back on your own success. If you want to stick to the gravedigger you must be careful not to make a success as Hamlet.

   That is all there is to it. Surely you dont believe that nature intended you to play comic blusterers like Baudricourt. You almost persuaded the audience to take him at his own valuation; and although that gave a certain weight to the scene that had its effect it was not exactly the effect I wanted. Whether your *remplaçant* was any nearer to the part I cannot say, as I have not seen the revival and dont know who he is; but I certainly told Casson to experiment with someone else if he could find a likely man. I had no idea that the engagement was of any importance to you: I thought you were up to your neck in film work doing sympathetic leading characters. To me it was a case of a new man vice S.G. promoted; and you must not suppose that any disparagement of you was involved: quite the contrary.

   I was abroad when your first letter arrived. All my correspondence had to await my return. I hoped to see the revival before answering; but that has not yet come off. Meanwhile do not feel slighted: the change bears quite the opposite construction.

                                                            faithfully
                                                            G. Bernard Shaw

135 / To Lillah McCarthy   Ayot St Lawrence. Welwyn. Herts.

8th June 1931

[APCS: HRC]

The new play Too True to be Good, *begun in the Mediterranean on 5 March as Shaw returned from a visit to the Holy Land, was not completed until 30 June.*

Alas! the new play is no use for the Haymarket, and hasnt a part you would look at! Just two young and very rowdy girls and one silly old woman. No tragic beauty anywhere: a perverse farce. Age is telling heavily on me.

G. Bernard Shaw

136 / To W. Nugent Monck   [Ayot St Lawrence. Welwyn. Herts.]

23rd June 1931

[ALS: Monck Estate]

Nugent Monck, requesting permission to schedule Arms and the Man *at the Maddermarket Theatre, had apparently sent a brochure indicating a production of John Webster's* The Duchess of Malfi *(1614) by the Norwich Players. Shaw had seen the William Poel version, by the Independent Theatre, 1892, and the Phoenix Society production at the Lyric, Hammersmith, 1919.*

Yes, by all means go ahead.

The D. of M. is the worst tragedy ever written, not that it is badly written, but that it shews an utter want of theatre sense. It is readable; but on the stage it is ridiculous. I have seen it tried twice.

G. Bernard Shaw

137 / To H.K. Ayliff   Malvern Hotel. Malvern

6th August 1932. After the show

[TLS: Hofstra]

Too True to be Good *was presented at the Malvern Festival that evening, directed by H.K. Ayliff, who appeared as the Elder.*

My dear Ayliff

Well, you have pulled it off – the double event: production and imper-sonation. Desmond McCarthy has just left me: he was enchanted with the Elder. So was I.

The curtain was late in Acts II & III. It should fall like a guillotine on Nature – NEVER. I gave the wrong cue – 'preach' – for the last curtain. It should start creeping down on 'surely perish'; so that it may reach the floor whilst Cedric has still two or three words to say.

The doctor was a complete failure. He is there solely to express the audience's impatience of Mrs Mopply and thereby make it a quality instead of a fault; but he simply made her a bore instead of supporting her. But it is no use telling him. There is nothing to be done but get rid of him as soon as possible.

Make Scott take an eggcup full of laudanum while he is off the stage in the second act. He *will not* slow down impressively for his curtain, damn him! He muffed it so completely that when the curtain hung fire Sweetie tried to fill up by laughing at him: a ruinous expedient: tell her on her life not to stir nor utter a sound, though it served him jolly well right.

For the rest it was success all the time. Leonora gave an astounding exhibition of power and authority in the fertilizer scene. I knew she would be good, but had no idea how much she had up her sleeve, and how completely independent she is of her good looks. Tell Barry to engage her at once for seven years.

ever

G.B.S.

Desmond **MacCarthy** (1878–1952) was a dramatic critic (one of the most discerning in London) and theatre historian. Cast members included **Cedric** Hardwicke as the burglar Aubrey, Barrie Livesey (1904–?) as the **Doctor**, Margaret Halstan as **Mrs Mopply, Scott** Sunderland (1883–1952) as Tallboys (muffing the Act II curtain line: 'Humanity always fails me: nature never'), Ellen Pollock (b. 1903) as **Sweetie**, and **Leonora** Corbett (1908–60) as the Patient.

138 / To H.K. Ayliff   Malvern Hotel. Malvern
                                             25th August 1932

[TLS: Hofstra]

Following the Malvern season Too True to be Good *was transferred to Birming-*

ham for additional performances and much tinkering before the London opening on 13 September. One immediate decision was to recast the Doctor, with Donald Wolfit (1902–68) assuming the role in London.

My dear Ayliff

I enclose another alteration besides all those which I have sent direct to the victims. I have told Miss Halstan and Livesey and Scott about these. I am getting decidedly old: I never before left such a lot of loose ends in a play.

I dont know how it is at the Birmingham house; but I think that here you did not allow enough for the remoteness of the Elder in that cave. There was a marked difference between the cave and the center in the delicacy with which your inflexions came across. I am convinced that the cave speech should convey the effect of being roared in the wilderness. If not, it seems like a rehearsal of the supreme tragedy speech. You were afraid of seeming to roar, and became more and more pathetically beautiful. Try the effect of roaring like a madman, or at least making the audience believe that you are the prophet Micah, whose speech was that of a lion and a dragon. The supreme tragedy speech will completely clear you of being able to do nothing else. A difference, as marked as possible, between the two great speeches is needed to shew that you have two strings to your bow. At all events experiment a bit. It does not matter if you wreck a performance or two. I somehow feel as if I had not shewn you off enough through your full range; and I think it can be done by getting that first speech addressed more to a universe of desolate sands and hopeless seas and less courteously to the sergeant and Sweetie. They should be astounded at the apparition rather than interested in the old gentleman.

Cedric and Leonora came over on Tuesday and said that you had a great success on Monday; so you will perhaps ask what more I want. But I always feel guilty if I have left any actor with an unexploited possibility.

I wont press the point about 'for which more martyrs have perished than FOR all the creeds put together.' You have got 'than all the creeds' firmly into your head; and nothing will ever dislodge it. It doesnt matter: it's a perfectly intelligible ellipsis.

If I can get Lawrence here some Thursday or Saturday I will bring him along to a matinée.

your troublesome
GBS

The Elder's **cave speech** on 'the supreme tragedy of the atheist who has lost his faith – his faith in atheism' is in Act III. The **Sergeant** was performed by Ralph Richardson (1902–83), who on the 23rd received a note of enthusiastic praise from Shaw. T.E. **Lawrence** (1888–1935) was Shaw's model for Private Meek.

139 / To Ellen Pollock   Malvern Hotel. Malvern

25th August 1932

[TLS: Ellen Pollock]

Ellen Pollock, who played the nurse Sweetie, was another of Shaw's favourite performers. He cast her the following year as Aloysia Brollikins in On the Rocks, *and licensed her to produce touring productions of a number of his plays, including* Candida, Pygmalion, The Devil's Disciple, Village Wooing, *and* Mrs Warren's Profession, *many of which she directed. In September 1950 she appeared in his last produced play,* Farfetched Fables.

Dear Ellen Pollock

A vulgar name would jar, unless it were quite unaffectedly common, like Susan Simkins. But just try the effect of saying 'My name's Gwendolen Anastasia St John Griffith-Evans, with a hyphen if you please.' Dont tell them beforehand; and you will have the fun of drying up the entire company. Let me know how it works.

It is a mistake to repeat Hell in the first act; and you dont get it quite right the first time. It should come out sharp, like a pistol shot: 'HELL I will.' You may not be familiar with the locution (an author never knows how much bad language an actress is accustomed to); but it goes like this. If Mops said 'Will you be our chaperone?' you would reply 'Will I Hell.' But as she says 'You will be our chaperone' you reply 'Hell I will.' However, I think we can do better. Instead of 'Hell I will &c.' say 'Chaperone! Well, you have a nerve, you have.' And at the cue 'doesnt that tempt you?' say 'Tempt me HELL. I'll see you further first.'

And now, another matter. The dress in the first act is very ineffective:

that washy blue in the dark room is no use. Just look at the enclosed photographs of the American production. Dont you think that the surgical get-up of brilliant white is rather a success? As measles are highly infectious there is nothing wrong in an antiseptic overall. The blue looks insignificant and almost invisible.

By the way, you have upset the relationships with your foreign accent, though I started it with the foreign title. She can't be Aubrey's sister if she is a Frenchwoman. Make them speak of you as Aubrey's half step-sister. His widowed mother might have married a Frenchman with a daughter married to a Count.

ever

GBS

140 / To J.T. Grein

'Empress of Britain'

At sea. World cruise

1st February 1933

[ALS: Boston University]

My dear Grein

I write this on the way to Singapore from Java, where I lunched with your father-in-law at the Hotel des Indes in Batavia. He was very friendly and much interested in you. Also in poetry and horse breeding.

As to your suggestion of a revival of Widowers' Houses, it has been anticipated by Barry Jackson. He revived it recently at Malvern with Cedric Hardwicke as Lickcheese and Marjorie Mars as Blanche. Bashville, with Gwenn Ffrangcon Davies as Lydia, was added as an afterpiece, making a very strong bill. Barry Jackson lent the production in London to the Stage Society, stars and all; and after this there would be no novelty about a new production, even if we could cast it as well.

This, I think, puts it on the shelf for the moment.

Besides, I am tired of being an intruder in West End theatres. It was bad enough thirty years ago, when George Alexander complained to me that his expenses at the St James's had reached such a figure that he could not keep a play on unless it drew a thousand a week. Well, my last play was drawing more than a thousand a week when it was taken off as a failure. Managers cannot get on with less than sixteen or seventeen hundred. Such figures from anything like our sort of drama are out of the question except in large theatres with low prices and three hours entertainment, with the West End audience practically excluded.

There is nothing really new in this; for though the figures have changed, London has always ruined every actor and entrepreneur in the long run. Bancroft, who invented the West End theatre by abolishing the old pit and charging half a guinea for a stall, cleared out in time, but at the cost of giving up his profession and becoming a man about town long before he and his wife were past their work. Irving, who made a great deal of money for the Lyceum landlords, was finally beaten back to the Provinces. Barry Sullivan, who deliberately turned his back on London after his great Hamlet success at the Haymarket, and exploited Australia and the Provinces and America, died worth £100,000.

However, this is a story of which you must be pretty weary. Its applications go far beyond the theatre. In all the professions there is nothing so deadly as a London success. All the arts and sciences are kept alive, not by the big fees of fashionable London, but by the half-crowns and florins and sixpences of the Provinces and suburbs.

In the seventeenth century fifteen shillings a week was quite an ordinary salary for a good London actor. But he was 'a player,' never troubled with the social pretensions of Bancroft and Irving. And his annual income was even bigger than that of modern actors, whose salaries are prohibitive.

I wonder why the devil you and I, being respectable men of fair abilities and reasonable conduct, should have succumbed to the craze for the most absurd and disreputable of human institutions.

faithfully

G. Bernard Shaw

J.T. Grein's **father-in-law** was Ernest Greeven. Grein's wife, Alix Augusta Greeven, wrote professionally as 'Michael Orme.' *The Admirable Bashville* is a verse play adapted by Shaw in 1901 from his novel *Cashel Byron's Profession* (written in 1882). Gwen **Ffrangçon-Davies** (1896–1992), who played Eve in the Birmingham Repertory production of *Back to Methuselah*, was a distinguished actress and singer who graced the stage for several decades. Shaw's **last play**, *Too True to be Good*, survived in London for 47 performances.

141 / To Katharine Cornell　　　　　　　4 Whitehall Court SW1
30th June 1933

[TLS(p): NYPL Theatre Collection]

Katharine Cornell (1893–1974) first played Candida *in 1924. Nine years later she sought a licence to include the play in an extended tour under her own management, in repertory with* Romeo and Juliet *and a new play by Rudolf Besier (1878–1942),* The Barretts of Wimpole Street *(1930). Diplomatically she requested Shaw to set whatever terms he thought right and asserted that* Candida *was 'a play I hope I may act until age makes it impossible' (TLS, 16 June 1933: HRC). Shaw responded with a licence for as many performances as she desired, until Spring 1934, at his standard scale, enclosing a statement of 'Terms and Conditions for Professional Productions' of his plays.*

My dear Katharine Cornell

Will the enclosed do? As you see, they are my ordinary terms – practically the same I had forty years ago from Richard Mansfield.

I dont think I was ever so astonished by a picture as I was by your photograph. Your success as Candida, and something blonde and expansive about your name, had created an ideal suburban British Candida in my imagination. Fancy my feelings on seeing in the photograph a gorgeous dark lady from the cradle of the human race, wherever that was – Ceylon, Sumatra, Hilo, or the southernmost corner of the Garden of Eden! If you can look like that it doesnt matter a rap whether you can act or not. Can you?

yours, breath-bereaved
G. Bernard Shaw

142 / To Lillah McCarthy　　　　　　　　Gregynog Hall
N^r Newtown. Montgomeryshire
(until Tuesday morning)
26th August 1933

[ALS: HRC]

The role Shaw was offering to Lillah McCarthy was that of the mysterious lady in grey robes at the end of Act I of On the Rocks. *It went, finally, to Fay Davis (1872–1945). The London production opened, not at the Prince's Theatre, but at the Winter Garden, in November.*

My dear Lillah

Are you really earnest about this? If Van Druten's play prove a success Sybil may not be available; and you could make the big effect (such as it is: it's only a trifle) as well as she. And failing both of you I dont know where to lay my hand on a substitute.

But would you really go through with it? The part has only 48 speeches, mostly two or three words to feed the leading man (nobody else on the stage), at the end of the first act; and she does not reappear. All she has to do is to convey an impression of being an extraordinary person. Macdona will appreciate the advertisement of your book; but he will offer you three and sixpence a week with a share in the very problematical profits, that being the system at the Prince's, with its five shilling stalls free of tax, and its shilling gallery.

And suppose the darned thing catches on and runs for months and months and months like The Apple Cart. Can you stand going back from being comfortable Lady Keeble at Hammels or exploring the Andes to the old professional drudgery of London lodgings and eight shows a week and Freddy deserted and in great danger of being res-cued by some Brazilian beauty who has lost her heart to him on the ship or elsewhere?

If the play got going irresistibly you could chuck your part after, say, six or eight weeks without checking the run. Probably all Macdona's stars reserve the right to do that if anything better turns up.

Anyhow, let me know whether you have considered the matter realis-tically, or have risen to it only on the wings of impulse.

G.B.S.

The play by John **Van Druten** (1901–57) was *The Distaff Side*, in which Sybil Thorndike was to appear. McCarthy's **book** was the just-published autobiographic *Myself and My Friends*, for which Shaw had provided 'An Aside' by way of an introduction. Having divorced Granville Barker in 1918, she wed (1920) Sir Frederick Keeble (1870–1952), a professor of botany and fellow of Magdalen College, Oxford. Shaw's reference to **Freddy** may be an unconscious comparison with Barker, paralleling Higgins and Freddy in *Pygmalion*!

143 / To George Cornwallis-West   [4 Whitehall Court SW1
                                                19th January 1934]

[Holograph note: BL 58432, f 147]

*George Cornwallis-West (1874–1951), estranged husband of Mrs Patrick Camp-
bell, sent Shaw a copy of his play* The Woman Who Stopped War *for criticism.
Shaw replied at length, enclosing a two-page typescript of a revised scene – and
an undated, red-inked comment on stage eating.*

Meals on the stage are a fearful bother. The stalls, full to the neck, hate
the smell of them and cannot sympathize with a display of appetite.
The pit and gallery are seldom hungry enough to be tantalized. The
actor *may* be hungry – I have known one who bargained for a stage
meal; but that was at Margate – but a London actor should not be
obliged to swallow a dictated meal which he may loathe. Banquets with
property viands and goblets are quite in order; but unless (as in You
Never Can Tell) a real meal has funny or interesting dramatic accompaniments, it is to be avoided.

I should take Tim and his meal off the stage, and get rid of page 9
with its disgusting steak and stout. Consider the vegetarians & teetotal-
lers in front!

It seems impossible to do this, as Tim must be on the stage to explain
the plot. But there are two ways of doing it. 1. Avoid the meal altogether by making Tim explain that he has dined already, conveying, if
you like, that he really has no appetite. 2. Postpone the meal until the
end of the act. This is easy.

144 / To Theresa Helburn   R.M.S. Rangitane
                                            Wellington NZ to London
                                                27th April 1934

[ALS: Yale]

On the Rocks, *presented by Charles Macdona at the Winter Garden Theatre,
London, on 25 November 1933, lasted only for 41 performances. The Theatre
Guild rejected the play, as they did all of Shaw's new plays that followed the
quick failure in 1935 of the Guild's production of* The Simpleton of the Unexpected Isles.

My dear Tessie

Your letter of the 6th Feb. did not reach London until after my departure for New Zealand; and its pursuit of me was long and tortuous.

I take it that I may now deal with On The Rocks as discarded by the Guild and free to find shelter wherever it can. In London it flopped in the most annoying manner: huge first night success, unanimously good press (for once) presaging an unlimited run, audiences apparently delighted by every line, AND receipts £400 a week! I had insisted on an experiment at half the regular theatre prices; but this involved a slightly out-of-the-way new theatre, and the general playgoer would not come, though the fans came over and over again. In short, it was a magnificent success with the people – say 5000 or so – who are interested in politics. To the others it meant absolutely nothing. After the first few weeks it settled down to £400; and the shutters had to go up before the management was quite cleaned out.

During this voyage I have written one full length play and begun another; but the finished one is so fantastic, and in great part so hieratical, that it is useless except perhaps for a Festival performance at Malvern (two or three shows only). I am writing myself off the theatrical map, partly through senile decay, partly because I am no longer interested in the sort of thing that has any commercial value in the theatre. Consequently unless I can find a fresh set of desperados, standing where the Guild did in the days of Heartbreak House and Jane Clegg, I am out of the running.

Is there such a thing? If so, dear Tessie, give it the address of your superannuated

G. Bernard Shaw

The **full-length play** was *The Simpleton of the Unexpected Isles*; the one **begun,** *The Millionairess.* **Jane Clegg** is an error for St John Ervine's later play *John Ferguson,* produced by the Theatre Guild in 1919.

145 / To Floryan Sobieniowski   4 Whitehall Court SW1
21st January 1935

[TLS: HRC]

Floryan Sobieniowski was translating The Simpleton of the Unexpected Isles, *produced by the Theatre Guild in New York on 18 February 1935 and scheduled for Malvern in July.*

Dear Sobieniowski

The matter is quite simple. The four young creatures, in their exquisite dresses, never utter a word naturally. They declaim, their speech is musical, rhythmical, artificial in the last degree. When Maya is making love she coos like a dove. Their attitudes are all deliberate poses, beautiful and dignified, but as natural as the poses of a dancer or tragedian.

Pra and Prola are distinguished by their Eastern dress and measured gravity of demeanour: they speak English (Polish) quite easily and pleasantly, but still as an acquired foreign language.

The others, in modern European dress, play and speak just as they would in a modern comedy. Lady Farwaters and her husband are distinctly upper class: their tone is that of the embassies. Mrs Hyering is pleasantly vulgar, with the selfconfidence of a pretty woman. She may have been a shop assistant in a west end shop.

All this is as easy as A.B.C. The parts are written to suit the various styles of delivery.

The stage directions are quite mechanical, mostly to shew the actors where to sit; but the final scene has a certain hieratic aspect: for example, though the persons take tea, they must not loaf about and smoke cigarettes as if they were having a holiday on the Riviera.

The third scene in the prologue presents a mechanical difficulty which I confess I have not solved. The change of scene must be practically instantaneous: any long interval would [be] fatal. If you have a revolving stage, or any of its equivalents, it is easy enough: if not, the quick change must be contrived as best it may. . . .

> faithfully
> G. Bernard Shaw

146 / To Maurice Colbourne   4 Whitehall Court SW1
                                        12th July 1935

[TLS: Theatre Museum]

Apparently the Colbourne-Jones tour of Canada in 1932 lost money and no royalties were paid.

Dear Maurice

Very ingenious nonsense; but you can't put nonsense over on me. I take it that you didnt pay the Guild, you didnt pay me, and you and B.J. drank my fees.

May I take it also that the tour did not pay and that the liquor was tea and its consumption a matter of vital necessity and not a debauch?

That being so I shall not dun you; for 'Where there is nothing, the king loses his rights'. Still, as I also have to live, it is Miss Patch's duty to call attention to oversights. She has now given you up as hopeless; so you may enjoy Malvern with a light heart.

faithfully
G. Bernard Shaw

The Theatre **Guild** served as a sub-licenser and collection bureau for Shaw in America. Blanche **Patch** (1879–1966) was Shaw's secretary, a post she had held since 1920. Her responsibilities included the posting of royalty payments in the accounts books and drawing Shaw's attention to significant delinquencies.

147 / To Victor Barnowsky   4 Whitehall Court SW1
                    26th September 1935

[TLS: Cornell]

The political climate in Germany in the 1930s resulted in a mass exodus to London of German and Austrian Jews and anti-Nazis: stage directors, managers, actors, playwrights, dramatic critics – many of them associates of Shaw and Siegfried Trebitsch for nearly three decades, and almost all of them needing assistance. One of these was Victor Barnowsky (1875–1952), Berlin theatre manager, who staged a number of Shaw's plays, with varying success. His production of Back to Methuselah, which nettled Shaw, was divided into two evenings: Parts I and II on 19 September 1925, which achieved a run of 92 performances, and Parts III to V, on 26 November 1925, which ran for 15 performances. All five parts were drastically scissored.

Dear Mr Barnowsky

All the directors who have suffered in the abominable persecution in Germany have come to me believing that I could help them in establishing themselves in London, if possible in connection with productions of my own plays. I can do nothing. The persecution is not confined to directors of theatres; and its relief is far beyond the means of any private individual.

As to taking a financial share in a theatrical enterprise that is not my business. I take money out of the theatre (when there is any); I never put any into it; and I strongly advise you to make the same rule.

I remember your production of Back to Methuselah very well. Your running the Lloyd George–Asquith section and dropping all the rest was a shocking breach of contract; but I hope it brought you in a sub-stantial revenue; and I have of course long since forgiven you for suc-cumbing to what must have been an irresistible temptation.

faithfully
G. Bernard Shaw

148 / To Sydney W. Carroll

4 Whitehall Court SW1
22nd June 1936

[TLS: Cornell]

Sydney W. Carroll (1877–1958), actor, journalist, and dramatic critic, became a theatrical manager in 1931. Two years later he created the Open Air Theatre in Regent's Park, London, where in July 1934 he presented Shaw's Androcles and the Lion *and the première of* Overruled. *Nothing came of the* Back to Meth-uselah *suggestion.*

My dear Sydney Carroll

Have you ever asked yourself this momentous question? Why is it that old Shaw, who has been in the theatre business for 44 years, is not an inmate of Fulham workhouse? The instructive answer is that he has never lost sight of the fact that it is the business of a playwright to take money out of the theatre and not under any circumstances put money into it.

I have carried out this policy strictly in the Open Air Theatre. You have lost £10,000; and I have had some of it.

Where did you get the ten thousand? Certainly not by criticism: I have been a critic myself; and I know. I cleaned out Miss Horniman in 1894 with my first commercially produced play. That was tea money. When the famous Vedrenne-Barker management was dissolved after its adventure in the Shaw business, G.B. pawned everything short of reducing himself to nudity and I disgorged much of my royalties to make a solvent ending. Even Barry Jackson, with the Maypole Dairy company behind him, was finally panicked, though his last production of Back to Methuselah [*1928*] actually made a profit of £25. Who is to be the next victim? If you can pick up ten thousand pound notes and spree them on the newest and biggest change in managerial policy in my time you are clearly eligible.

How would the Adam and Eve scenes from Methuselah, followed by the Comedy of Errors, do for Regent's Park? I can pocket Shakespear's royalties all right. Any thing that will tempt a shark is good enough for

Yours until the times do alter
G. Bernard Shaw

149 / To Hugh Beaumont   4 Whitehall Court SW1
23rd February 1937

[TLS: Colgate]
Hugh Beaumont (1908–73) was managing director of H.M. Tennent, Ltd., Britain's most powerful theatrical management, whose West End revival of Candida *had opened on 10 February. Wendy Hiller (b. 1912) played Liza in the Malvern Festival* Pygmalion *in August 1936. Film production did not commence until 11 March 1938.*

Dear Hugh Beaumont

I have made up my mind as far as it is capable of being made up that I will not have an old stager in the next Pygmalion revival. At present I want Wendy Hiller. Unfortunately she is to make a film of it in June and will be busy at the studio making other films to put her well on the map first. And the film may kill the play. A horrid muddle.

Except for my contract with Cochran for The Millionairess I have no West End management on hand: they seldom wake up to an opportunity in less than five years or so. Anyhow there is no competition for the moment.

faithfully
G. Bernard Shaw

C.B. **Cochran** (1872–1951), a leading British showman, at the urgence of Edith Evans took an option on Shaw's play *The Millionairess* (1934); but no production eventuated. In 1940 Tennent's obtained rights and sent the play on a pre-London tour with Evans; the West End engagement was cancelled after its intended venue, the Globe Theatre, was blitzed.

150 / To H.K. Ayliff Ayot St Lawrence. Welwyn. Herts.
18th April 1938

[APCS: Hofstra]

Ayliff engaged Elisabeth Bergner (1900–86), former favourite of Vienna and Berlin audiences, who played Saint Joan in 1924, to recreate her role at the Malvern Festival in August 1938. Shaw detested the gamin quality she affected in her roles, as in the play Escape Me Never *by Margaret Kennedy (1896–1967), which she played in London in December 1933; after he witnessed her performance at Malvern he refused her the film rights.*

I spent all yesterday, Easter Sunday, over that copy of Joan. There can be no question of retaining the German prompt copy, because the whole play will have to be learnt over again in English.

What the little devil has done is to cut out all the unfeminine and unladylike speeches so that she can give a pathetic repetition of her Escape Me Never stunt.

What *I* have done is to fill the margins of her changes with my explanations of them and my opinion of her in the very reddest of red ink. She will receive it tomorrow morning. So if you hear that she has drowned herself in Virginia Water you will know why.

But not she: she is as tough as a Brazil nut.

GBS

Bergner first settled in England in the town of **Virginia Water**, N.W. Surrey, which had an artificial lake.

151 / To H.K. Ayliff 4 Whitehall Court SW1
30th June 1938

[APCS: Cornell]

Paul Shelving (1889–1968), principal designer of the Birmingham Repertory Theatre, conceived of Herr Battler in the forthcoming Malvern Festival production of Geneva *as wearing Lohengrin's winged Tarnhelm (the magic helmet – a wishing cap – that renders him invisible or transforms him).*

I strongly approve of the Lohengrin idea. Let Paul proceed accordingly.

Never heard of N.W. Why did Clunes chuck the best part in the play from the point of view of publicity?

I hear that the journalist is translating his part into Americanese. Let me have his alterations as soon as convenient, as I may have to order some more copies from the printer.

You mustnt call BBDE Bombardini, which is a diminutive. He is Bombardoni, which is hyperbolical. The distinction is important in Italian.

GBS

N.W. was Norman Wooland (1905–89), who was replaced by Walter Hudd (1898–1963) as Battler (a satirized Hitler) in the transfer to London in November. Alec **Clunes** (1912–70), a young actor who would become a major figure in British theatre, appeared in three of the Festival plays that summer; he was Dunois in *Saint Joan*. The **journalist** in *Geneva* was Wilson Barrett (1900–81), who established a successful repertory company in Glasgow and Edinburgh in 1940. Shaw is referring to more rehearsal **copies** of the rough proof. **BBDE** is Shaw's abbreviation in the printed text of the play.

152 / To H.K. Ayliff   Ayot St Lawrence. Welwyn. Herts.
                                              11th December 1938

[TLS: Cornell]

Shaw attended a performance of Geneva *at the Saville Theatre the previous evening. Despite his dissatisfaction with what he saw, the production settled in for a profitable London engagement of 237 performances.*

Dear Ayliff

What a horrible horrible play! Why had I to write it? To hear those poor devils spouting the most exalted sentiments they were capable of, and not one of them fit to manage a coffee stall, sent me home ready to die.

The first scene was beautifully lighted: I cant imagine what that idiot was thinking of.

Begonia petered out in the third act. The reason was that she and the betrothed kept up their spooning all through. They should straighten up when the judge tells them that the world is looking on, and put on their best behavior until the end. Begonia should change her accent to a refaned hawhaw. The betrothed, being disciplined socially, should wear his best wedding garments, and not be indistinguishable from the

American journalist. He, by the way, should be smarter, not only because he is a stetson hatted American but also a special correspondent and not a Fleet St free lance.

The Commissar is too young to be picked up by the bishop, and not Russian enough in his get-up. It is quite right that he should be very well dressed; but he should be made up like Litvinoff. This would make him less like the Jew.

Hudd's imitation of H's bursts of oratory were astonishingly good, and his performance generally most remarkable; but he threw away the word Machiavelli by just muttering it. This was natural; but as the audience dont know the word or are not prepared for it he had better listen with the deepest suspicion and hurl the name MachiaVELLLLLLLI at Thesiger. He also unaccountably drops the all-important word Messiah – one of his old tricks. It should be the climax. All the rest should play to it.

The widow does not remember that her dream, which is the tip top of her part, and starts a new hare, is a keyword of the first importance. The sentence beginning 'In my dreams night after night' is a terrible one; but she runs on without picking it out in the least. She should end the previous sentence with anguish in her voice and then stop and cover her eyes with her hands. Then 'In my dreams – night after night – she comes to me and begs me to forgive her; and [MADLY] I have to kill her again.' This is necessary not only to get the new horror across, but to give Battler a sufficiently strong cue.

I dont think Hudd has a pet dog: his 'my little doggie' was not heartbroken enough.

The widow's 'I shall dream and dream and kill and kill' should be much more Siddonsy.

The judge is admirable; but he must work up his last line into a regular curtain speech. It is his triumph and the moral of the play.

I still think Thesiger should play his charm more in the second act and make up more beautiful. The suggestion of Joseph is out of character: and the remonstrance with the secretary can be quite goodhumoured and 'my dear fellow' ish. Except for this he is perfect. Why should he have to change the impression from Austen to Joseph at first, since Austen is the man?

I think that's all. The production is as right as rain.

GBS

208

Maxim **Litvinov** (1876–1951) was the Russian commissar for foreign affairs 1930–8. **Hudd** was imitating Hitler. Ernest **Thesiger** (1879–1961), one of Shaw's favourite actors, physically modelled his character (Sir Orpheus Midlander, British foreign minister) after Joseph Chamberlain (1836–1914), Liberal MP and political reformer. Shaw's preference for a model was Sir Austen Chamberlain (1863–1937), son of Joseph, a Conservative MP, Chancellor of the Exchequer 1917–21, and a pacifist, winner of the Nobel Peace Prize in 1925. The brackets are Shaw's in '[**MADLY**].' Sarah **Siddons** (1755–1831) was queen of the London stage in her day. The **judge** was played by Alexander Knox (b. 1907).

153 / To Roy Limbert   Hotel Esplanade

Frinton, Essex

17th September 1939

[ALS: HRC]

Roy Limbert (1895–1954) was co-founder and joint-manager (with Barry Jackson) of the Malvern Festival.

Dear Roy

The declaration of war is the making of Geneva, which has always lacked a substantial climax. I have heard nothing from Cyril Gardiner; but I have written a new scene – the arrival of the news of Battler's attack – which will just do the trick. I have also sent for a copy of Geneva to run through and fit the new scene in. Miss Patch has the shorthand draft of it. Her typescript will reach me on Tuesday. It should be in your hands before the end of the week.

I held up America for you until you said definitely that you had given it up. At all events you have enough on your hands at present without Canada. You must console yourself with the likelihood of Colbourne being torpedoed.

If you will give me an estimate of what your gross receipts must average weekly to make the tour possible I will consider whether I cannot alter my terms in such a way as to lighten the loss if the result is complete flop and abandonment.

G. Bernard Shaw

Britain had declared **war** on 3 September. Cyril **Gardiner** (1897–1949), played the League of Nations secretary in *Geneva*. Maurice **Colbourne** was scheduled to open his new tour (which included *Geneva*), in Toronto on 16 October. The crossing was made uneventfully.

154 / To C.B. Purdom   4 Whitehall Court SW1

18th November 1939

[TLS: Cornell]

Charles Benjamin Purdom (1883–1965) was a journalist, author, and stage director, who at one time operated a theatre in Welwyn Garden City.

Dear Mr Purdom

I have to thank you for the copy you have sent me of the proposal for an Actors' Theatre as part of the work of Equity. I have read it attentively.

Equity is a Trade Union; and the history of Trade Unionism is a warning against such schemes. They have been tried, and have always failed. The job of Equity is to prevent the sweating of actors by their employers, not to provide employment for them, which is a completely different and highly speculative business. They should be kept entirely separate. If Equity becomes itself a speculative employer, not only will all its time and energy be taken up with its theatrical enterprises, but its point of view will change from that of the employee to that of the employer. It will not be 'under the control of actors who understand what they are doing and what the public requires,' because (a) there are no such actors, and (b) if there were they would be making colossal fortunes on their own account, and not slaving for £3 a week in an Equity Theatre.

What is needed is a scheme like that of the late Federal Theatre of the United States, now unhappily abandoned under the pressure of influences partly of Puritan hostility to the theatre as such, and mostly by the indifference to cultural institutions and the objection to taxation of the common Philistine. While it lasted I placed all my plays at its disposal on easy terms on condition that the price of admission to the performances should not exceed half a dollar. It greatly relieved unemployment in the profession and had some marked artistic success. Now that we have a British Council for handling such a scheme Equity might quite properly approach it and urge the establishment of a British experiment on the same lines for the relief of unemployment. But if the suggestion were adopted Equity would have to look after its treatment of its employees just as sharply as after commercial managers.

In short, my opinion is that though Equity may quite properly and usefully suggest the experiment to the British Council, and agitate for its adoption as a measure to relieve unemployment, it must on no account undertake the scheme itself.

faithfully

G. Bernard Shaw

British Actors' **Equity** Association was founded in December 1929. The American **Federal Theatre** project was established by an Act of Congress in 1935. Under the guidance of its indefatigable director Hallie Flanagan (1891–1969) it flourished until 1939, reaching millions of Americans, when conservatives in Congress, distressed by its blatant left-wing political slant, succeeded in abolishing it. The **British Council** was founded in 1934 'to promote a wider knowledge of the United Kingdom and the English language abroad' (Phyllis Hartnoll, ed., *Oxford Companion to the Theatre*, 4th ed., 1983). It expanded in 1937 to include a Department of Drama, one of whose chief functions was to negotiate foreign tours for leading British theatre companies.

155 / To Herbert Marshall   4 Whitehall Court SW1

12th August 1940

[TLS: present source unknown]

Herbert Marshall (1906–91), who became director of the Old Vic later that year (he should not be confused with a film star of the same name), staged Thunder Rock, a pacifist play by American dramatist Robert Ardrey (1908–80), which Shaw attended at a matinee on 10 August as a guest of the management.

Dear Herbert Marshall

I owe you a word of explanation for breaking away on Saturday afternoon, and avoiding a meeting with the company. I was afraid of discouraging them after all their hard work, and especially of disillusioning M.R. about his part – if he has any illusions about it. Much the best thing in the play is your lighthouse; and I could not but admire the desperate ingenuity with which you have exercised every producer's trick to persuade the audience that the play is Hamlet and Faust rolled into one, instead of being a very American budget of the pessimistic commonplaces of the eighteen-seventies compèred by an unfortunate actor who has to pretend that he is a leading tragedian when he has absolutely no part at all, bar that of *compère* [*master of cere-*

monies]. The success of your attempt to keep the audience listening to those two appalling bores in a breathless belief that something great is coming, and to get them out of the house before they realize that they have been completely duped, stamps you as one of the great producers of the age.

But the show must not be given away; so let this be a dead secret between us. I hadnt the heart to let M.R. and R.S. know what I thought of their parts. They worked like Trojans.

The author has some talent. The inspector is really a good part. And the Chinaman who says nothing but Okay has at least an easy one.

Congratulations on the box office. But what a damfool audience!

always yours

GBS

M.R. was Michael Redgrave (1908–85), who played the central role of a lighthouse keeper. **R.S.** was Robert A. Sansom, who died in 1945 while in military service.

156 / To William Armstrong

Ayot St Lawrence. Welwyn. Herts.
29th August 1941

[APCS: present source unknown]

Gabriel Pascal (1894–1954), Hungarian film director to whom Shaw had entrusted a number of his plays for screen treatment, was frustrated by an inability to obtain a saleable actor for the lead in a film version of Arms and the Man. *Shaw's first choice, Alec Guinness (b. 1914), joined the Royal Navy in 1941. His second choice, Rex Harrison (1908–90), enlisted in the Royal Air Force in 1942. The project was abandoned.*

Garrison tours dont matter. I am against full dress metropolitan [productions] of any play of mine during the war, because taxation makes me a mere collector for the Government with a negligible commission of a few pence in the £.; but minor business goes on as usual. I should like Rex Harrison to have a go at Bluntschli, as he is to play him in the film. So when the time for action comes there will be no difficulty that I can foresee. Use my country address: I skulk there from the bombs these times.

G.B.S.

157 / To Irene Hentschel   Ayot St Lawrence. Welwyn. Herts.
                                            25th February 1942

[TLS: present source unknown]

Irene Hentschel (1891–1979), daughter of Carl Hentschel and one of very few successful female stage directors in Britain at this time, was staging a West End revival of The Doctor's Dilemma *for H.M. Tennent, to whose blandishments Shaw had apparently succumbed after earlier asserting that war taxation made production unfeasible for successful dramatists. With Vivien Leigh (1913–67) as Jennifer, the Haymarket production achieved one of the longest runs (474 performances) of any Shaw play in London.*

Dear Irene Hentschel

Vivien is absolutely right. She must play the beautiful romantic heroine for all she is worth. The least touch of comedy, the faintest suggestion of a sense of humor in Jennifer would ruin the play.

Nevertheless I agree with you most heartily. Women (or men) who live in a false world and sincerely believe in it, who never for a moment look facts in the face or see people as they really are, are to me unbearable: I detest Jennifer, and much prefer Minnie Tinwell, whose part is one of the best in the play brief as it is. It was first played by the daughter of an American bishop (Mary Hamilton if I recollect aright); and the way she managed to convey in two minutes that she was quite open to an adventure with any of the doctors was so delicious that Lewis (the original B.B.) slipped his card into her hand as she went out.

I suggested to Catharine Cornell that she should double the two parts as a *tour de force* of acting! Pass it on to Vivien.

Now you share my dislike of Jennifer; and you want to use the last act to *expose* her. Not on your life, Irene. Let Vivien alone: the exposure of Jennifer is another play. The name of that play is Jitta's Atonement, which I translated (to put it mildly) from the German for its author Siegfried Trebitsch, who said that my translation was marvellous but that I had *almost* changed his tragedy into a comedy.

I am writing to my publishers to send you a copy if all the copies have not perished in the blitzes. Vivien might make another success in it if a first rate comedian could be found for the husband, and Nancy Price would play the old woman. Someday you must produce it for me.

I have not seen the D's D for many many years, and shall probably never see it again.

GBS

Mary **Hamilton** (1877–1945) was the daughter of the Archbishop of Ottawa. She performed for Vedrenne-Barker mainly as an understudy at the Royal Court and toured in their companies before settling in Boston, Mass. Eric **Lewis** (1855–1935) specialized in comic roles. Katharine **Cornell**, who added Jennifer to her repertoire quite successfully in 1941, did not heed Shaw's *doppelgänger* suggestion. Nancy **Price** (1880–1970), veteran character actress, was the founder of the People's National Theatre, to which Shaw gave his blessing.

158 / To Patrick Crean

Ayot St Lawrence. Welwyn. Herts.
25th March 1942

[TLS: Stelco Library, Shaw Festival]

Patrick Crean (b. 1911) was a young actor in repertory at York, appearing as Bohun in You Never Can Tell. *In Act IV, one night, he was inspired to blow a whistle he wore around his neck as part of his 'Harlequinade' costume, to silence the bickering Clandons instead of shouting as rehearsed. Though it garnered a huge laugh, his director vetoed the business as cheap clowning. The aggrieved actor sought Shaw's opinion. In later years Crean joined the Dublin Gate Theatre, moved on to Canada, and eventually became a celebrated fight director at the Stratford and Shaw festivals.*

Dear Mr Crean

Obviously the whistle will get a laugh. I should probably join in if I were in the audience; BUT I should at once class you as a crude low comedian and not as a serious actor. An actor can always get a laugh in the theatre by doing something absurdly silly; but whether it pays him to do so depends on whether he desires to get future engagements as a clown or as a serious comedian. Clowning is very good business both artistically and pecuniarily: I enjoy it myself as much as anybody; but I should not engage a clown, however gifted, to play any part in You Never Can Tell; and if I were in command of Stratford-on-Avon I should cast him, not for Macbeth, but for the porter. So make up your mind which line you hope to excel in. If you choose clowning blow the whistle by all means, though the waiter will probably resent your spoiling his entrance with the jingling tray, and stealing the stage center from him when he is clearly entitled to it.

It is, however, not wise to quarrel with a producer, an author, or a manager until you have achieved a reputation so great that they cannot afford to do without you no matter how much they dislike you. It is they who cast plays: your livelihood depends on them at present. Your producer has probably blacklisted you; I, the author, know nothing about you except that you lost interest in Bohun, one of the most effective parts in the play, because you were not allowed to blow a whistle in it. That is not a prudent beginning. I advise you to stand the producer several drinks and tell him you feel, every time you play the part, how right he was about it. Write me to say that now that you have got into the skin of the part you would like to play it every night for six months it is so interesting.

Anyhow, get on the right side of the producer. Producers have much to do with casting, and do not love those who give them trouble.

faithfully

G. Bernard Shaw

Geoffrey Staines was the **producer** (that is, director) of *You Never Can Tell.*

159 / To Hugh Beaumont

Ayot St Lawrence. Welwyn. Herts.
30th June 1942

[APCS: Colgate]

The Millionairess *was broadcast by the British Broadcasting Corporation in two parts, on 28 and 29 June, with Edith Evans as Epifania. Beaumont did not listen to the performance, but, as Shaw informed Evans on 7 July (Bryan Forbes,* Ned's Girl, *1977) he 'heartily agreed' to scrap any further plans for a production after receiving Shaw's reaction.*

They made such a horrible mess of The Millionairess on Sunday that I gave it up for dead. However, I sent in a 1000 lb bombshell on Monday; and the second broadcast was quite decent.

But the lady played farce instead of tragedy, and slurred all her keywords so carelessly that I see she has not really caught on to the part; and I am not keen on a London production. The play will not bear underplaying or half playing.

In fact I am decidedly cool about it now. How did it strike you?

GBS

160 / To Herbert Marshall   [Ayot St Lawrence. Welwyn. Herts.]

18th October 1942

[ALS: present source unknown]

Herbert Marshall, who was becoming an expert on Russian theatre and cinema, re-quested Shaw to record a brief introduction to a film 'of unprecedented heroism' on the defence of Leningrad, for which he could arrange to send a sound van to Ayot.

No, damn it, I write the play: I dont bang the drum outside the booth.

WALK UP
BY
BERNARD SHAW

How would that look? No, Herbert, no.

I am not accessible at present, as my village has no train service nor any buses. And I am so old that I am hardly fit to be seen. But we shall meet when the war is over.

GBS

161 / To Sean Power   Ayot St Lawrence. Welwyn. Herts.

11th November 1942

[APCS: Boston University]

The Earl of Longford's Company at the Gate Theatre, Dublin, had compensated for the Abbey Theatre's current disinterest in Shaw by staging productions of seven of his plays between 1938 and 1942, including Saint Joan, *the full-length* Man and Superman, *and in September 1942 a production of* Getting Married. *Sean Power was the Gate's box-office manager.*

– Private –

Dear Sir

Someone has sent me one of your programs in which my name is given as George Bernard Shaw. Will you be good enough to see that the George is omitted in future. Professionally my name is Bernard Shaw. In all my agreements there is a clause specifying this form for all printed matter dictated by the management. It is more convenient everywhere; but in Ireland in particular my Hanoverian Christian name is super-fluous.

faithfully
G. Bernard Shaw

162 / To Hugh Beaumont Ayot St Lawrence. Welwyn. Herts.
30th November 1942

[TLS: Colgate]

Tennent was casting a production of Heartbreak House, *presented at the Cambridge Theatre on 18 March 1943, starring Robert Donat (1905–58), who stubbornly insisted on playing Shotover, though Shaw, who thought he was too young for the role (as subsequently confirmed in performance), wanted to cast him as Hector. Others cast in the production were Edith Evans (switching from Ariadne, which she had performed in 1921 and 1932, to Hesione), Isabel Jeans (1891–1985) as Ariadne, Deborah Kerr (b. 1921) as Ellie, and J.H. Roberts (1884–1961) as Mazzini Dunn.*

Dear Hugh Beaumont

Surely Robert Donat is too young for Shotover, and just the right age for Hector, who is the juvenile lead. The part has never yet been played with the proper romantic air and D'Artagnan make-up which makes his fascination for Ellie credible. Donat could pull that off. Tell him fifteen years hence it will be time for him to play old character parts. Failing Hardwicke, the obvious choice for Shotover is Cecil Trouncer, who is by far the best heavy man now on the stage. He was quite equal to the part at the Westminster, where he played it a few years ago.

Harcourt Williams wants to play it; but his voice is not right for it: he would be intelligent enough but he has not the proper sea dog bark and bite.

What has become of Eric Maturin? He was perfect as the man about town in the original production; and his age does not matter if he still keeps his figure. At all events the part needs somebody in his line. A bad casting would hamper Edith terribly.

I have not seen Isabel Jeans since she played in the revival of The Country Wife by the Pioneers [*error for Phoenix Society*] a longish time ago [*1924*]. She is not big enough to look like Edith's elder sister; but she had, I thought, the quality to play the irresistible enchantress Hesione. The real difficulty therefore is Ellie, who, whatever else she may be must be virginal, and have no sexual glamor. No woman in the cast should compete with Hesione in that department. Ellen O'Malley, an Irishwoman for whom I wrote the part, was perfect in it; and Eileen Beldon got away with it successfully; but the combination of real youth with power to take a strong lead and a virginity that makes her mystic union with the old captain wholly spiritual is not easy to find. S.S. I have never seen; and I am not sure that Deborah could stand up to Isabel with the necessary force.

Roberts is, or used to be, too smart and crisp a comedian for the mild old foozle Mazzini Dunn. Can't you get O.B. Clarence? He would be perfect.

Mangan and the burglar are easy parts to cast. There are dozens of actors who could play them.

If You Never Can Tell has anything of a run Maude will probably get tired and drop out of the cast after a few weeks. It will not matter once the play has settled in; for Cyril Maude is not a bit like the waiter and never was. What upset the old Haymarket venture was my not making him play the juvenile lead instead of wasting his youth on old character parts (let this be a warning to Donat). To replace him I am not sure that Clarence would not be your best choice. Anyhow he must be silky, soft and charming, not in the least like C.M. The boy Phil should be very elegant, very smart and selfpossessed and is beautifully dressed: he and Dolly should have the charm of a pair of porcelain figures. The traditional rendering of the part is all wrong. Roberts could play McComas and Trouncer Bohun or Crampton. Donat is on the heavy side for Valentine; but he could play it successfully. Mrs Crampton is important: she must be ladylike, quiet but very determined. Gloria and Dolly will have a fight for the star part: I am too hopelessly out of date to be able to suggest anyone.

This place is very inaccessible unless you have plenty of petrol; and my wife is ill and cannot bear much company; but if you will give us a few days notice whenever it suits you and can manage the journey we shall be glad to see you. I will send you printed directions as to how to get here by car. I note that this is a matter for next year. Enterprizing of you to venture as far as Gib[raltar] under the circumstances.

faithfully

G. Bernard Shaw

Shaw's loyalty to players who had enriched earlier Shaw productions is evidenced in his casting suggestions. Cecil **Trouncer** (1898–1956), described by Shaw as the best heavy lead in London, had recently appeared as Bombardone in *Geneva*. Harcourt **Williams** (1880–1957) created Count O'Dowda in *Fanny's First Play* (1911), played Valentine in *You Never Can Tell* and Larry Doyle in *John Bull's Other Island*, and, as manager of the Old Vic (1929), added Shaw's plays to the Shakespeare repertory. Eric **Maturin** (1883–1957) was Randall the Rotter in the 1921 *Heartbreak House*. Eileen **Beldon** (1901–85), who played Ellie in 1932, was Nell Gwynn in *In Good King Charles's Golden Days* (1939). **S.S.** may be Sophie Stewart (1908–77). O.B. **Clarence** (1870–1955) was a brilliant Inquisitor in the 1924 *Saint Joan*.

Cyril **Maude**, who retired in 1933, did not return to the stage for *You Never Can Tell*. The contemplated Tennent revival was shelved until 1947, when the Waiter was portrayed by Harcourt Williams. Beaumont's **Gibraltar venture** was as tour manager of a concert party visiting military installations in 1943 for the Entertainment National Service Association, popularly known as ENSA.

163 / To Hugh Beaumont

Ayot St Lawrence. Welwyn. Herts.

8th December 1942

[APCS: Colgate]

I did not understand that Edith is to change her old part for Hesione. Isabel can play Utterword on her head. Deborah played in the Barbara film and met me at Cliveden, where we were both visiting. I cannot suggest a better Ellie. What about Jean Cadell for Guinness – a Caledonian Guinness?

All right for Shotover: let R.D. try him; but if his health is still precarious he should have a strong understudy.

Roberts by all means, failing O.B.

GBS

Cliveden was the home of Lord and Lady Astor. Jean **Cadell** (1884–1967) was a Scottish actress who will long be remembered for her Mrs Pearce in the film version of *Pygmalion*

(1938). Robert Donat's **health** failed him during the ten-month run of *Heartbreak House*; he was succeeded by John Laurie (1897–1980).

164 / To George Orwell Ayot St Lawrence. Welwyn. Herts.
26th December 1942

[TLS: BBC Written Archives]
George Orwell (1903–50), a talks producer in the Indian Section of the British Broadcasting Corporation, in its Eastern Service, was preparing a six-part series Calling All Students, *broadcast for University of Calcutta students enrolled in the B.A. English Literature course, and dealing with set texts, one of which was* Arms and the Man. *The extract broadcast on 22 January was the third-act scene suggested by Shaw in his letter.*

Dear Mr Orwell

. . . [Y]ou must not broadcast any of the first act of Arms and the Man.

In the third act the scene where Raina and Bluntschli are alone together for the first time since his return, beginning 'You look ever so much nicer than when we last met' and ending with 'Oh, I wish I had never met you,' prefaced, of course, with a sketch of the story of the play up to that point, would be possible; but if the course is on English literature something from my prose works, or a piece of oratory such as Cæsar's first soliloquy, or the Devil's speech of death from the third act of Man and Superman, or the prologue to Cæsar and Cleopatra spoken by the god Ra, would be more suitable. The dialogue in Arms and the Man has no special literary pretensions. The passages I suggest are deliberately rhetorical.

faithfully
G. Bernard Shaw

165 / To James Bridie 4 Whitehall Court SW1
11th September 1943

[ALS: National Library of Scotland, Acc. 9887/22]
James Bridie (1888–1951), a Scottish physician turned playwright, was the author of A Sleeping Clergyman, *produced at the 1933 Malvern Festival, and* Mr Bolfry, *which had been playing at the Westminster Theatre, with Alastair*

Sim in a memorable performance, since early August. Charlotte Shaw died the next day.

Many thanks. I have noted the address; but at this moment it looks as if the patient were beyond all professional help. The end cannot be far off for either of us (she 86: I 87); but it seems very close now for the younger.

I saw the play at the Westminster, and remarked to Roy Limbert that I was glad to know that if I had [done] nothing else for the drama I had at least made the production of such stunners as Bolfry possible. I enjoyed it all except the servant's part, of which not a word got across, because she had not been warned that dialect has to be articulated as clearly and artificially as blank verse. She thought only of imitating it successfully.

G. Bernard Shaw

166 / To James Bridie . 4 Whitehall Court SW1
4th December 1943

[APCS: National Library of Scotland, Acc. 9887/22]

The government was encouraging wartime 'educational' entertainments through tax exemptions to managements.

This notion that plays can be classified as educational and non-educational is such utter thoughtless nonsense that there is nothing to be done about it but stick to our royalties and let the managers take their luck in getting exempted. Argument is impossible: it may be worthwhile to humbug the competent authority into passing your Jonah as a scripture lesson, or my King Charles as a table of logarhythms and a page of history; but there is no logic in the business: it wont stand stirring-up.

Waiving royalties does no good whatever. Professionally it is blacklegging. Are you a member of the Society of Authors? You ought to be.

G.B.S.

Bridie's play was *Jonah and the Whale* (1932); Shaw's was *In Good King Charles's Golden Days* (1939).

167 / To Lawrence Langner

4 Whitehall Court SW1

9th July 1945

[TLS: Yale]

Dear Lawrence Langner

. . . My plays are mostly too long for radio; and the art of producing plays invisibly is a special one in which the choice of contrasting voices (the vocalists may be as ugly as Satan) is all important. I doubt whether you will find it possible to run the two distinct businesses together, and shall not commit myself to it until my doubts are resolved one way or the other.

Your news of the renovation of the Guild is very welcome. I had written it off as moribund.

> [*Handwritten*] In great haste – I am
> overwhelmed with business on the
> verge of my 90th year –
> G. Bernard Shaw

The Theatre **Guild**, near to insolvency, suddenly struck it rich with its production of *Oklahoma!* (1943) and *Carousel* (1945). In 1945 it also launched the Theatre Guild on the Air, sponsored by U.S. Steel, which was broadcast for eight years, then transferred to television.

168 / To Cecil Gray

4 Whitehall Court SW1

31st January 1946

[ALS: BL 57786, f 46]

Gilles de Rais (1404–40) was a French soldier, member of Joan of Arc's guard and (in 1429) Marshal of France, who subsequently was convicted of Satanism and hanged for the murder of some 140 children. His name became associated posthumously with that of the fictional 'Bluebeard' in Charles Perrault's Tales of Mother Goose *(1697). Cecil Gray's unpublished play* Gilles de Rais *was privately printed in an edition of 250 copies for the author by the Favil Press. In a postscript to the book Gray stated that in Shaw's* Saint Joan, *'the character and role of Gilles are completely misunderstood, misrepresented, and absurdly minimised.' This, he added, should not be construed as a criticism of the play, which was 'a masterpiece if ever there was one,' but 'merely as a justification of the claim that in all essential respects the foregoing play is strictly accurate in its his-torical foundation in fact.'*

Dear Cecil Gray

I have just read Gilles de Rais, which, as I learn from the card enclosed in it, you sent me last October. That is what happens to books that arrive without a separate letter to announce them. There are piles of them, mostly unreadable, and they join the heap, neglected and unread. My discovery of Gilles was a happy accident.

First, before we come to the play as a work of art, a few vulgar consid-erations. You must change the name; for nobody will ask for a book if they cannot pronounce its name. You will have to call it Bluebeard: Friend of St Joan. And you have perpetrated the most appalling stage direction ever written. A great flame is to shoot up on the stage, and the curtain to be dropped instantly. The audience would conclude that the theatre was on fire; and the death roll would make the play a hor-ror and a hoodoo for years. You must cut that out, or at least make the bishop stir up the fire with a very large poker first.

I approve highly of your references to me in the postscript; but why do you call the pile of literary rubbish which Anatole France put for-ward as a life of Joan 'monumental'? It was his only failure. Hamlet with Hamlet left out would be a masterpiece in comparison. [*The next four sentences were added in the left margin.*] A.F. had XIX century limita-tions. He could not believe that a woman could have military ability and political leadership. To him wome[n]'s place was not even in the home: it was the bed. His book is a compilation of unmemorable and finally unreadable twaddle about nobodies: hack work by his assistants mostly.

The main defect about Gilles as the subject of a biographical drama is that which has broken all plays with a major historical figure as a minor role and a defeated character as the hero. Masefield's Pompey, Drinkwater's Robert Lee, Harris's St Paul etc. etc. are all spoilt by the overwhelming claims of Cæsar, Lincoln, and Jesus to the leading part even if, as in the cases of Macbeth and Antony, final victory is denied them. I had to make Gilles a nobody lest he should for a moment, as Bluebeard, divide the interest with Joan, or even with the Dauphin or the Bastard [*Dunois*]. The slightest reminder of his tragedy would have been a ruinous mistake.

But you have vanquished this difficulty by making it possible for a sufficiently attractive actress to make enough of her two small parts [*scenes*] to save them from seeming insignificant. That was no small feat.

I think you have succeeded with Gilles. I saw in the fellow but a pathological case like those of Hitler, Nero and Tsar Paul, an average man with his head turned by enormous wealth and power. But you have brought him to life in tragic magnitude, and achieved a perfect portrait by telling all we know about him, giving it the magic of a work of art at the same time. It is good history and good drama, daringly free from theatrical shoppiness.

Many thanks for sending it to me. Send me the next one too.

G. Bernard Shaw

[*Handwritten*] Forgive all these blots and blunders. I am very old.

The works Shaw cites are the Anatole France (1844–1924) *La Vie de Jeanne d'Arc* (1908), the John Masefield (1878–1967) play *Pompey the Great* (1910), John Drinkwater's *Robert E. Lee* (1923), and Frank Harris's fictional *Stories of Jesus the Christ* (1919).

169 / To Katharine Cornell Ayot St Lawrence. Welwyn. Herts.

22nd July 1946

[ALS: NYPL Theatre Collection]

Katharine Cornell, following her fourth and last revival of Candida *in April, was seeking another suitable Shavian role, but found nothing. The Millionairess had a try-out at Lawrence Langner's Westport Country Playhouse, in Connecticut, in the summer of 1938, with Jessie Royce Landis (1904–72) as Epifania, but there had not yet been a major American production.*

Dear Katharine Cornell

Granted you are not quite right for The Millionairess, and will not be until you conceive her as a tragic figure behind the comedy dialogue.

Face the fact that Major Barbara is not a star play for Barbara, whose youth must be genuine, not acted, however ably.

Then why dont you try Captain Brassbound's Conversion, a star play written for Ellen Terry when she was just at that stage in her career that you have reached?

Why have you never thought of it, though it has been staring you in the face all the time?

G.B.S.

Edna Best (1900–74) brought *Captain Brassbound's Conversion* back to life briefly in New York in 1950.

170 / To M.E. Barber   [Ayot St Lawrence. Welwyn. Herts.
c. 16 December 1946]

[ALS: BL 56631, f 160]

The Phoenix Little Theatre (Arizona) had requested permission to give a royalty-free performance of Arms and the Man. *Shaw's American agent Samuel French Inc. passed the request on to the Society of Authors, which in January 1946 had undertaken, on a commission basis, the licensing of Shaw's works for publication and performance and the collecting of royalties and fees. M. Elizabeth Barber (1911–79) was assistant secretary of the Society.*

No plays should be royalty-free, absolutely.

Authors who violate this rule should be expelled from the S. of A. They are starving their fellow authors.

Charity and business should be kept in separate compartments.

G.B.S.

Companies which cannot afford a shilling in the pound of their takings should peel potatoes instead of performing plays.

171 / To Maurice Evans   Ayot St Lawrence. Welwyn. Herts.
25th February 1947

[TLS: Hampden-Booth Memorial Library]

Maurice Evans (1901–89), who came to the United States in 1935 as leading man to Katharine Cornell, playing the Dauphin in Saint Joan, *later made an enormous reputation in Shakespearean roles (Richard II, Hamlet, Falstaff, Malvolio, Macbeth) before gaining a comparable reputation in the Shavian repertoire (Tanner, Dudgeon, Magnus, Shotover). His production of* Man and

Superman, *in October 1947, ran for 295 performances in New York, and 242 more on the road.*

Dear Maurice Evans

I cannot alter my royalty terms because if I do it for one I must do it for all. I must not have favorites. Langner and Gertrude Lawrence want a flat rate of 10%; but that is too much for the little ventures, and not enough for the big metropolitan successes. The big metropolitan flops get off with 5% (village terms); so that they have nothing to complain of. I have not changed my terms for 50 years, though all salaries and all other theatre expenses have risen sky high, to say nothing of war taxation which leaves me only sixpence in the pound over my living expenses.

Subject to these terms, which must be regarded as unchangeable, you are in the same position as any other actor manager, and are not bound to the Theatre Guild in any way, nor are they bound to you. Loraine made an enormous success as Tanner half a century ago in America and lost it all in London by undercasting and holding on too long. I see no reason why you should not repeat the first half of that adventure. And you have your licence to play Tanner in repertory on tour just as you can play Hamlet.

Ann is very important: Loraine collapsed by miscasting her in London; but I am too old to know anything about casting nowadays; so I must leave that to you. I never heard of Celeste.

The field is open to you as a manager exactly as it is to anyone else; and you have a tremendous appeal as a star actor.

G. Bernard Shaw

Gertrude **Lawrence** (1898–1952) starred in a scintillating production of *Pygmalion* in New York in 1945–6. The **Theatre Guild** was empowered by Shaw to license amateur and stock productions of his plays for a commission, but he continued to control the licensing of major productions. **Celeste** Holm (b. 1919), famed as Ado Annie in *Oklahoma!*, would have been miscast as Ann Whitefield; the role went, eventually, to Frances (later Fanny) Rowe (1913–88), adroit British comedian, who was at the moment performing in London in the Arts Theatre production of *Back to Methuselah*.

172 / To The Society of Authors   Ayot St Lawrence. Welwyn. Herts.

29th March 1947

[APCS: BL 56631, f 184]

The London fringe production of Pygmalion *at the Lyric, Hammersmith, in June 1947, had a first-rate Higgins in Alec Clunes, who in 1959 would perform the role musically in the London production of* My Fair Lady. *Mervyn Johns (1899–1992), who was not a comic, was the dustman Doolittle in the same production.*

– Pygmalion Revival –

Do not license this unless fuller particulars are given about the cast. No presentable actress can fail as Eliza, though real youth greatly adds to the charm of the play. But the part of Higgins must not be treated by and as a juvenile lover; and the dustman needs a first rate comedian, and is a principal part.

I regard the play as worn to rags, and will sanction a full dress West End revival only if the cast is very interesting and not old and stale.

G.B.S.

173 / To Maurice Evans   Ayot St Lawrence. Welwyn. Herts.

15th September 1947

[TLS: Hampden-Booth Memorial Library]

Shaw here appears to be confusing Frank Reynolds of Letchworth, who occasionally collected amateur fees for him, with the New York literary agent Paul Reynolds (1864–1944), whose firm had handled American literary business for Shaw since 1912. Maurice Evans, in his autobiography All This . . . And Evans Too! *(1987), published what ostensibly was an extract of the third and fourth paragraphs of this letter. It was, in actuality, pruned and rephrased.*

Dear Maurice Evans

What on earth is all this stuff that you have written to Miss Patch? I am dreadfully old; but I am still able to run my business much better than your solicitor. I am in no difficulty whatever about management: all I wanted to convey to you was that using the Guild as my agent is open to the objection that as it wants all my plays for itself (just as you do) it can hardly be expected to encourage full dress revivals by its competitors. But I have at my disposal the Frank Reynolds firm, which has been in the business for fifty years and acted for me when I was a beginner.

But you need not bother about my affairs. You can pay royalties direct to me. When I die you can pay them to the Society of Authors, 84 Drayton Gardens, London, S.W. 10.

Somebody has told me that at the end of Man and Superman you altered my stage business by making Ann sit down and distract the attention of the audience from yourself, thereby stealing the end of the play from you. She and everybody else on the stage should not stir a finger during your speech about the wedding presents and be entirely forgotten until she gives you the cue for the last word 'Talking!'

If you really made such a blunder you are hopeless as a producer. Engage a competent specialist, and stick to acting, which is your job. And sack him if he changes my business in any essential particular. My plays flop in the hands of duffers who think they know better than I do.

What do you mean by a reduced royalty? I never reduce: if I did that for one I should have to do it for all: an author must have no favorites. A change from the sliding scale to a flat rate or a share in the profits is not a reduction.

The Guild has no exclusive rights, nor any rights at all. They are in the field, like any other management, just as you are.

I must not now dictate casts: I am too far out of date. The names you mention mean nothing to me: you must do the best you can.

G. Bernard Shaw

174 / To F. Aicken [Ayot St Lawrence. Welwyn. Herts.
c. 1 December 1948]

[*Belfast Telegraph*, 11 December 1948]

When Arms and the Man *was presented at the Larne Dramatic Festival by the Larne Grammar School Dramatic Society, the adjudicator suggested the approach to the play was wrong, that Shaw was writing 'with his tongue in his cheek,' and that the players' acting should have been done in like manner. The director of the production, F. Aicken, communicated this to the author.*

I never write with my tongue in my cheek. Your view of Arms and the

Man is correct. Played farcically for the laughs, they will not come; and the performance will be a failure. Played melodramatically it will be dull and ridiculous and disappointing. Played sincerely as serious 'anti-romantic' comedy it never fails. Even Raïna's operatic posing is sincere; she believes devoutly in it.

[*unsigned*]

175 / To Cedric Hardwicke   Ayot St Lawrence. Welwyn. Herts.
                                                   9th May 1949

[TLS: present source unknown]

Sir Cedric Hardwicke (knighted in 1934) negotiated with New York producer Richard S. Aldrich (1902–86) for a production of Cæsar and Cleopatra, *which was presented on 21 December 1949 with Hardwicke and Lilli Palmer (1914– 86) in the title roles. It was Shaw's third consecutive Broadway hit in four years, following Aldrich's* Pygmalion *(Gertrude Lawrence was his wife) and Evans'* Man and Superman.

Dear Cedric

Of course if you will undertake a Broadway production of Cæsar for a regular run you have every claim to my most friendly consideration. But you must make me a proposal before you engage a company or commit yourself in any way. I have nothing to do with your engagement of anybody but yourself as Cæsar. But would it not be wise to have a try-out somewhere before you venture, on condition that if it was success-ful you would guarantee the company a Broadway engagement? They would probably agree to this. The parts, including Cleopatra's, are not difficult; but Apollodorus, Rufus, and Septimus (especially Septimus, short though his part is) must not be mere utilities or they will belittle Cæsar.

Ftatateeta might be played by a negro, if he were extra tall and a good female impersonator.

But you must not produce as well as act. You can of course tell the producer all about the original stage business; but producing is the ruin of an actor: instead of thinking of his own part he watches the oth-ers all the time and ceases to be an actor. That is what happened to Granville-Barker.

229

As to the scenery you will be up against the Pascal film: a bad film except for the scenery; but you must contrive quick changes with only one long interval; and that will take some doing. Otherwise the play will be too long and its acting damagingly interrupted.

This is all I can say so far. Do not get into the American habit of supposing that a first rate production can be arranged by cable within 12 hours. The contract must be either with you solely and personal, or with a bank backing. Nobody must have a mere rake-off for nothing.

[*Handwritten*] I have just heard that Miss Palmer wishes to back herself financially as Cleopatra. Nothing could be more objectionable. Even if she were just right for the part (which is strongly denied) I would not put her in sole command of the production to this extent. She is not indispensable: you are.

G. Bernard Shaw

By '**Rufus**' Shaw means Rufio. Shaw's suggestion that Ftatateeta be performed by a male **negro** in drag was one he had earlier made to Forbes-Robertson in 1903 after seeing the incomparable American comedian Bert Williams (1876?–1922) in the London production of *In Dahomey*. Gabriel **Pascal**'s film version of *Cæsar and Cleopatra* was released early in 1946. The New York critics were more appreciative than Shaw of Lilli **Palmer**'s appropriateness to the stage role, Brooks Atkinson in the *New York Times* (22 December) lauding her 'limpid, girlish, roguish Cleopatra' as 'nothing short of ideal . . . a superb exposition of character.'

176 / To Roy Limbert 4 Whitehall Court SW1
27th May 1949

[TLS: HRC]
Roy Limbert found sufficient financing to bring the Malvern Festival back to life in August 1949, its bill including the first British production of Shaw's last full-length play Buoyant Billions *(begun in February 1936 but abandoned in August 1937; re-begun in August 1945 and completed in July 1947), directed by Esmé Percy; a revival of* In Good King Charles's Golden Days *(produced as a new play in the 1939 final pre-war Festival); and* The Apple Cart, *directed by Matthew Forsyth (1896–1954), who had staged a production of* Good King Charles *at the People's Palace, London, in October 1948. Despite Shaw's admonition Ernest Thesiger remained as director of* Good King Charles.

My dear Roy

I am really sorry to bother you so much; but you are heading for a failure through bad production and not grasping the difference between Festival and ordinary occasions. The Malvern Festival must be like the Bayreuth Wagner Festivals: people must go to it as they go to church; and the plays must be given without the omission of a comma, like the church service. Yet you let your producers write to me asking me to make cuts all over the plays. You must at once give a general order that there are to be no cuts absolutely, and that any producer proposing them will be replaced.

Next as to choice of producers. On no account should any player both act in a play and produce it. Percy may very exceptionally produce and act in B.B. because he knows my game and appears in the last act only, the part of Old Bill being played in the earlier act by the other characters. He does not appear: they talk about him.

But Thesiger must not produce King Charles. He must think about his own part, and not keep watching and thinking about the others, and trying to reduce their parts and magnify his own. I am being pestered to cut and minimize the part of Kneller (Forsyth's mistake). Kneller has to pick up the play when the audience has had enough of the others. He must be splendidly dressed, and fanatically and thunderingly assertive of his aesthetic religion against Newton, whom he would burn alive if he could. Naturally Thesiger would like to extinguish him. Another of your people is on the same tack, understanding nothing of esthetics or mathematics or philosophy, and thinking the part dull because it is not police news. He writes to me as if he were producing. Drown him.

All this is so likely to wreck the plays that I am driven to make a suggestion that you will think desperate. Theodora Winsten has a sister, Ruth Winsten, who has graduated with credit as a producer at the R.A.D.A., and brought off a public performance successfully. She is in every way a desirable person in the theatre, and understands that my plays are essentially religious and serious, however entertaining they may be, and no matter how many laughs they may get when the actors dont play for them. I could trust her to produce much more hopefully than these 'Where's your murder?' chaps you seem to hit on. As a matter of experience women are better producers than men.

Forsyth should understudy Thesiger, in case ——

Remember, no cuts, and all accompaniments on the cathedral, NOT the barrel, organ.

G.B.S.

The **Winsten** sisters were daughters of the writer Stephen Winsten (1893–1991) and his artist wife Clare (1894–1989), neighbours and friends of Shaw at Ayot. Theodora (b. 1917), a Prizeman in Stage Design, who won a scholarship to the Slade School of Art, designed the well-received settings for *Buoyant Billions.* Her sister Ruth (b. 1920), who later was awarded an O.B.E., directed a much-praised RADA production of J.B. Priestley's *An Inspector Calls*, with fellow-students Robert Shaw and Peter Barkworth in the cast, and won a RADA one-act play competition in the same year.

177 / To Cedric Hardwicke   Ayot St Lawrence. Welwyn. Herts.
27th May 1949

[TLS: present source unknown]

Shaw's allusion to 'the big success of the film' of Cæsar and Cleopatra *was exaggerative. Though Shaw received his full royalties, Pascal's extravagances resulted in financial failure for the film, and the withdrawal of his principal backer, J. Arthur Rank (1888–1972), from further participation in Pascal productions. Hardwicke would later perform in the Charles Laughton (1899–1962) First Drama Quartet version of* Don Juan in Hell *(1951) and in* Too True to be Good *(1963), but the 1956 revival of* The Apple Cart *was produced by Maurice Evans, with Signe Hasso (b. 1915) as a delectable Orinthia.*

Dear Sir Cedric

I am sending by the same mail as this a shattering letter to Richard Aldrich to say that I will have nothing to do with financiers who make a poor mouth of a golden opportunity like a revival of C. & C. People who cannot put up $100,000, and ask me to reduce my extremely reasonable terms because they must underpay their actors and skimp the production with the few dollars they can beg from door to door are of no use to me or you.

A revival of C. & C. with you as Cæsar is the nearest thing to sure fire in the market; and after the huge success of the film (between ourselves a bad one which made nothing of Cæsar) and the sensational success of Maurice Evans's revival of Superman, I'll pay no attention to backers who think I stand where I did fifty years ago.

I strongly advise you to take the same attitude. In any contract I may make I shall make your engagement of its essence and thus enable you to make your own terms without risking a cent or cheapening yourself by a dollar. So just sit tight and wait.

The Apple Cart will be equally sure fire if it comes after a big success in Cæsar; and Miss Palmer will be riper for Orinthia, who cannot, like Cleopatra, be played by an ingenue.

I need say no more now. Your letter is very interesting and I have taken it all in. I am quite agreed as to the advisability of a try-out.

G. Bernard Shaw

178 / To R.G. Walford   Ayot St Lawrence. Welwyn. Herts.
31st May 1949

[TLS: BBC Written Archives]

R.G. Walford (1913–75) was Assistant Head of Copyright. The 'recent broadcast' of The Devil's Disciple *by the British Broadcasting Corporation, on 13 December 1948, was a repeat performance first broadcast on 21 January 1947. As Shaw rarely professed to have enjoyed radio performances of his plays, his reaction in the present instance was not surprising. He was, however, rather unusually incensed by the poor quality of the musical performance on the recording for the final act, which he described to the Society of Authors as 'disgracefully feeble' (internal memo, 'Shaw and the B.B.C.,' Society of Authors, 14 November 1950). Despite Shaw's scepticism he eventually authorized a telecast of the play, presented on 26 July, his 93rd birthday.*

Dear Mr Walford

The Society of Authors has sent me your letter about televising The Devil's Disciple. I have not a television set: it is bad enough to have to listen-in without having to look-in as well. But I will not license performances like your recent broadcast on any terms. I hope you have destroyed the record of it.

The personality, voice, and accent of Swindon must be in the strongest contrast to Burgoyne's, and much less agreeable. The Sergeant must be a first rate character actor with his class well marked. Dick must be from the first a tragic foredoomed figure dressed in black, like Buckingham in Henry VIII. At the end of the second act Anderson's explosion at the óath 'Bloodanouns!!!' must be an atom bomb. In the last act there must be a great display of uniforms, Hessian and Brunswick as well as British.

But the music, horribly messed in the record, must be tremendous in the last act. The Dead March from Saul, at first heard off, must burst into full splendor when the band enters; and it must be played as only the International Staff Band of the Salvation Army can play it.

When the British march off at the Sergeant's stimulating order, the side drums must start them with three thundering rataplans before striking up British Grenadiers. When the ragged Americans come in afterwards playing Yankee Doodle they must play it on fifes, a cheap drum, and a couple of accordions: musically very amateurish, but with the quickstep well marked. The town clock must be as impressive as Big Ben. Without all this the play will go to pieces at the end, as it did in that damned broadcast. It is a full blooded melodrama, not a farcical comedy. But dont therefore shout it from beginning to end.

Christy, by the way, must be a comic zany, not an actor fancying he is playing Hamlet.

Can you get the idea? I doubt it; and unless you can convince me I will have no television and no more broadcasting.

G. Bernard Shaw

179 / To Frances Day   [Ayot St Lawrence. Welwyn. Herts.]
10th November 1949

[APCS: present source unknown]

Frances Day (1908–84), an American cabaret and film performer, pleasantly surprised critics and playgoers in her 'legit' debut in Buoyant Billions. *The BBC was negotiating for a televised performance, which Shaw eventually authorized after it became apparent that the production, about to be evicted from the Prince's Theatre, couldn't hope to survive without Day, who was committed to a Manchester pantomime season. The principal performers and their director Esmé Percy had travelled to Ayot for a rehearsal with Shaw on the lawn of the Winstens' house before the Malvern Festival opening.*

I have not a television receiver. It is bad enough to have to listen: to watch would be intolerable. I have not been to see B.B. I would not cross the street to see one of my own plays, though a Punch & Judy would hold me for half an hour. Five minutes at Winsten's were enough to convince me that you have the indispensable fire in your inside.

The Piccadilly is a queer theatre in its design; but it is unquestionably West End, and much better for B.B. than the Princes. But as 9 plays out of 10 are failures (bar pantos) there will soon be other theatres available.

G.B.S.

180 / To Cedric Hardwicke Ayot St Lawrence. Welwyn. Herts.

10th January 1950

[TL & ALS: present source unknown]

The Hardwicke Cæsar and Cleopatra *omitted both the original Act I, Scene I, and the 'Ra' substitute prologue Shaw had provided for Forbes-Robertson's farewell season 1912–13. The request that the omitted scene be restored 'at once' was ignored.* The Dark Lady of the Sonnets *was to receive its first American professional performance on 29 January in the third ANTA Album benefit for the American National Theatre and Academy, at the Ziegfeld Theatre, with an all-star cast of Peggy Wood (1892–1978) as Elizabeth, Rex Harrison as Shakespeare, Lilli Palmer as Mary Fitton, and Francis L. Sullivan (1903–56) supplanting Hardwicke as the Warder ('Beefeater'). Apparently Shaw failed to grasp that this was a single charity performance and that Harrison was already cast as the Bard.*

My dear Cedric

Lord bless you, the Ra prologue was never meant to be played with the original version. I never dreamt of such a thing. It was a *pièce d'occasion* written to enable Forbes-Robertson to omit the first scene and the third act. But the difficulty of getting a big enough actor for Ra, and the success of the third act in Germany, where it nearly killed the rest of the play, scrapped all that; so everything is in order . . .

It occurs to me that you may be omitting the first scene. That is a mistake. The audience does not know where it is or who is who; and you have to start unheralded and at sea level instead of on top of a set of utilities with the audience informed and expectant. If the scene is cut, restore it at once and you will feel the difference.

You positively must not play the Beefeater. It is Shakespear or nothing. Burbage did not play Bernardo or Marcellus in the middle of the first run of Hamlet. Rex Harrison will do quite well. Anybody can play the B. And almost anybody can produce. You must not at this climax of your eminence as a great actor take on these tupennyhapenny jobs.

GBS

Richard **Burbage** (*c.* 1567–1619), creator of most of Shakespeare's tragic roles, played Hamlet in 1602.

181 / To Val Gielgud   Ayot St Lawrence. Welwyn. Herts.
5th May 1950

[TL (u): BBC Written Archives]

Val Gielgud (1900–81) was Head of Television and Sound Drama for the British Broadcasting Corporation. Shaw's first television exposure had been a production of How He Lied to Her Husband *on 8 July 1937, followed by eleven additional performances in 1938–9 of seven of his plays, including* Androcles and the Lion, Candida, *and Act III of* Geneva, *the latter relayed from the stage of the St James's Theatre. On 7 June 1946 the official postwar re-opening of BBC Television was marked by a performance of* The Dark Lady of the Sonnets. *From 1946 to 1950, the year of Shaw's death, fifteen more productions were offered, of eleven Shaw plays, including* Saint Joan *(in two parts),* Arms and the Man, The Devil's Disciple, Widowers' Houses, *and* Buoyant Billions *from the stage of the Prince's Theatre two nights after the final performance on 12 November 1949.*

Dear Mr Gielgud

The difficulty about Television is not artistic but economic. The more convincingly you assure me that the acting will be first rate and the play uncut the less I can afford to let you do it. And with every improvement in color, size, price of receiving sets &c, my objection will be intensified. For the better the performance the more surely it will strike the play dead in the theatre box office from which I get my living. Nobody who can see an adequate performance for nothing in comfort at home with his family will dress up, leave his fireside, and pay guineas for theatre stalls and taxis.

But this does not extinguish television. It applies only to live plays, not dead ones. Now all but a very few plays and books are stone dead in

18 months. Even very successful plays, after a run in London and a tour in the provinces, are dropped for years. It is to these that you must look for television. But my plays neither sleep nor die. They are in continual use, to which television would put a stop.

There is one exception: the play called Jitta's Atonement, which nobody will touch because it purports to be a translation from the German of Siegfried Trebitsch. The first act, though good theatre, is Trebitsch: the rest is Shaw, with three first rate comedy parts. If you care to look it up, I should not object to its television for Trebitsch's sake as well as my own. That is all I can suggest.

[unsigned]

182 / To M.E. Barber   [Ayot St Lawrence. Welwyn. Herts.]
25th July 1950

[TLS: BL 56633, f 48v]

The Arts Council of Great Britain, founded in 1946 as an outgrowth of an earlier Council for the Encouragement of Music and the Arts, was Britain's principal channel for distribution of public money to the theatre and other arts. The Council in 1950 requested a licence to present Cæsar and Cleopatra *as one of four special plays for the two companies being specially formed for the 1951 Festival of Britain, to run for the full eight weeks of the Festival after a break-in tour, with an all-star cast headed by Vivien Leigh. Laurence Olivier (1907–89) eventually was signed to play Cæsar. John Fernald (1905–85), American stage director, ran the Liverpool Playhouse 1946–9; he later became principal of RADA, 1955–65.*

The Arts Council must write to me about this, and tell me exactly what they want. The B.B.C. is clamoring for a television of SAINT JOAN, and claiming that they are acting with the Arts Council.

I will not have the part of Cæsar acted by their best utility man, and directed by a producer who thinks that if he can get Vivien Leigh in the bill the rest doesnt matter. If Olivier will play Cæsar, and the Mr Fernald who lately produced Heartbreak House for the Arts Theatre will direct, I may consider it.

Anyhow they must be more explicit as to where, when, how often &c.; so you had better turn them on to me.

GBS

The production of Cæsar and Cleopatra, *the last with which Shaw was professionally associated before his death on 2 November, opened to unanimous approval on 10 May 1951. Directed by young Michael Benthall (b. 1919), who had done notable opera stagings at Covent Garden and several Stratford productions, its cast included, in addition to Olivier and Leigh, Robert Helpmann, Wilfrid .Hyde White, Niall MacGinnis, Maxine Audley, Jill Bennett, Norman Wooland, Elspeth March, Esmond Knight, and Henry Oscar.*

Index of Correspondents

Index